GRIZZLY**WARS**

EASTERN WASHINGTON UNIVERSITY PRESS

GRIZZLY**WARS**

THE PUBLIC FIGHT OVER THE GREAT BEAR

DAVID KNIBB

Foreword by
Lance Craighead

13 12 11 10 09 08   5 4 3 2 1

Cover photograph by Michael Quinton.

Jacket design and typography by A. E. Grey.

Library of Congress Cataloging-in-Publication Data

Knibb, David G.
   Grizzly wars : the public fight over the great bear / David Knibb.
      p.   cm.
   Includes bibliographical references and index.
   ISBN 978-1-59766-037-2 (alk. paper)
   1. Grizzly bear—Conservation—Government policy—North Cascades (B.C. and Wash.) 2. Wildlife
recovery—Government policy—North Cascades (B.C. and Wash.) 3. Grizzly bear—Conservation—
Government policy—Rocky Mountains. 4. Wildlife recovery—Government policy—Rocky Mountains.
I. Title.
   QL737.C27K595 2008
   333.95'9784097—dc22
                                                                        2008019737

Eastern Washington University Press

Spokane and Cheney, Washington

CONTENTS

ILLUSTRATIONS

FOREWORD

Grizzly Wars: The Public Fight over the Great Bear chronicles in careful and admirably unbiased detail the events surrounding the listing of grizzly bears as a threatened species under the Endangered Species Act and the progress that has been made toward the recovery of these populations. Knibb tells the story of how these events unfolded with a compelling immediacy, almost as if he were there in the conference rooms, meetings, public hearings, offices, and chambers where the fate of these wild creatures was negotiated by those both sympathetic and hostile to their continued existence. Weaving the ongoing events into a coherent whole, Knibb imparts a keen sense of the implications of this struggle, which concerns more than just the question of what to do about a dangerous animal living on the borders of our civilization. The story of the grizzlies raises the fundamental issue of man's place in nature—of whether we can learn to live in balance with what remains to us of our planet.

Our intellect tells us that human beings are superior creatures, a species somehow separate from the rest of the animal kingdom. And yet we are all part of the intricate web of life on earth. We drink the same water, breathe the same air, and capture energy for survival, growth, and reproduction from the same sources that grizzly bears do. Allowing grizzlies to disappear might free up a few additional resources for a few more humans, at least in the shorter term, but the demise of the species would ultimately have a greater and longer-lasting impact than many of us imagine. And it would be a terrible shame.

The Endangered Species Act and the recovery process are not perfect solutions to the problem of imperiled species, but they are a big step in the right direction. If threatened grizzly bear populations are ever effectively recovered, the Endangered Species Act will be the main reason why. Recovery plans—for which the US Fish and Wildlife Service is responsible—are in effect twofold. They provide blueprints for nature reserves, intended to ensure population persistence, and they lay out policy guidelines for the appropriate management of these reserves. Recovery plans for grizzly bears have fallen short on both counts. In part, this has happened because the science of reserve design and the study of population viability are in their infancy, and both must cope with a great many variables and unknowns. However, uncertainty need not hinder progress if we allow ourselves a wide enough margin of error.

Recovery areas for grizzly bears have been a subject of controversy ever since the government first created these reserves. As Knibb explains, central to this controversy has been a sometimes contentious debate over whether to base recovery plans on a population's numbers alone or whether also to take into account the changing dynamics of bear habitat. Many scientists, including myself, feel that our approach too often overlooks critical issues of habitat and that an inadequate margin of error exists in some of our present plans. This became apparent in the March 2007 decision to remove the Yellowstone grizzly bear population from the list of threatened species, thereby ending federal protection. Plans for managing the newly delisted bears fail to provide a sufficient buffer against the crises this population potentially faces: climate change, loss of habitat, unreliable food sources, disease, a decline in genetic variation, and more numerous confrontations with human beings. The reasons for this shortfall are primarily political. Providing extra space for bears to move into, either as their numbers increase or as other habitats disappear, incurs economic, social, and political costs that decision makers do not wish to assume.

In the meanwhile, grizzlies in the lower 48 states have become prisoners on islands of habitat surrounded by seas of humanity. As Knibb reminds us, biologists and conservationists have argued from the very beginning that the government's preoccupation with recovery areas ignores the crucial need for territory through which bears can move from one area to another. Such territory is known as connectivity habitat. As it stands, it is no easy matter for a bear to travel between reserves. The designated recovery areas are surrounded by roads, highways, and railway lines, including a busy east-west thoroughfare that runs through southern British Columbia, effectively acting as a fence. The mountain regions in the vicinity of these reserves are often crisscrossed by logging roads that are popular for off-road vehicle use, and the drivers of these vehicles are apt to carry hunting rifles. Homes are sprinkled throughout hills and valleys, and livestock graze on grassy slopes. There are also plenty of towns, whose residents are not likely to be very tolerant of adventuresome bears. These roads and developments are like minefields for young male grizzlies—the ones most likely to strike off on their own.

But, assuming enough food exists in a reserve to supply a minimum viable population, why do grizzly bears need to travel anywhere at all? Why *do* bears cross the road? The answer: to get their genes to the other side. In order for a species like grizzlies to survive, individuals must move around. Like elk, lynx, wolverines, and other wild creatures, grizzlies need secure patches of habitat to live in—areas where they are unlikely to be disturbed by human activity. But they also need habitat through which they can roam. Dispersal permits new genes to be introduced, and gene flow is necessary for long-term population persistence. In short, grizzlies need to travel to ensure their long-term genetic variability and ultimately their survival as a species.

Barriers to travel obviously prevent new genes from coming into one population from another. The Yellowstone grizzlies, for example, are like the residents of a small town, consisting of maybe six hundred individuals who have been interbreeding for about a century. By 1975, after the park closed its garbage dumps, there were probably fewer than 250 grizzlies left in Yellowstone, which produced something of a genetic bottleneck. Although numbers have since increased, this reproduction has resulted in some degree of inbreeding, and the bears have begun to suffer the effects, much as people isolated in a small town would experience. One of these effects is inbreeding depression, a condition that lowers the reproductive rate. The Yellowstone grizzlies may not yet have reached a crisis point, but they need an influx of new genes. The retained genetic heterozygosity of grizzly bears in the Yellowstone population is estimated to be about 75 percent, which is less than zoos manage for, and the inbreeding coefficient is 0.125, as it would be in the offspring of a marriage of first cousins.

The best way to maintain genetic variation and sustain healthy populations is to allow these bears some territory that would permit them to move into and out of the Yellowstone Ecosystem. The current management solution, which consists of dropping an occasional transplanted grizzly bear into the Yellowstone population, will do little to solve genetic problems. The transplanted bear may never reproduce, and, even if it does, its genes are not likely to be as well adapted to survival as those of a bear who had managed to travel to Yellowstone by itself. In the opinion of many scientists, transplanting bears to augment gene pools amounts to short-circuiting natural selection—and experience should tell us that you don't mess with Mother Nature. Under ordinary circumstances, the best genes would find their way to Yellowstone, and likewise to other reserves, by themselves.

As Knibb observes, grizzlies are generalists: habits and needs vary considerably from one individual to another. Beyond allowing for gene flow, habitat connectivity enables individual bears to satisfy their requirements for feeding, mating, denning, and movement within and between habitat areas. At the level of a metapopulation—a large population of connected subpopulations—dispersal between population centers is important for population persistence. Providing for dispersal between local populations also allows for immigration and emigration in response to epidemic disease, outbreaks of insects that destroy food sources, climate change, or large-scale fires that could wipe out one or more local populations. Historical evidence supports the existence of a true metapopulation structure for grizzly bears in the contiguous United States. Rather than treat each grizzly population as if it were a separate entity, which is what the Yellowstone delisting decision does, we should regard each group of bears as one population center in a regional metapopulation and manage accordingly—and sound management includes providing for gene flow within the metapopulation.

Historically, the Greater Yellowstone grizzly population was linked to the west and north through the Centennials to the Selway-Bitterroot, to the Cabinet-Yaak, and ultimately to Canadian populations. Another route of connectivity led from Yellowstone to the Northern Continental Divide Ecosystem through Montana's Big Belt Mountains or, further west, through the Tobacco Root, Highland, Champion-Thunderbolt, and/or Elkhorn mountains. Currently, enough secure, wild areas remain on private lands to provide effective connectivity habitat through these mountain ranges and other such stepping stones on public lands. What is lacking is the public willingness to encourage grizzly bear movement beyond the spaces in which they are presently confined—that is, into places that, while still remote, are not quite as far away from us.

In 2001, the governors of Montana, Idaho, and Wyoming appointed a fifteen-member citizens' roundtable to review the Draft Conservation Strategy for the Grizzly Bear in the Yellowstone Area, developed by the Interagency Grizzly Bear Committee. One of the recommendations of the panel, echoing the language of the document, was to "support the expansion of grizzly bears beyond the Primary Conservation Area, into areas that are biologically suitable *and socially acceptable*" (my emphasis). The phrase "biologically suitable and socially acceptable" was subsequently incorporated into the final grizzly bear conservation strategies of each of the three states. No equivalent language exists in the Endangered Species Act, however: recovery criteria are based entirely upon biological factors—and rightly so. Notions of social acceptability have no precedent in federal law, and the inclusion of such language interjects a significant element of subjectivity, and hence the potential for bias, into the recovery process. It allows politics to intrude into matters of science.

Of course, any process designed by human beings and implemented by governments is inherently political. As Knibb forcefully argues, however, policies made in Washington DC have a profound impact on grizzly recovery in the Northwest. The key to ensuring the recovery of endangered and threatened populations—to maintaining biodiversity and safeguarding ecosystems, which are the life support for the planet and all its inhabitants, and ultimately to finding a sustainable balance between human populations and the rest of the biosphere—is the public will. If the citizens of a democracy strongly support a particular cause, the political will to accomplish the needed objectives should soon follow. Concerns about clean air, clean water, and other public health issues that are a function of natural ecosystems have been steadily growing over the past decades, and such causes are likely to receive even greater emphasis in the future. Grizzly bears, like few other species, are clear indicators of the health of these ecosystems—ecosystems that also sustain human beings. It takes a complex web of life, from air to soil to water to plants to herbivores to omnivores, to support a single grizzly bear. In a real sense, then, the fate of threatened grizzly bear populations is a touchstone of our public health and well-being.

Grizzly Wars should go a long way toward bringing this fact home to all of us. It offers a clear-sighted account of our priorities in regard to grizzlies and, in so doing, points to how poorly we understand grizzly bears. As a society and as individuals, we need to realize that the survival of the grizzly bear and the future we are leaving to our children and grandchildren are deeply intertwined. Unless we work to preserve healthy wild ecosystems, the life support systems for all forms of life will start to fail. To secure our own future, we must understand that, like any other species, grizzlies *are* socially acceptable.

—*Lance Craighead*
Bozeman, Montana
March 2008

ACKNOWLEDGMENTS

Many of the people who helped with this book are mentioned in it, so the book itself is an acknowledgment of their support. In addition, I want to thank four biologists whose contributions went beyond what I have attributed to them. They provided important insights, answered follow-up questions, and pointed me toward new and useful sources. These kind folks are Wayne Kasworm, from the US Fish and Wildlife Service in Libby, Montana; Jon Almack, who was with the Washington Department of Fish and Wildlife; Bill Gaines, from the Wenatchee-Okanogan National Forest; and Ann Braaten, from North Cascades National Park. My special thanks also go to Doug Zimmer, from the US Fish and Wildlife Service office in Olympia, Washington, for his valuable perspectives.

In Canada, Matt Austin was a continuing source of information—sometimes frustrating but always useful. I am grateful to him and to Dennis Pemble, who took the time to describe his experiences with Winston, British Columbia's best-traveled grizzly bear.

My thanks also go to the staff at Eastern Washington University Press. Ivar Nelson's interest in this project persisted despite his move from one university press to another, and he gave me vital advice on how to focus this book. Pamela Holway was the take-charge person who always led the way through what seemed to me the byzantine process of turning a manuscript into a book. Both would say they were just doing their jobs, but that in no way lessens my appreciation. I am also grateful for the early support of Pat Soden at the University of Washington Press.

Finally, I appreciate the encouragement and enthusiasm of my friends Michelle Dewey and Art Campbell and, most of all, my dear Wendy.

GRIZZLY**WARS**

INTRODUCTION
"I Won't Say It Wasn't"

Entering Napeequa Valley is like passing through a portal into a lost world. A dark gash of a canyon slices through a mountain wall, a shortcut carved by an ancient accident. A hundred centuries ago the Napeequa flowed on down its hidden valley and out the far end. But then a landslide plugged it and the river backed up. Like a flood looking for a weak spot in a dike, this new reservoir found a crack in the side of White Mountain and started to spill out. Quickly it ripped this canyon through the mountain wall and escaped in a thunderous roar.[1] Without its stream, the inner valley was left high and dry. Where the river once flowed, all that was left was a pair of lakes. Wendy and I are headed for those Twin Lakes.

Spring in Washington's Cascade Mountains is like dodging snow squalls; the season varies from one peak or valley to the next. Along the crest fifteen miles to the west, everything is still deep in snow. Here, the sun is burning holes through clouds fresh from the Pacific. They will evaporate as the wind carries them east into sagebrush country. Crook Mountain, forming the far wall of Napeequa Valley, still glistens from sunlight on steep clean snow, but the valley floor has started its annual warm-up and dry-out. Fern fiddleheads soft and green are starting to unfurl. The river, full of snowmelt, growls through the gorge. We head up a squishy trail that clings to the canyon side.

We are entering Glacier Peak Wilderness, which straddles the crest between Stevens Pass and North Cascades National Park. From their south end in California, the Cascades are volcanic all the way up through Oregon—a landscape of lava, basalt, and snow-

3

covered cones. These volcanoes march up into Washington, pushing up smartly every forty to sixty miles. But the range takes on a new character here near its northern end. Indeed, it is almost two distinct ranges. One is composed of high, isolated volcanoes—Adams, St. Helens, Rainier, Glacier, and Baker. The other is a jagged uplift of granite, gneiss, and schist that forms a tangle of sharp peaks, hanging ice, and roadless valleys. The orderly march of volcanoes turns, like a plan that fell apart, into mayhem in this wildest, most rugged part of the Northwest.

Flat lands depress me. As a lad in southwest Virginia, I loved the Alleghenies. A summer job brought me west and introduced me to these Cascades. Since then, despite my complaints about gray Northwest winters, I have never wanted to live anywhere else. For thirty years, Wendy has been tramping these mountains with me. They will never be as dear to her as the coastline of her native Australia, but she has come to appreciate my Cascades as much as I now enjoy her beaches.

We pass through the canyon gateway into Napeequa Valley. How quickly we transition from roads and ranches to a wild, hidden valley. It is as if we entered a cathedral off a busy street. Our trail is now the only mark of man, an aisle cushioned with needles through living columns of cedar and fir. As we pad along, both we and the river are hushed.

At a spot where trillium bloom under maples that are just starting to leaf, we turn away from the river and switchback up toward Twin Lakes. Here in the shade of conifers, crunchy snow covers our path. Sprinkled with dead fir needles like chocolate flakes on a white cake, it shows few tracks. We are among the first to visit the lakes this spring.

We circle close to the lower lake and reenter dark forest for our final climb. Fifteen minutes later we emerge from the shade on a carpet of needles into a vista that is quintessential Cascades—a long, dark lake filling a V-shaped valley, rimmed by slopes that rise in near-symmetry. The Rockies look more rugged because they are bare and exposed; the Cascades conceal their secrets under a dark blanket of trees. An unbroken canopy of conifers grows from lakeshore up two-thirds of each slope, then splits into vertical strings of trees that mark the edges of avalanche chutes. Above those, both ridges tilt up to rock and ice. This is the kind of scene that sells Sierra Club calendars.

The lake is glass-smooth except for a breeze stirring ripple patches, like wispy clouds crossing the face of the moon. We are gazing at what is left of the old Napeequa River. In this part of the North Cascades, this is the inner sanctum. In another month Twin Lakes could be crowded. They're not that far, nor that hard to reach. Yet, by pushing the season, today we are alone.

We look for a place to sit and savor the view over lunch. Like most mountain lakes, the outlet is clogged with floating gray logs, the remains of trees that fell into the lake and drifted down to its mouth. We hop these bleached bones, less confident than youngsters on a railroad track, looking for the right spot. Close to water's edge, we settle on one, shed packs, and sit down. I start rummaging for a sandwich. Wendy is scanning uplake with her binoculars. I have just taken my first bite when she says in a quiet, urgent voice, "There's a bear!"

"Where?" I ask. I stop chewing.

"It's really big!"

"Where?" I repeat.

"Right over there," she replies, pointing with one hand as she keeps the glasses to her eyes with the other.

I've put down my sandwich and start digging in my pack for the other binoculars. As I dig, I look where she's pointing. I don't need binoculars to see it. A big tawny bear has stepped out of the brush onto a grassy point just around a curve in the lakeshore from us. It is less than a football field away.

Now we are both staring through binoculars, speaking in semi-whispers.

The bear is grazing on new plants growing lush along the shore. If our noses were as good as the bear's, we would smell it. The breeze is blowing from the bear toward us. Otherwise, it certainly would have heard or sensed us.

My first reaction is awe—such a big wild animal! It is bigger than any black bear I have ever seen, and I have seen many. Awe turns quickly into a sense of nakedness. Because of the curving shore, there is water between us and the bear. But around that shore the only thing separating us is an alder patch, which would slow down a bear about as much as traffic cones would slow down a runaway truck. I don't know what the bear might do if it saw us, and I don't know where we would go if it did.

As vulnerable as I feel, I start to study the animal. That is my nature. More than once something has startled me in the woods, but I always regained my wits and reverted to my analytical self. I notice that the bear's fur is thick but mangy, as if it had just come out of hibernation and started trying to rub off a winter coat. I suspect it's a grizzly because of its size and color, but I'm not sure. The bear is the tawny color common with grizzlies, yet I see no silver glisten to its outer fur and no distinct hump across its shoulders. That is supposed to be a grizzly's giveaway. Maybe because of the way it is standing, or because of its heavy fur, its hump isn't so obvious. Besides, as I say to Wendy in a hushed voice when the bear lifts its head, "Look at that distinct forehead. No black bear has a face and eyebrow like that."

I know black bears can be tawny too—in fact we've seen some— but lighter colored black bears are usually in drier country.[2] We are on the dry side of the Cascades, but still close enough to the crest that the habitat here is much like the west side, too wet for such a light-colored black bear. And it's so big, and it doesn't have the baleful, straight face of a black bear.

After explaining all this to Wendy, I declare, "I think it's a grizzly." Saying that gives me a shiver.

The bear grazes on around the point, moving away. To improve our line of sight, we need to move to our right, away from the bear but across the outlet of the lake. With glances over our shoulders, we hop logs, turn to look, hop some more, look some more, until finally the bear is completely out of sight.

My pulse still pumps. We almost tiptoe back to our packs. The view has not changed—the breeze is still pushing ripples down the lake, the snow-topped ridges still guard the valley. The quintessential Cascades scene looks the same. But that itself is disquieting, for now we know this scene also includes a huge primeval presence. It may look the same, but it is different. We have heard for some time that grizzlies may still inhabit the Cascades, but we have been all through these mountains and never seen one. Until today, grizzly bears were like spirits. We longed to see one, but until we did, we could not be sure what was fantasy and what might be real.

Now, as we forgo lunch, pack up, and start down the trail, we watch and look. Our heads jerk at every sound. No longer do these mountains seem so familiar. Something big and strong has been here much longer, knows this land better, and is still here. The Cascades seem taller and more lonely, the gorge deeper and darker, and the river more thunderous. That big bear has added a wild dimension to this landscape. We see it with new eyes.

Lee Stream, biologist for the Washington Department of Fish and Wildlife, calls me from his Yakima office. He has just returned from Upper Twin Lake, where he went to investigate my report. Instead of hiking up through the gorge as we did, he and a colleague entered the valley from the far end of the lake. Stream has both a Forest Service key to a locked gate and a boat, which gives him quicker access to the place I tried to describe over the phone.

"That's good bear habitat," Stream starts. He tells me about the plentiful horsetails and cow parsnip, two spring delicacies if you're a bear.

"Bears den high up on the mountain," he says. "When they come out in the spring," he explains, "the males head downhill right away, looking for new plants." The mothers with cubs stay around their den several more weeks, he says, because they need to avoid the males. "The females don't come down till the brush in the avalanche chutes starts to green up."

"I think I found the point on the shore that you described," he says. "There were plenty of bear tracks, but I didn't find any grizzly tracks."

He explains that a Forest Service crew in the area a week earlier had seen "a big cinnamon-colored black bear."

"Do you think that was it?" I ask, somewhat sheepishly.

"Maybe," Stream replies. After a pause, he adds, "I didn't see any grizzly tracks, but I won't say it wasn't a grizzly."

I thank him for calling. We hang up. I wonder if he added that last point mainly to make me feel better. I wonder if he actually found the same spot on the lakeshore where we saw the big bear. My report will go in the state record of grizzly sightings as a class 3. Class 1 is definitely a grizzly; class 2 is probably. Class 3 means it could be either a black bear or a grizzly, but there is not enough evidence to say. I am glad my sighting was not graded class 4—definitely not a grizzly.

I would like to think it was a grizzly. At the time, I was mostly scared, but now I remember what a majestic animal it was. Bragging rights are not important, but I feel it would be a privilege to see such a symbol of the wild and know, for a moment, that I shared space in a wild place with that awesome animal.

It would be a privilege or it was a privilege? Just how privileged can I feel about seeing something when I'm not even sure what I saw? Lee Stream won't say it wasn't a grizzly, and I take some comfort in that, but he won't say it was. I sense some of the frustration of Jon Almack, the biologist who led the fieldwork on grizzlies in the Cascades, who set bait, traps, and cameras in an effort to capture or photograph a grizzly and prove to all the skeptics that, yes, they are still here. His cameras snapped photos of surprised black bears, coyotes, raccoons, even cows, but no grizzlies.

Scientists suspect that ten to twenty grizzlies still live in the Cascades. They base this mostly on class 1 and 2 "sightings"—which are more about tracks, hair, and scat than actually seeing bears— plus the historic presence of grizzlies and the abundance of good bear habitat.

Ten to twenty bears in a sea of mountains the size of Maryland! No wonder Wendy and I, even though we regularly tramp trails and scan hillsides with binoculars, have not seen a grizzly before. They are like ghosts, relics of a past age, slipping through the shadows beyond our consciousness, sticking to valleys without trails, living out their days in loneliness.

Officially, America is committed to saving its grizzly bears. In the Lower 48, they are listed under the Endangered Species Act, entitled to protection, and the subject of a federal recovery program. Yet Americans remain ambivalent about this effort. Grizzlies, after all, are wild and dangerous.

This book chronicles the effort—always contentious—to recover or restore elusive populations of grizzlies in the North Cascades and Northern Rockies. Once the stuff of legends throughout the American West, the grizzly bear is now, in the words of *National Geographic,* "cornered," lurking in wild pockets of its former range.[3] The wild Cascades of Washington and British Columbia are one of only a handful of places the great bear still has and the only one in the lower 48 states outside of the Rockies.

The Cascades lag the farthest behind of all the grizzly recovery efforts on America's agenda. For this reason they illustrate most of the challenges and frustrations that face the entire recovery effort. The Cascades are the wrinkled old-timer who can say with the experience of years, "I've seen nearly everything."

These Northwest mountains have also been a stepchild to grizzly bear recovery elsewhere. They symbolize a broader debate over national priorities—a debate that has taken a paradigm shift away from wildlife in the past decade. With too little money to go around, officials play God and choose where and what to save and where they need to show success.

This book reviews the status of grizzly bear recovery throughout the West, but starts with the North Cascades because they typify most of what the grizzly wars are about. And wars they clearly are. Chris Servheen, grizzly coordinator for the US Fish and Wildlife Service, describes them with the voice of a veteran: "Conservation is like warfare. Without a strategic and proactive approach, a management program [for grizzly bears] continuously responds to ongoing conservation threats. Such a defensive and reactive approach is doomed to failure. To quote Napoleon, 'The only logical end to defensive warfare is surrender.'"[4]

PART 1
HISTORY AND HABITAT

1 | AN END TO THE KILLING

When comic strip character Frank asks his ne'er-do-well partner what he means by "making progress," Ernest proudly replies that "I've slowed down the rate at which I'm falling behind." By this measure, progress for grizzly bears in the North Cascades started at an improbable place called Fisher Creek Basin. You can see it from Easy Pass—either a misnomer as a place or someone's idea of a joke. From the 6,500-foot summit of this tough scramble, you can peer down the west side, hard under the flank of Mount Logan, into the wild valley of Fisher Creek. Talus slides and avalanche chutes scar its sides. At the head of this steep valley, under the corner where Ragged Ridge and the crest of the range join, lies Fisher Creek Basin, the Cascades monument to grizzly bears.

When the North Cascades highway was still a mere gleam in an engineer's eye, Fisher Creek Basin was in the wild heart of the North Cascades, twenty miles from road's end. To reach it in September 1967, Rocky and Lenora Wilson drove up through the Skagit River gorge, a foreboding gateway into the high country. On the shore of Diablo Lake they unloaded horses, loaded packs, and disappeared into the dark forest heading up Thunder Creek. When they left their truck, they already were deep in the mountains.

Shadowy forests enveloped them like an eight-mile foyer into a dark cathedral. Where Fisher Creek joins Thunder Creek, they stopped for the night. Next morning they broke camp and turned east up Fisher Creek. Twelve miles later, the Wilsons reached the valley head. From truck to basin, they had climbed three thousand feet from a deep mossy forest to a brush-and-boulder basin ringed with rock walls. Fisher Creek Basin is one of those holes typical of the west Cascades—deep, flat-bottomed, and enclosed by cliffs.

Rocky and Lenora were no strangers to this country. They lived off this land, prospecting, hunting, and fishing. They worked a pick-and-shovel silver mine on the Cascade River. For forty years they had packed into places like this. Fisher Creek Basin was a favorite during the "high hunt," when deer season opened in the high country ahead of anywhere else.

The Wilsons had set up camp, built a fire, and were watching the sunset burn the top of Ragged Ridge a bright orange. Just as a commercial fisherman still marvels at the sea, the Wilsons, who made their hardscrabble living from the hills, were comfortably settled into camp enjoying the evening glow. It was already dusk in the basin. Lenora was about to start supper when they saw a big bear, seemingly unaware of them, come ambling out of the brush on the far side of the creek. In an instant, the Wilsons stopped admiring scenery and reverted to their more prosaic reason for being there.

Rocky grabbed his rifle, already loaded, took aim in the fading light, and fired. The rifle roared; the horses jerked back on their ties; the bear dropped. While the sound of gunshot echoed back and forth across the basin, Rocky and Lenora stood for a moment and watched. Then, with rifle ready, he cautiously approached. That was when he first noticed that the bear lying in a heap before him had the big shoulders and frosty coat of a grizzly.

Events sometimes earn their significance from what happens after them, as when explorers later proved that Christopher Columbus had not discovered the coast of Asia. Shooting a bear was not especially significant to Rocky Wilson. It became significant for reasons he had no way to foresee. More than a century had passed since a surveyor named Henry Custer had shot a grizzly in the western foothills of the Cascades. Between then and Fisher Creek Basin, white men had orchestrated a massacre. Rocky Wilson could not have known that he would be the last of them to kill a grizzly in the Cascades.

Since then, hunters elsewhere in the West have killed other grizzlies, usually by mistake or in self-defense. But no human has killed another grizzly in the Cascades of Washington or British Columbia since that evening. The echo of Rocky Wilson's rifle ricocheting off the walls of Fisher Creek Basin was a requiem for all those bears who had died.

The Wilsons skinned their bear, packed it out, and reported the kill. Grizzlies were rare, but there was no law against shooting them. Ellis Bowhay, state game official, measured the hide at six feet ten inches, nose to tail. One left front claw measured 3.25 inches. The Wilsons took the hide to Morgan's Taxidermy in Yakima for tanning, then showed it around local schools. It ended up on display at a sports shop in Mount Vernon, Washington.

A year after Rocky Wilson shot his grizzly, Congress created North Cascades National Park. That ended hunting in Fisher Creek Basin. Four years later, the North Cascades highway opened. Instead of a twenty-mile hike, Fisher Creek Basin is now only a one-day scramble over Easy Pass. Even so, gazing down from that high vantage, you can imagine why a grizzly bear seeking a redoubt deep in the Cascades might pick Fisher Creek Basin.

A year after the North Cascades highway opened, President Nixon signed a bill with far broader implications for wildlife than the one creating a national park. It was the Endangered Species Act.[1] At first few realized its potential. Under this new law, the US Fish and Wildlife Service listed the grizzly bear as "threatened" in the lower 48 states on July 28, 1975. For starters, that made killing a grizzly, except in self-defense, a federal crime.

A ban on killing does not equal recovery, but it is a big first step. From the bear's perspective, it was the first step in the right direction for nearly two hundred years.

Up to one hundred thousand grizzlies once roamed western North America. Their homeland stretched from the Great Plains west to the Pacific Ocean, from the Yukon south to Mexico's Sierra Madre. Grizzlies thrived on the rolling prairies east of the Rocky

Map 1. Historical grizzly bear range

Mountains, in the valleys carved into the Rockies, and in the mountains themselves.

They did not care so much for the intermountain desert,[2] but they thrived in the Sierra Nevada and Cascades. West of these ranges, California grizzlies roamed free in the grasslands and chaparral within sight of the sea. In the Northwest, bears congregated around salmon streams, but they did not like the rain forests of the western Cascades or Pacific Coast. For that reason they avoided Washington's Olympic Peninsula and British Columbia's Vancouver Island.[3] Apart from those preferences, the smart and adaptable brown bear was equally at home in grasslands, river bottoms, ridgetops, and alpine meadows.

Grizzlies have been here for fifty thousand years—before, during, and after the last Ice Age. They walked across the Bering Strait land bridge from Asia, where they were part of a larger brown bear family.[4] Today that family includes a remnant population in northern Japan,[5] the brown bear of Eurasia, whose range spans Eurasia from Siberia to Scandinavia, and two subspecies within central and western Europe.[6] A North African subspecies was wiped out a century ago.[7] Our North America emigrant also evolved into two subspecies—the giant Kodiak bear, which lives on Kodiak, Shuyak, and Afognak islands off the coast of Alaska, and the mainland grizzly bear.[8] Some evidence also suggests that polar bears are an offshoot from grizzlies or their Asian cousins.

In the centuries after the first humans reached North America, man and grizzly reached something of a truce. In the Northwest the views of Native Americans toward the bear varied with the tribe. The fish-eating Nooksack along the coast revered all land animals. The plateau tribes east of the Cascades hunted, fished, and occasionally killed grizzlies. Like other tribes of the Mountain West, however, they held the grizzly in high esteem and prepared for any hunt with ceremony.

Native Americans viewed killing a grizzly as different from the routine slaying of other animals for food or hide. It was almost a religious rite. Hunters used special weapons. They spoke to the bear before killing it. They spoke to its spirit after killing it. They skinned and dressed the carcass with much ceremony. They prepared and ate the meat according to strict ritual. They viewed the bear as having sacrificed itself, and its spirit as having returned to a special place. According to legend, women especially could morph into grizzly bears and vice versa. The relationship between Native Americans and grizzly bears was steeped in symbolism and respect.[9]

Thirteen thousand years of coexistence ended when Europeans reached the Northwest by land. The first to do so was David Thompson and his North West Fur Company brigade. In 1800 he crossed the Rockies into what is now British Columbia and began to explore the region for its fur-trading potential. Four years later, Lewis and Clark started west to investigate America's Louisiana Purchase.

These explorers had no comprehension of grizzlies. Stumbling through strange country, they often surprised the great bears at close range. Foolishly, they even chased them. Some grizzlies instinctively charged, and the explorers instinctively shot. Clark wrote in his journal, "These bear being so hard to die rather intimadates us all. I must confess that I do not like the gentlemen."[10] In one confrontation, two members of his group leaped off a cliff into a river to escape a charging grizzly. The bear finally died from eight rifle balls. The killing had started.

Within a decade, it had been commercialized. Three fur companies from St. Louis set up dozens of trading posts along the Missouri River and its tributaries. Overland caravans bearing furs would rendezvous with boats to haul their loads downriver to St. Louis. Beavers attracted trappers as far south as New Mexico and west to the Sacramento and San Joaquin rivers of California. They even trapped golden beavers in the deltas of San Francisco Bay.[11] Fur traders and trappers were the first white explorers in much of the West, finding the routes later followed by wagon trains of emigrants.

Within the Northwest, two British and one US company competed to build posts and trade in furs. By 1810 the Astorians (US) had built trading posts or forts at the mouth of the Columbia River and at the junction of the Columbia and Okanogan rivers. The British companies merged under the Hudson's Bay name, and built posts at

Vancouver, Nisqually, Colville, Walla Walla (called Fort Nez Perce), and on the Thompson River at what later became Kamloops. At that stage, there was no boundary delineating what was British or American. The Northwest was a commercial free-for-all.

Fur trading everywhere relied on Native Americans to do the dirty work. They already knew the animals. It was a lot easier for them to hunt, trap, skin, and pack furs to the trading post. Except for a few "mountain men," the Europeans mainly stocked the trading goods and shipped the furs away. This business was mostly about beavers, but no fur-bearing animal was exempt. Mink, fisher, muskrat, lynx, deer, elk, and bears were all fair game.

Fur trading introduced tribes, attracted by strange and wonderful goods, to materialism. In contrast to the swap meet or potlatch, which natives had known for generations, the trading post must have seemed like a fully stocked Wal-Mart.

"We did not inherit this land from our forefathers; we have borrowed it from our children," goes an old Native American saying. The fur trade replaced this ethic with a concept of nonsustainable use. The land's abundance had rarely been an issue before.[12] But the more pelts you took to the trading post, the more goods you could bring home. It was a new economy. In his pioneering account of the fur trade, Hiram Chittenden observes: "By far the larger part of the fur was taken by the Indians and came into possession of the traders only by exchange. . . . From this starting point the two races gradually came into closer contact until finally the Indian became dependent upon his white brother, relinquishing little by little his former way of life, acquiring new wants, becoming corrupted by new vices, and drifting insensibly into that intricate relationship with the United States government."[13]

Whatever the effect of fur trading on Native Americans, its effect on wildlife was like the Holocaust. In a tide of destruction, tribes began to wipe out local wildlife. As the idea caught fire, they exploited an animal community they had lived beside for longer than legends.

No more ceremonies and talking to spirits. The fur trade knocked grizzlies off their pedestal. Chittenden writes, "The fur of the grizzly bear did not have high value, although it was generally saved, as opportunity afforded, and sent to market."[14]

In the Northwest, grizzly killing on the west side of the Cascades was light because there were so few bears to kill. But in the drier, savannah-like country east of the mountains, the story was different. Okanogan, Methow, Spokane, and Nez Perce tribes became proficient bear hunters. Between 1827 and 1859 three Hudson's Bay posts in what was later Washington and one in what was later British Columbia shipped 3,788 grizzly bear hides.[15] Fort Okanogan, operated by the Astorians, left no records. But one can estimate from Fort Colville's records that Fort Okanogan, which occupied similar terrain, had only a slightly lower intake of grizzly hides than Fort Colville. If so, the number of grizzly skins delivered to all the forts around the Cascades would have been about four thousand. Four thousand grizzly bears killed in three decades!

Fur traders left no record of where bears died, but we can generally tell based on which posts shipped the hides and what we know about the country around them. Perhaps 15 to 20 percent of those four thousand grizzlies came from the North Cascades region ringed by the Columbia and Okanogan rivers on its east and the Similkameen and Fraser rivers on the north.

Bears in the river bottoms would have died first. Those closest to humans were most vulnerable. Because of better habitat, they were also the biggest. The survivors were the ones lucky, smart, or shy enough to hide in the hills. From an original population of perhaps a thousand grizzlies in the Cascades and the valleys around those mountains, by 1860 only 350 or so survived.

Elsewhere in the West the story was much the same. Bears died from surprise encounters with fur trappers perhaps as often as from outright hunting. A Rocky Mountain trapper named George C. Yount claimed, "I have often killed as many as five or six [grizzlies] in one day."[16]

Fur trading declined as tensions grew between Native Americans and Europeans. As waves of white people kept coming into the land, tribes felt more threatened. In sight of Oregon's Blue Mountains, a band of Cayuse in 1847 lost patience, attacked, and destroyed the Whitman mission, signaling a start to open warfare. For the next decade, Northwest wildlife gained a reprieve while humans were busy hunting and killing each other.[17] When the smoke and bloodshed ended, the victorious whites relocated the Indian survivors to reservations, and Henry Custer, a surveyor for the United States–Canada boundary, became the first white man to report killing a grizzly in what later became Washington State. He shipped its hide back to the Smithsonian Institute.

The fur trade never rebounded. Instead, the end of the Indian Wars brought a new breed of men to the West. Mining started along Washington's Skagit River in the 1860s, and word spread that the Cascades contained gold. That brought a throng of new and different people. Makeshift and often temporary towns sprang up. As reports or rumors of gold strikes circulated, prospectors dashed from one place to another. By the mid-1890s more people lived in the Cascades than ever before or since. Only word of the Klondike gold strike in Alaska emptied the mountains.

Log cabins with caved-in roofs and rusty machinery still commemorate the era of the prospector. They left names all over the landscape, ranging from the lovelorn Big Bosom Buttes to the whimsical Three Fools Peak. Bears were a common theme—Big Bear Mountain, Silver Tip Peak, Bears Breast Mountain. Thanks to the prospectors, we now have Grizzly Mountains, Grizzly Peaks, and Grizzly Creeks all over the Cascades and Northern Rockies.

Unlike the fur trade, which concentrated in the valleys and foothills, the search for mother lodes lured prospectors into the high country. Some of these miners were locals, but most were like "Mighty" Joe Morovits, a legendary figure in the Mount Baker area, of whom it was said, "As with many miners of his time, no one seemed to know how he came to the Pacific Northwest nor where he went when he left."[18] Miners left few records of their encounters with bears, but one can imagine what happened when well-armed fortune seekers entered grizzly country. Based on population estimates before and after the mining era, prospectors in the Cascades probably killed about two hundred grizzlies.

The echoes of prospectors had faded, the grizzly was almost a ghost, and a forlorn Native American was trying to sell an orphaned cub on the streets of Olympia before bear killings attracted much notice. The first sign of concern came in 1892, when residents of Chelan became upset about the shooting of local grizzlies and mountain goats by eastern and European sportsmen.[19]

Yet one final wave of killing was still to come. Mostly it was to make the world safe for domestic sheep. The US government opened much of the Northern Rockies and eastern Cascades to grazing in the earlier 1900s. By the 1920s sheepherders and the packers who supplied their camps had taken over the alpine meadows and declared war on all predators.

Grizzlies are not efficient predators. They are not designed to run down long-legged deer and elk. In the hunt for protein, bears are more opportunistic. They focus on fish, newborn ungulates, and winter kill—none of which move very fast. Sheep can run too, but they lack the survival smarts of their wild cousins.

For bears, wolves, and coyotes, introduced sheep were too easy. The flocks were like a moving feast. Sheep also brought diseases that wiped out other native prey, such as bighorn sheep, and left predators more dependent on imported meat. Sheepherders preferred the high plateaus with open meadows, which were also prime grizzly habitat. The result was inevitable.

Sheepmen might have worried more about other losses. A 1921 Forest Service study of 11 sheep outfits in the Cascades reported that out of 30,000 sheep, bears killed only 35. Wolves and coyotes killed 60, 150 sheep died from eating the wrong plants, and 500 simply "strayed."[20] Yet the government sided with stockmen against the bears. During the 1920s predator control hunters hired by the federal government shot some of the largest grizzlies. Pete Peterson, a government hunter, killed a grizzly near Hart's Pass that weighed 1,350 pounds. Three years later someone found bigger tracks in the same area. The biggest was probably a 1,400-pound grizzly shot in the early 1940s by a hunter in Horseshoe Basin.[21]

Between 1900 and 1960, thirty-five grizzly killings were recorded in the Cascades. All but three were on the US side of the border. A dozen were killed in the 1920s, four in the 1930s, five in the 1940s, and ten (including three in Canada) in the 1950s.

During World War II, workers built an emergency airstrip in the Pasayten Wilderness. Some Methow Valley residents recall that men on that project shot a number of grizzlies they never reported. The Cascades grizzly is now extinct, they claim, because the airstrip builders dealt grizzlies the final blow. More likely, it was just another in a series of blows that reduced the bear to where it is today.

The last sheepherder to kill a grizzly did so right before Rocky Wilson packed into Fisher Creek Basin. Olie Anderson shot one while herding sheep south of Hart's Pass. Anderson did not report his kill until a year after the news of Wilson's grizzly. The bear Rocky Wilson shot was the fourth in the 1960s. The following year, 1968, was the first in 157 years when the guns fell silent and no human killed a grizzly bear in the Cascades.

In other parts of the West, where the mountains did not afford such a wild and remote retreat, persecution of grizzlies was more effective. When the shooting stopped in most places, it was only because there were no more bears to shoot.

If we lined up all the maps showing grizzly range in the western United States from 1800 until now, and then flipped through them, it would be like watching a slow-motion movie of melting ice. Grizzly range started as a solid sheet, broke into pieces, and then each piece began to shrink.

Texas killed its last grizzly with a pack of fifty-two dogs in 1890. By the start of the twentieth century, the last grizzly was gone from the Great Plains. Nevada's final one died in 1907. In 1922 a rancher shot the last of California's great bears—prompting some recent suggestions that California replace the grizzly on its state flag with a sports utility van. A year later, a sheepherder killed Old Ephraim, Utah's last grizzly. Boy Scouts later built a monument to him in Logan Canyon. In 1931 a government trapper killed the last grizzly in Oregon's Wallowa Mountains, hard against Hells Canyon and the Washington State border. The last of the great bears in Arizona and New Mexico were shot in 1933 and 1935.[22]

Unconfirmed reports of other grizzlies trickled in after these killings, but they gradually died out as any survivors themselves died out. Only in Colorado's San Juan Mountains have reports of grizzlies persisted since the last one was supposedly shot in 1979.[23] But even those are fading.[24]

Outright killing makes the news, but habitat loss and fragmentation can bring delayed extinction—a lag between the destruction of habitat and an animal's actual extinction.[25] Railroads and the fires they sparked, logging and the roads it built, dams and the salmon they blocked all worked against the grizzly. Today only fragments of grizzly country remain, mostly along the Canadian border. Within the coterminous United States, the grizzly's range has shrunk from 1.5 million square miles to 32,000.[26] Less than 2 percent of the grizzly population today survives on 2 percent of its former range.

Bruce McLellan, British Columbia's most senior bear biologist, worries that the southern edge of this range keeps creeping north. He writes: "Because people settle, farm, and build roads and railroads in the valleys, the southern fringe of brown bear range is gradually becoming a series of islands isolated from each other. . . . Human development in bear habitat operates like a ratchet; it tightens in stages but has little ability to slacken."[27] The Cascades and Yellowstone now mark the southern end of grizzly bear range. Will they halt their withdrawal here in these wild mountains or, like the melting edge of a glacier, keep retreating north?

Substitute Canadian lynx, timber wolf, or woodland caribou for grizzly bear and the story is much the same. Humans came and killed, randomly or systematically. We took the best habitat as our own. We fragmented what was left, separating remnant populations into subgroups too small to survive on their own. We introduced livestock and pets and then justified more killing to protect them. Even now that we realize the consequences, some of us resist change because change would make things harder, more expensive, less consistent with our own needs. Quietly, the subgroups start to wink out.

This is extinction while we watch. The story of the grizzly differs from the others only because the great bear makes it harder for itself by placing greater demands on us.

2 | A TENTATIVE START

One afternoon a fisherman watched the weather change. All morning a raw wind had blown in from the southwest, churning the water angry and dark, dragging in a parade of low clouds. But early in the afternoon he felt the wind ease. Then suddenly it stopped. For a quarter of an hour all was calm. No clouds moved; the water surface turned to glass. Then, just as suddenly, the wind started again—but this time out of the north. It blew just as consistently—if not as hard—as it had earlier from almost the opposite direction. Within another half hour the clouds had blown away, the water was sparkling blue, the afternoon was warm and sunny. In that fifteen-minute calm, everything had recalibrated and set off on a new course.

The same thing happened with grizzly bears in the mid-1970s. For over a hundred years, grizzlies had been chased, trapped, poisoned, and shot. Their habitat was in shambles and their population dwindling when the federal government adopted the Endangered Species Act in December 1973. The act was intended "to provide a means whereby the ecosystems upon which endangered species and threatened species depend may be conserved, to provide a program for the conservation of those endangered species and threatened species, and to take such steps as may be appropriate" to make it happen. It defined an endangered species as one "in danger of extinction throughout all or a significant portion of its range." A threatened species was one "likely to become an endangered species within the foreseeable future."

The US Fish and Wildlife Service, designated for the lead role with land species,[1] took its first tentative steps under this new law by compiling lists of endangered and threatened species. In July 1975, it designated the grizzly bear in the lower 48 states as a "threatened" species. It was here that the calm ended and the wind started to blow from a new direction.

Grizzly recovery began in the Northern Rockies. The Fish and Wildlife Service designated recovery areas in Yellowstone, the Northern Continental Divide area around Glacier National Park, the Cabinet-Yaak Mountains in northwest Montana, and the Selkirks, which straddle the border between Idaho and the northeast corner of Washington. Grizzlies still lived in all these areas, and all these areas were predominantly federal lands—either national parks or forests.

The Fish and Wildlife Service was comfortable with the idea of recovery areas for grizzlies. It had used this approach to manage other wildlife, notably through its network of wildlife refuges. It was comfortable with the concept.

Outside government, others argued that the idea of specific recovery areas for grizzlies was thinking too small. Recovery areas focused too much on isolated islands of habitat, they claimed, and ignored bears outside those islands. Even if grizzlies "recovered" within one area, they would still be cut off genetically from bears in other areas. Grizzlies needed bigger areas with safe corridors between them so they could move from one place to another.[2]

Biologically these critics were right, but Fish and Wildlife officials did not feel they had the clout to make the wholesale changes in land use and ownership needed to transform ranches and commercial forests into bear preserves with linkage zones between them. The government had to deal with conditions as it found them and spend its resources where it had the best chance of success.

Besides, the Endangered Species Act had been a delicate compromise. Skeptical conservatives in Congress had succeeded in limiting funding to three-year intervals so they could keep tabs on it. Those congressmen were not about to turn a federal agency loose to roll back the clock in favor of plants and animals. To play it safe, the Fish and Wildlife Service decided to stick with its recovery area idea and pick areas that were already federally managed and mostly roadless. That way, recovery wouldn't upset too many applecarts.

Officials insisted that the goal would still be to recover grizzlies throughout their range, rather than in specific areas. The designated recovery areas would be where this was most likely to happen because of good habitat and focused efforts, but if they managed to restore healthy populations within these core areas, bears would likely disperse into the surrounding country. Even if recovery areas were cut off from each other, a recovered population in one area still might be used to supplement a fragile population in another. In short, recovery areas were intended as pieces in a bigger picture, not as individual pictures on their own.

Having dismissed the criticism of its recovery-area approach, the Fish and Wildlife Service moved on to the issue of whether to consider recovery areas besides the four it had declared. It invited scientists to suggest other areas based on the presence of bears or habitat suitable for them.

A few biologists had already pondered these possibilities. Grizzlies had once lived in Washington's North Cascades, Idaho's Bitterroots, and Colorado's San Juans and maybe still did. All three of these rugged regions seemed the sort of big wild places where the great bear might have evaded detection and survived.

Jonathan Bjorklund, a biologist for North Cascades National Park, was the first to broach the subject publicly. Starting in 1978, he wrote three papers on whether the park and its two adjoining recreation areas could support a grizzly bear population.[3] He focused only on those parts of the Cascades run by the Park Service, but he started the discussion.[4]

A group of biologists and land managers from the state, federal, and provincial agencies around the Cascades met a year later and agreed that bringing grizzly bears back or saving those still there deserved more thought. Similar thoughts circulated among biologists and wildlife managers about Idaho and Colorado. Out of this emerged nominations to consider Washington's North Cascades, Idaho's Bitterroots, and Colorado's San Juans as additional grizzly bear recovery areas.

Map 2. Grizzly bear recovery areas

The San Juans were shelved, perhaps because they were so far removed from all other recovery areas. In 2007 they remain in the recovery plan as an area worthy of study, but no work is planned. It is the same dilemma of priorities—like the committee of doctors who must decide which patient gets the new heart—that comes up all the time in underfunded recovery work. The Fish and Wildlife Service decided to stick with the Northwest, specifically with the Cascades and the Bitterroots.

As the next step, graduate students with Fish and Wildlife Service support and university supervision combed the scientific literature to learn what they could about grizzlies in the Cascades and the Bitterroots. The key questions were how recently grizzlies had lived in these two areas, whether any bears might still survive, and whether there appeared to be enough habitat to warrant more study.

Both the Cascades and Bitterroots were important to the overall strategy of saving grizzlies in the lower 48 states. The four recovery areas already set up in the Rockies were separate from each other, and the Bitterroots could provide a key link between them. If grizzlies returned to the Bitterroots, they might eventually roam back and forth between Yellowstone and the other three recovery areas farther north. Besides being a recovery area itself, the Bitterroots could thus become the type of wildlife corridor that nongovernment advocates urged and government scientists conceded was critical to long-term grizzly survival.

The Bitterroots had one drawback: they were too much like the four other recovery areas. The Bitterroots were part of the Northern Rockies, and bears throughout the Rocky Mountains depended on much the same food. If the whitebark pine, for instance, whose nuts are an important source of high-energy protein and carbohydrates for bears, was killed off by a blister rust or by climate change, all grizzlies in the Rockies would lose an important food source. That made the Cascades, a separate mountain range with its own microclimate and plants, especially important. Indeed, that separateness itself could be valuable.

The new wind that signals a change in directions did not always blow with consistency or speed. The process of deciding how to manage recovery areas and how to evaluate the Bitterroots and Cascades moved like a glacier, partly because the Fish and Wildlife Service was feeling its way along. But it was also trying to work with a jumble of other agencies—the US Forest Service and Park Service, the Bureau of Land Management, and various state agencies. Government land management agencies have their own fiefdoms. The state agencies had chips on their shoulders about the feds usurping them. Every agency guarded its turf like a cougar guards its kill.

To overcome this, in 1983 the Fish and Wildlife Service finally convinced all the agencies to form an umbrella group, the Interagency Grizzly Bear Committee (IGBC). It brought together managers from all the federal agencies plus state wildlife agencies from Idaho, Montana, Washington, and Wyoming. This freed agencies from micromanaging projects and arguing about who should do what. The IGBC, like an international peace process, brought representatives from all the agencies into one room at the same time. If diplomats start by arguing about the shape of the table, early IGBC meetings were marked by posturing over federal versus state control. But once these people came to know each other and realized how much they shared the same goals, they started to think like a group. This was a huge step.

It broke the logjam. In 1984 the IGBC designated both the Bitterroots and North Cascades as evaluation areas. That meant both would be carefully studied to see if they had enough of the right conditions to support grizzlies. In 1985 Fish and Wildlife, the Forest Service, and the Washington State Game Department agreed on a five-year plan, funded mostly by Fish and Wildlife, to evaluate the Cascades. A similar program started in the Bitterroots. After years of delay, the Cascades and Bitterroots seemed poised to start down a track that would add both areas, each critical in its own way, to an overall plan to save the grizzly.

Sixty years earlier, federal hunters were shooting grizzlies in the name of predator control. Now that same government was taking its first tentative steps toward saving the survivors, faced with the challenge of how to reverse a century of antibear sentiment and the question of whether all the king's studies and all the king's men could ever put the habitat together again.

3 | WHO NEEDS IT ANYWAY?

The Endangered Species Act draws only one distinction between "good" and "bad" species: an insect officially designated a "pest" becomes an outcast excluded from protection. All other plants, fish, and wildlife within US jurisdiction are covered.

Though Congress made the policy choice to protect all native plants and animals, good and bad, following Aldo Leopold's advice that "no species can be 'rated' without the tongue in the cheek,"[1] that still does not stop people from arguing about it. Opponents of grizzly bears believe that grizzlies belong in a category of outcasts, along with rattlesnakes and sharks.

The law has no such category, but the debate rolls on, like lawyers vying for the last word. Opponents of grizzly recovery raise a host of arguments, ranging from economic concerns to personal fear, although they often devise proxy arguments for the latter. Naturalists and ecologists counter that grizzlies should be saved. Both sides seem unwilling to give Congress the final say.

Why, then, do grizzlies deserve protection?

We start, improbably, with mountain meadows. Those pleasant meadows full of wildflowers may be a byproduct of a grizzly's attraction to freshly dug glacier lily bulbs. Using those big front claws for their intended purpose—digging and plowing like the shovel on a backhoe—the bears alter the ecology of the meadow. Researchers find higher levels of nitrogen and water-soluble carbohydrates and twice as many seeds as in unplowed meadows.

What would change if grizzlies stopped plowing and those meadows disappeared? A lot, according to biologists. As trees replace grasses, animals that rely on meadows would suffer. "Edge" conditions, which favor species such as deer, would shrink. Researchers claim that grizzlies, in concert with several other species, maintain a mosaic of habitats thanks to their trampling and digging.[2]

Grizzly and black bears are also first-class plant distributors, transporting seeds in their fur and scat. In *Mark of the Grizzly*, Scott McMillion describes Utah bear biologist Barrie Gilbert, who calculates the number of seeds in a bear scat: "His math showed that a big bear can pass four hundred thousand berries through its body in a day, leaving behind it a trail of seeds encased in rich fertilizer."[3] These seed pellets, deposited in the right places, speed the recovery of plants on disturbed soil after a fire or avalanche.

In the same way, where bears still catch fish, they transfer nutrients from stream to forest. A group of Washington State University scientists estimates that grizzlies in the Northwest historically gained up to 90 percent of their carbon and nitrogen from salmon.[4] Their scat deposited these minerals in the right places and in a form more useable by trees.[5] Charlie Robbins, team leader for this research, says: "The gigantic old-growth trees that grew along the river courses that enriched the Northwest were likely produced not only because they were old, but because of the millions of salmon that died in the streams and were eaten by wild animals that then fertilized the trees."[6] The only place this still happens on a large scale is in Alaska and coastal British Columbia, because salmon runs in the Lower 48 have been hard hit.

Grizzlies exert other influences as effective predators of young ungulates. Grizzly bears are often called one of our top predators, "at the top of their food chain," and there are accounts of grizzlies in Yellowstone running down adult elk.[7] But the embarrassing truth is that grizzlies are more scavengers than predators.[8] Elk calves are one of the few ungulates they can catch. In elk country, grizzlies perform the same critical function as other predators in keeping the prey base on its toes and under control.

Cougars are far more efficient predators than bears, and grizzlies know it. A grizzly is not too proud to dine on venison provided compliments of a cougar. Sometimes the bear will simply help itself while the cat is away. More often the grizzly will chase the cougar off and claim the carcass. Occasionally a cougar will try to defend its kill, but that is not a smart thing for a 150-pound cat to do when faced with a 500-pound bear. The wise cougar calculates the odds, lays back its ears in annoyance, and moves on to an area where it can catch and eat its food in peace.[9]

This displacement of one wild animal by another is not widely understood, but bear biologist Jon Almack points out: "Grizzlies will take kill away from a cougar. Grizzlies will kick a black bear out of the best berry patch. Overall, the grizzly pushes rival species to less attractive food sources. But it doesn't displace them entirely unless there's not enough for both."

Studies show that black bears are more affected by grizzlies than by humans. Perhaps that says something about our place in the pecking order. Where grizzlies are active during the day, black bears turn nocturnal. If grizzlies are nocturnal, black bears take the day shift. Black bears stay out of berry patches or fishing streams while grizzlies are feeding. If grizzlies leave an area because of humans, black bears move in.[10]

"Black bears stick to forested landscapes," says another biologist. "In Alaska, if there are no trees, there are no black bears. They need trees to escape from grizzlies." So grizzlies influence the behavior of other mammals, both ungulates and other carnivores. The big bear keeps everyone alert and on the move. The impact is subtle. By stealing food from cougars, do grizzlies limit the number of cougars? Do cougars simply kill more to make up for it? If cougars end up killing to feed both themselves and grizzlies, does that limit the number of deer? Does the grizzly's food poaching encourage cougars to disperse, so that they kill fewer deer in one place? Is the net effect a better predator-prey balance throughout the entire ecosystem? Biologists know some specifics about the influence of grizzlies on their surroundings but almost nothing about these ripple effects.

Bill Noble, a Fish and Wildlife Service biologist, stresses this point: "The Cascades ecosystem evolved for ten to twelve thousand years with grizzlies as a part of it. We weren't able to see it when grizzlies were still a major factor, so we have no before-and-after yardstick to measure change. Moreover, we only see a small slice of the ecosystem.

"The changes may be too subtle for us to detect," Noble cautions. "But any ecosystem that has evolved for as long as the Cascades with grizzlies as a part of it will be different if they disappear."

Jon Almack puts it this way: "We don't know all the ways that the grizzly affects the ecosystem. We only know the bear and the ecosystem evolved together. If we remove the bear, we change the ecosystem in ways we can't understand."

The eastern United States illustrates what can happen. Cougars (regionally called mountain lions or panthers) were wiped out in all but the south tip of Florida and perhaps remote parts of Maine. Not only have deer proliferated to the point of becoming pests, but people have noticed a sharp decline in songbirds. Since cougars rarely bothered songbirds, how could this be? The main reason, it turns out, is that removing the top predator allowed mid-level predators such as raccoons to flourish, and raccoons raid bird nests.[11]

Coyotes assumed an unnatural importance in Yellowstone for a similar reason—elimination of wolves—with similar unexpected results. Bringing back the wolves was not popular with the coyotes, but it helped correct an imbalance that few had foreseen.

When we are short of knowledge, we use shortcuts to fill the gaps between what we know. Biologists still don't understand a lot about the web of life, so they rely on a dominant animal, such as the grizzly, to send signals about the health of lesser things. Then they use labels to describe those signals.

We know that grizzlies require mostly wild conditions. If the bears are doing all right, then it seems likely that a host of other animals and plants who also require wild conditions also are all right. Conversely, if the grizzly is suffering, we can expect these other species to suffer too. We call such a creature an "indicator," because it acts as a shorthand sign of ecosystem health. No self-respecting grizzly would appreciate the analogy, but it acts like the canary in the mine shaft.

Bill Noble notes that some people think the grizzly is not a very good indicator "because it is too much of a generalist." It is true that grizzlies can cover miles and find what they want in everything from an alpine meadow to a river in the rain forest. But Noble argues that this may make the bear an even better indicator than if its needs were more specific. "Because the grizzly is such a wide-roaming generalist," he says, "its survival means that the entire ecosystem is intact."

You can turn this idea around. If we protect enough different types of wildness for the generalist grizzlies, then myriad lesser plants and animals that require only pieces of that bigger wildness will also thrive. Depending on how you look at it, you could say these others ride the grizzly's imaginary coattails, or it holds a big umbrella under which they all fit. The latter metaphor has caught on; the big bear is often called an "umbrella" species because other plants and critters are protected by preserving grizzly habitat.[12] Wolverines, mountain caribou, lynx, pine martens, bull trout, and harlequin ducks all can thank the grizzly for this. They and many other animals survive where it survives. Thanks also from the water howellia and a host of other plants. Botanists say these plants remain because grizzly protection has made their homes off limits to the threats they face in other places.

The reasoning may seem a bit circular, but naturalists claim that a benefit of saving grizzlies is what else is saved with them. Not only does the grizzly umbrella protect many other species, but it also protects the landscape itself. People who have seen grizzlies in the wild recount both fear and awe at being in a place wild enough for such an unreformed animal. For many people, it is very special to live in or near an area that remains wild enough for grizzly bears.[13]

Some argue that protecting wildness brings economic benefits. In *Green-Collar Jobs*, Alan Thein Durning documents how a good environment and proximity to wilderness can boost a local economy: "In the Pacific Northwest, the natural resources that most matter to the economy are no longer the little-processed raw materials but the natural amenities the region offers to high-value industries. . . . [B]usinesses must compete for talented workers as well as markets, and attractive locations give would-be employers a leg up."[14]

Biologist Almack raises a related concern about the durability of wilderness without grizzlies: "The griz is the first line of defense against deterioration of the ecosystem. Take away the wildest, most dangerous creature out there and human expectations change. They come to expect the mountains to be safe. Next, they may want to purge cougars to make the mountains safer, and so it goes."

"So it goes" could someday mean acting on complaints like one left at a trailhead register in the Bridger-Teton National Forest: "The coyotes made too much noise last night and kept me awake. Please eradicate these annoying animals."

🐾 🐾

On British Columbia's central coast, seventeen rivers empty into a long lake. The Wanuk River drains from that lake into Rivers Inlet, part of Queen Charlotte Sound. The twenty-two rundown houses of Oweekeeno Village sit on the river's north shore, inhabited by members of the Oweekeeno tribe, which has resided there as long as anyone knows.

Every fall grizzlies came down from the surrounding hills and passed through this village on their way to the river. Bears and Indians respected each other; neither one bothered the other. It was just an annual event, marking the change of seasons and the return of the sockeye salmon.

But in the fall of 1999 something changed dramatically. Instead of passing through, the grizzlies stayed in town, scavenging around houses, climbing up on porches, clawing at windows. Even the dogs could not scare them off. Villagers did not want to kill the bears, but they could not leave their houses. They had to drive their children to school in cars rather than let them walk. Ultimately they designated one of the men to shoot those grizzlies that were most aggressive. No one was happy about it. The shooting started. School-children cried. By January, long after bears normally would have hibernated, villagers and provincial wildlife officers shot the last of fourteen grizzlies.

What had happened? People can still recall when 3.4 million salmon came to Rivers Inlet. Even within the past five years, 35,000 to 60,000 sockeye showed up—enough to feed bears and villagers alike. In 1999, however, only 3,500 salmon returned to the inlet. To make matters worse, timber companies had clear-cut many of the surrounding hills and sprayed the logged areas with herbicides to keep down the brush—elderberries, salmonberries, huckleberries, the very foods on which bears depend.

The bears were starving. No one knows how many died in the woods, how many failed to awake from hibernation, how many cubs were never born. We only know that a system that had func-tioned for centuries crashed in the blink of an eye. Through over-fishing, warming of coastal waters, overlogging, and herbicide use, man caused an ecosystem to collapse.

And the bears were among the first to go.

Defenders of biodiversity sound like evangelical preachers. We all have heard about the accelerating loss of species—how 20 percent of the world's species will be extinct within the next thirty years and at least half in the decades that follow[15]—and how diversity of life around the world faces a crisis. Most people who think about it sense this is wrong. With varying degrees of philosophical or moral revulsion, they feel frustrated about what they can do individually to stem this tide of death.

Leading a recent nature walk, a park ranger spoke to the group fol-lowing her: "Even if we have to defend biodiversity on cost-benefit grounds," she said, "we should think of it like an insurance policy.

"What if something happened to any of the four grains—wheat, rice, corn, and soybeans—that have fed humans since the dawn of time?" she asked. "If we destroy their wild substitutes, what can we fall back on if our domestic varieties fail?" Is this far-fetched? "Not at all," she said. "Look what happened in Europe, especially Ireland, during the 1840s. Blight wiped out the only type of potato they had. They had no substitutes. Over a million people died."

Northwesterners know that biodiversity is under threat not only in the Amazon. In the Northwest, the salmon crisis grabs the most headlines, but martens, murrelets, fishers, and Canadian lynx have almost disappeared. Perhaps fifty northwestern plants are endangered or threatened. And, of course, there is the grizzly bear.

In the Cascades and Northern Rockies, this leading indicator and umbrella species serves as one of the largest symbols of the biodiversity crisis. The wild Cascades are one of the few places in North America that still contain all their native species.[16] The grizzly is dangerously near to being the first to go.

Environmentalists cite other practical reasons for protecting biodiversity in general and grizzlies in particular. Medical research is eager to learn some of the grizzly's tricks. How, for example, can bears gorge themselves on twenty thousand calories every autumn day to store fat without developing artery or heart trouble? A grizzly's ability to recycle urea filtered from its blood while it hibernates for months could be a lifesaver for kidney patients who now depend on dialysis. Washington State University is studying the cardiac function of captive grizzlies during hibernation for clues that could help heart patients.

We know so little about a natural world that may hold many secret benefits. A decade ago foresters treated the Pacific yew as a weed tree. Then scientists discovered taxol, a cancer-fighting substance in its bark. Dogfish, a lowly shark, contains compounds in its liver that seem to starve cancer tumors by cutting off their blood supply. The saw-scaled pit viper of North Africa is a deadly snake with few fans, but researchers have learned that its lethal venom contains an anticoagulant that the Montreal Heart Institute predicts could save ten thousand lives a year.

The list keeps growing: hormones from lizards that may reduce Lyme disease, a poison from certain spiders that may treat epilepsy, and the immunity of some frogs to mosquitoes. Fifty-seven percent of the 150 most prescribed drugs today have their origins in biodiversity.[17]

In addition to biodiversity, grizzly bears have direct economic benefits. The bottom-line claim is not about gall bladders and bear paws smuggled to Asia as aphrodisiacs, but live bears in the hills chomping on cow parsnip and berries, fishing in streams, tearing up logs, chasing elk, and just being bears. In the economy of the new West, proponents say, ecotourism means money, and bear watching is a booming business.

It always has been big business around Yellowstone and Glacier national parks and in the parks along the Canadian Rockies. Every year millions of people visit these parks hoping to see a big bear. Some pay $500 to spend two days with biologists spying on grizzlies in Yellowstone and the Grand Tetons.

More than thirteen thousand camera-touting tourists watch grizzlies from an elevated platform each year at Brooks Camp in Alaska's Katmai National Park, not far from where Timothy Treadwell kept his dubious and mortal vigil with local grizzlies. Environmentalists and politicians are at odds over whether the number of visitors poses a threat to the bears. At McNeil River, more than two thousand applicants apply each year for 250 permits awarded by lottery to watch grizzlies at what has become a world-renowned site.

Entrepreneurs see money in bear watching. British Columbia's Knight Inlet Lodge, reached only by float plane, is one of the latest. The seventy-year-old lodge used to be a fishermen's hangout, but guests took such an interest in the local bears that the lodge built some elevated viewing stands along the Glendale River, where grizzlies come to fish. Now a growing crowd of visitors comes just to watch the bears. With only twenty rooms, the lodge is packed every autumn during the bears' fishing season. Through word of mouth and the Internet, many Europeans have discovered the lodge. Bear watching has mostly replaced fishing.

In the northernmost inlet of British Columbia's coast, BC Parks has agreed with local natives not to advertise Khutzeymateen Provincial Park for fear of what crowds would do. But the word is out about this off-the-beaten-track valley. Visitors pay C$1,000 per person to drift quietly in boats through the estuary, where grizzly bears come to feed.

On Alaska's Kenai Peninsula, outfitters operate a tent compound called the Great Alaska Bear Camp. Visitors pay anywhere from $350 to $4,500 for a safari-style adventure where they watch grizzlies fish and graze along Chinitna Bay.

With more than forty ecotourism companies advertising bear watching in British Columbia, guides are complaining that grizzly hunting is hurting their business. Dale Roberts, a member of the Campbell River Indian Band, which is working on plans to bring animal watchers into two local lodges, told a Vancouver newspaper, "Bears are worth a lot more alive than dead."[18]

The Alaska Department of Fish and Game did a study in 1992 on how much money people spend on bears. Surprisingly, they found that Alaskans spend more to see bears than to hunt them. On trips taken primarily to view bears, locals spent a total of $29 million, compared to $4 million for hunting. Nonresident bear hunters, the trophy hunters, spent $17 million. The survey did not count how much nonresident bear watchers spend, but it did find that Alaskans are willing to spend more money to see brown bears than any other wildlife.[19] Watching Alaskan bears has become popular enough to justify its own guidebook.[20]

≈ ≈

Ecosystem and economic reasons for preserving grizzlies are easier to measure than intangible benefits. But just as a company's good will may be worth more than its physical assets, the greatest value of grizzlies may lie in one intangible benefit: the challenge they pose.

As a group of Canadian biologists writes: "In the end, grizzly bears may prove to be the ultimate challenge in whether humans can coexist with nature."[21]

Man and the grizzly share power. Man is capable of destroying the grizzly by destroying its habitat. But if the two meet by chance in the wild and the human is unarmed, the grizzly has the upper hand. In their own ways, man and bear are capable of destroying each other. In this sense they are equals. Some people have a problem with that. Others see it as a virtue. As Doug Peacock, the high priest of grizzly advocates, says, grizzlies are "a reawakening to the possibility of other worlds and orders—even dangers."[22] "Hiking unarmed into Griz country can provide us with a unique opportunity to experience the humbling power of nature," Peacock says. "And in being humbled we're reminded of our original and proper place in the natural world."[23] So far, neither man nor bear has shown much willingness to accommodate the other. In the words of Peacock, the grizzly bear is "a lot of trouble, a massively inconvenient animal."[24] Yet humans can adapt a lot more than grizzlies.

Grizzly recovery thus rests with humans, not grizzlies. They are our big test. If we insist that animals serve some end, the grizzly's ultimate value and purpose may be to test our willingness to share part of Earth with a wild and fearsome creature that remains as intolerant of us as we have been of it.

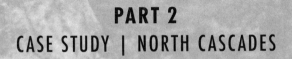

PART 2
CASE STUDY | NORTH CASCADES

4 | SAVE IT SOMEWHERE ELSE

To appreciate why the North Cascades might be a homeland for grizzly bears, tramp up one of its long timbered drainages to the steep walls that typically encircle a valley head. Scramble up through a boulder and heather basin, through snow patches that linger into July, and find your way to the top of the ridge.

When you reach the crest, you step into a wide-open panorama unlike anything you expected. As if walking onto a bright stage, you emerge from snow and dark forest into sunshine and a park-like alpine meadow.

If your view opens to the south, the meadow may tilt away in front of you down into another valley full of shadows. And across that chasm, the jagged north faces of snow-covered peaks may rise on the other side. They seem to go on forever. If the view behind you was a lullaby, this would be the Mormon Tabernacle Choir—a panorama of snow-mantled summits, each a sharp, distinct wave in a frothy sea of white.

Blue, green, and white are the colors of the North Cascades.

Anyone who has trouble seeing a forest for its trees will have double trouble seeing the Cascades for its peaks. This is especially true gazing up at one or two mountains from a valley. Only when you climb into the high country do you see what the Cascades really are. Then the valleys shrink away to punctuation marks in a bigger book.

Starting near sea level on their west side, the Cascades rise through deep, mossy rain forests to alpine meadows and tundra. Clouds scudding in from the Pacific rise with them, condense as they cool, and dump up to ten feet of rain and snow on the side facing the ocean. The Cascades form a barrier that holds back the rain. East of their crest, the range gradually dries out in a mosaic of grassy slopes and pine-fir forests, which give way finally to a desert country of bunchgrass, bitterbrush, and sagebrush along its flanks. The east slope has the look and feel of the interior West.

The Cascades are also a mosaic of different management areas. Until the 1960s, nearly all of it was national forest. Then part became North Cascades National Park and two national recreation areas run by the US Park Service. The state of Washington controls about 5 percent around the edges. Perhaps another 5 percent is private.

The only formal wilderness back in the 1960s was what the Forest Service had declared on its own in the Pasayten and around Glacier Peak. Later, Congress gave binding status to both under the Wilderness Act in 1964. Since then, other areas—Alpine Lakes, Boulder River, Henry Jackson, Lake Chelan-Sawtooth, Mount Baker, and Noisy-Diobsud—have also become wilderness. Still other roadless areas are managed as "dispersed recreation," where roads and most logging are off limits.

Regardless of the labels, the North Cascades remain one of the biggest, wildest domains in the lower 48 states. With ten thousand square miles of mountains, three-fourths of it free of motor vehicles, this is big-time wilderness.

When the Interagency Grizzly Bear Committee named the Cascades and Bitterroots evaluation areas, that was only the first step. The next was to evaluate these areas, which were only sketched on a map, and decide which parts, if any, might qualify as grizzly bear recovery areas.

Evaluation areas differ from recovery areas in several ways. An evaluation area is halfway between nowhere and a nomination. It is a potential recovery area, a candidate. Biologists still must study it and the IGBC must decide based on their findings if the area qualifies to become a recovery area. In an evaluation area, biologists are looking for suitable habitat. Thus, in the Cascades and the Bitterroots, they would ask:

Is there enough room for grizzlies to roam without conflicts with humans, roads, garbage dumps, crops, or livestock?

Are there enough den sites, spring range, and key food sources in adequate amounts and variety to sustain bears throughout the seasons?

Biologists would also look for resident bears. Management differs if bears are already there. Then, if the area is otherwise suitable for recovery, it becomes a question of whether to bring in more grizzlies, what age, what sex, and how many. If all the bears are gone, it is a matter of starting from scratch.

Surviving bears also raise legal complications, as illustrated by the reintroduction of wolves in the Northern Rockies. When wildlife agencies decided to put wolves back into Yellowstone and the mountains of Idaho, the secretary of the interior declared them an "experimental" population, as allowed under the Endangered Species Act.[1] That meant any wolf caught killing calves or sheep could legally be shot. Without that designation, killing it would be a federal crime. The experimental label provided greater flexibility in managing reintroduced animals.

Two federal courts of appeals upheld this decision. The court of appeals for the Ninth Circuit in San Francisco conceded that Canadian wolves imported for reintroduction became threatened or endangered under US law as soon as they entered the United States, but the Fish and Wildlife Service (through the interior secretary) could still reduce their protection to "experimental" if the agency concluded that would help the reintroduction effort.[2]

In a second case, which confronted the issue of preexisting populations, the Farm Bureau took the secretary of the interior to court in 1996 over the "experimental" designation for wolves in Yellowstone. It argued that Yellowstone already had naturally surviving wolves. Not many, but the Farm Bureau insisted there were some, and the Fish and Wildlife Service could not refute that possibility. As there was no way to tell a native wolf from an imported one, the Farm Bureau argued, calling the whole wolf population "experimental" deprived native wolves of protection they had enjoyed under the Endangered Species Act. Despite the irony of the Farm Bureau, which is more conservative than most ranchers, suddenly becoming a champion for native wolves, it argued that the secretary, through the Fish and Wildlife Service, could not downgrade their status so that it became legal to shoot a native wolf that previously was protected.

Some biologists and environmentalists shared this concern, and for a while court-watchers witnessed the odd specter of several biologists and the pro-environment Audubon Society joining the antienvironment Farm Bureau in a federal lawsuit challenging wolf reintroduction in Yellowstone. All probably concurred with Russian violinist Jascha Heifetz, who said: "No matter what side of an argument you're on, you always find some people on your side that wished you were on the other side." Ultimately it was too much for Audubon and it withdrew from the case, but a federal district judge agreed with the Farm Bureau and in 1997 declared the wolf reintroduction program illegal.[3]

In 2000, however, the US Court of Appeals for the Tenth Circuit based in Denver reversed, ruling that the interior secretary, through the Fish and Wildlife Service, had the discretion under the Endangered Species Act to declare an entire population experimental, even if that effectively downgraded protection for individual animals who were there before the reintroduction. The agency could lawfully do this if it decided such a designation would further its goal of recovering the species as a whole. In sum, the court explained, the Endangered Species Act was intended to save threatened or endangered species, not individual animals.[4]

The same argument resurfaced in the Bitterroots when Fish and Wildlife proposed to treat grizzlies that it planned to bring into that area as experimental. The last local bear had been killed in 1956, according to the agency, and the Bitterroots no longer hosted any resident grizzlies. But the Great Bear Foundation, a nongovernment probear group from Missoula, insisted that a few still prowled the backcountry, and treating them as experimental so that they could be shot legally would be at least a tragedy and at most a violation of the Endangered Species Act. The Great Bear folks found funding to mount a search in support of their claim that grizzlies still lurk in the Bitterroots. Their hunt came to be called "the Great Grizzly Search."

It seemed misguided. Even if they found grizzlies, it is unclear where they could go with their argument in view of the Tenth Circuit's ruling. The Tenth Circuit is not the only federal court of appeals and another one might see the issue differently, but the Ninth Circuit had already reached a similar conclusion and the Tenth Circuit's decision was articulate and carefully reasoned. Between them, these two circuits cover the American West.

What this demonstrates is that the presence of surviving bears can spark arguments, angst among environmentalists, and even lawsuits. That means wildlife managers, like hikers studying maps before choosing a route, need to know what they are dealing with from the start.

The Bitterroots and the Cascades differed from other recovery areas in another crucial way. A few grizzlies still live in the Cascades, and maybe the Great Bear Foundation will find some in the Bitterroots, but few people ever see them in either place. Folks do not realize bears are there. Contrast that with the residents of western Montana.

Doug Zimmer, a Fish and Wildlife Service officer based in western Washington, grew up on a Montana ranch. People there, he says, take grizzlies in stride. "My mom, who still lives on the home ranch, talked to me this weekend," he says. "She had a grizzly bear in the backyard last week. She has apple trees, so she's going to have bears. She just leaves the gate open at night so they don't knock down the fence."

Studies confirm this link between familiarity and tolerance. In Montana's Mission Valley, where grizzlies come down each spring from the Mission Mountains to summer in the valley, local ranchers and residents actually appreciate the bears. According to a poll, 55 percent of the local residents feel that having grizzlies as neighbors contributes to their quality of life. Significantly, those locals who know the least about grizzlies are the ones who admit they are most likely to shoot.

Another survey in the North Fork of Montana's Flathead Valley, just west of Glacier National Park, shows that 84 percent of the users, mostly locals, want to keep grizzlies in their valley, while 81 percent say they would not avoid an area because of grizzlies.[5] As one resident told a reporter, living anywhere else is just "a watered-down experience."[6] A study in Alaska showed similar results. Two-thirds of all Alaskans in the early 1990s said they did not avoid the woods because of grizzlies. Both voters and resident hunters opposed trophy hunting. About half of both groups were tolerant of bears in urban areas.[7] Familiarity apparently spawns some level of acceptance, maybe even appreciation.

As sure as snow lingers longer on a north slope, however, the opposite is also true—ignorance breeds fear. Ironically, because people around the Cascades and the Bitterroots lack firsthand experience with grizzlies, they are more afraid and thus more likely to oppose. That may not be their only objection, but it is a big one. As one official complained to the IGBC Cascades subcommittee: "It is hard for people who lack experience with bears to get over the fear." Hank Fischer, former Defenders of Wildlife representative for the Northern Rockies, noted this after a particularly stormy public meeting in Idaho. "Once we get bears on the ground, a lot of those fears will be alleviated."[8] Chris Servheen, grizzly coordinator for the US Fish and Wildlife Service, observes: "People who live in grizzly country tend to shrug it off. To them, grizzlies are no big deal. In other places there's this mythical view that grizzlies are hyperdangerous, that they'll come killing schoolchildren at bus stops or breaking into your house. People seem to feel besieged. It's a hysterical reaction."

Evaluating an area for grizzly recovery can itself put things on a collision course. This is especially true in the Northwest, which has been one of the nation's richest timber-producing regions. In parts of the North Cascades, the Forest Service was on a mission to punch logging roads into every valley, log the high-risk trees, and convert old-growth timber stands into managed forests. Every town in the Okanogan Valley had at least one sawmill. The smell of fresh saw-dust wafted on the wind. The Biles Coleman mill in Omak, where every logging company trucked its pine logs, was the county's biggest employer.

Calling the Cascades an evaluation area set off alarms. If biologists and land managers concluded that the Cascades should become a grizzly recovery area, that had big implications for timber management. Logging is only a temporary disturbance for grizzlies, but they are extremely sensitive to road traffic,[9] and timber management in the Northwest means roads—lots of them.

Unlike black bears, which hardly seem to care, grizzlies start to avoid roads driven by only ten vehicles a day. As few as fifty vehicles per day can segregate female home ranges.[10] Researchers in Montana found that radio-collared grizzlies double their distance from closed roads if those roads are reopened.[11] As road density grows, grizzlies retreat.

The bigger problem is that roads bring people, including those with rifles mounted in the back windows of their pickups. Almost half of all human-caused grizzly deaths are within one mile of a road.[12] A Yellowstone study found that secondary roads raised the risk of grizzly mortality by five times over what it was in roadless areas.[13] Some people shoot for the hell of it, others because they can't tell a black bear from a grizzly. Then there is the poacher who sells bear paws and gall bladders on the black market in Asia and leaves orphaned cubs to starve beside Mama's carcass.

Theoretically it is possible to close roads after logging, but that draws howls from folks who use them and is hard to enforce. Drivers of off-road vehicles have a knack for finding their way around locked gates. A study in Montana found that gates stopped vehicles only 29 percent of the time. Permanent barriers, such as earth berms and boulders, were slightly more effective, but 57 percent of them still failed to stop motorized trespass.[14] Unless culverts are pulled and bridges removed, roads tend to be forever.[15]

The changes in business as usual would not be limited to timber if the Cascades became a grizzly recovery area. Ranchers had long-term permits to graze livestock in the high country each summer. Cows mostly had replaced sheep, but even cows and grizzlies do not mix. Ski area operators on national forest leases could face more restrictions. Even recreation managers would need bear-proof dumpsters in campgrounds, warning signs, and public education about travel in grizzly country.

Before the Cascades became an evaluation area, very little went bump in the night. People roamed the hills with scant attention to the black bears and cougars, which actually deserved more respect than people gave them. Apart from that and the risks inherent with inexperience or stupidity, the Cascades seemed about as safe as a city park. Grizzlies would certainly change that perception. The very mention of grizzly bears causes some hikers and horsemen to go berserk.

Yellowstone and Glacier park rangers knew about these concerns. Near roads and campgrounds, human-bear conflicts had dropped as they enforced cleanliness and weaned bears away from garbage dumps that had once attracted as many bears as tourists. But after 1980 the number of backcountry hikers hurt by grizzlies remained steady in Yellowstone[16] and even climbed in Glacier.[17]

The problem was more hikers, leading to more encounters, leading to more injuries. Parks in Canada and Alaska noticed the same thing. Recreation managers in the Cascades knew that if one of ten thousand monkeys tapping on ten thousand typewriters could eventually compose "God Save the Queen," then some poor soul among the growing horde of hikers and campers would eventually be mauled and perhaps killed.

Federal land managers in the Cascades were more skeptical of grizzly recovery than their peers in the Bitterroots, mainly because the Bitterroots were already mostly wilderness. The Cascades, by contrast, had a wide range of land categories and uses. Depending on how boundaries were drawn, recovery areas could include federal and state lands managed mostly for timber and grazing, plus a lot of private lands. Because these mountains are so close to urban centers, they also attract more recreationists than any place in the

Rockies. Hence, grizzly recovery in the Cascades had the potential to step on a lot of toes.

In any face-off between grizzly recovery and other land uses, grizzlies are their own worst enemy. They are so ornery and intolerant, so unadaptable, so trouble-prone. Saving them in places like the Cascades means changing how land managers do business. But if grizzly recovery didn't require change, there wouldn't be any need for recovery. It is our status quo—our business as usual—that has already backed bears into a corner.

Washington Irving compared change to stagecoach travel, where "it is often a comfort to shift one's position and be bruised in a new place." But those who managed the Cascades preferred old bruises to new ones. In 1986 Chris Servheen, coordinator for grizzly recovery, and Jon Almack, the new project leader for the North Cascades grizzly evaluation, found this out.

Servheen oversaw grizzly recovery for the entire United States, which effectively meant the Northern Rockies and Cascades. He was based in Missoula, in the heart of grizzly country. What set Servheen apart from other good scientists was that he also understood how bureaucracies work and how much grizzly recovery depended on public acceptance.

Almack was one of those biologists who had earned his masters degree studying potential evaluation areas. His fieldwork was on grizzly sightings in the Selkirks, but he also had done a "quick-and-dirty" study of Cascades habitat. He moved to Washington State to lead the more comprehensive evaluation in 1986. The state Game Department hired him, but US Fish and Wildlife would reimburse most of his salary.

Almack was a sandy-haired fellow with a boy's face, but he was as tough as granite. He had been a Navy Seal in Vietnam. As a biologist, he already had a reputation for attention to detail. He had a lot greater interest in science than in people's opinions, which some saw as a weakness. Almack already knew more about grizzlies than any other biologist in Washington State.

Servheen and Almack set up a meeting in Wenatchee. They invited biologists and resource managers from all federal and state agencies who had a stake in the North Cascades. They wanted to reach a consensus on boundaries for the new evaluation area. This brought the forces of change and resistance into the same room for the first time.

Their May 1 meeting had barely started when those forces collided. A resource manager for Wenatchee National Forest interrupted the preliminaries. Why, he demanded to know, had he been asked to attend? It was those people at North Cascades National Park who wanted to bring back grizzlies, he claimed, so what did this have to do with the Forest Service? Evaluation for grizzlies, he insisted, should be limited to areas in the national park.

If Servheen and Almack wanted a debate, they certainly got one. The question sparked immediate argument. Forest Service managers were skeptical of this grizzly business; the Park Service people were all for it. Bad blood had persisted between these agencies ever since Congress carved the North Cascades National Park and two national recreation areas out of national forests and transferred control of those lands from the Forest Service to the Park Service. Whenever these agencies spoke of each other's management practices, it was clear that they saw each other as rivals.

Servheen and Almack tried to explain that the IGBC wanted to look at a bigger area, that the park itself might not be big enough to qualify as a recovery area. For that reason, a study limited to the park might be a waste of time. It was better to include too much than too little. Besides, an evaluation was simply that. If a decision was made later to go ahead with recovery, boundaries for the recovery area could be different from those used in the evaluation.

Their view prevailed. Begrudgingly, the group agreed to include in the evaluation area all state and federal lands from Interstate 90 north to Canada. But that initial spat warned of a deeper resistance, like a troubled volcano that would erupt again and again. The Forest Service managed forests for multiple uses; that was its mandate. If this grizzly business got too serious, it could trump everything else. Doug Zimmer, who became the evaluation team's spokesman, recalls with a strong dose of understatement: "The perception that grizzly bear recovery might add restrictions to resource management, both timber and recreation, greatly concerned some of the agencies and agency heads."

This was not unique to the Cascades. Some national forests in Idaho and Montana already had a reputation for ignoring the habitat needs of grizzlies. At the time, the Targhee and Flathead led the list (although they have since improved). In the Cascades, Almack soon found that two of the three forest supervisors were hostile. They wanted the revenue from timber sales to fund other programs and to keep county commissioners happy. Bears threatened those goals. When Almack met with one supervisor to discuss garbage controls, the man refused to talk about it and insisted that he leave.

It took four years of haggling to agree on the color and wording for a warning sign about bears. According to Almack, the final version was watered down from one used in the Rockies. Then one forest supervisor refused to post it at campgrounds or trailheads. It might scare people. Besides, acknowledging the possibility of grizzlies could be self-fulfilling. Hence, no signs, no bears.

Federal agencies could not opt out. The Endangered Species Act directs them to cooperate. For the first time in half a century, federal land managers in the Northwest were forced to consider grizzly bears. Most were concerned about how the bears would change their work. Within the Forest Service, no one seemed enthusiastic. Only a hazy line separated a pretense of cooperation from thinly disguised foot-dragging.

5 | THE CASCADES BECOME OFFICIAL

When the US Fish and Wildlife Service decides to protect threatened or endangered species, it relies on other government agencies to do much of the work. Fish and Wildlife acts as a manager or coordinator; its role is to set direction and priorities. It is responsible for making the Endangered Species Act work for land species, but it has nowhere near the staff to do that alone. It relies on other federal agencies, like the Forest Service, which is already managing national forests, to manage in a way that protects wildlife.[1] Whether the Forest Service actually does so is another matter—initial signs around the Cascades were not encouraging—but this is the way the system is designed to work. Generals direct wars, they do not fight them.

This is also where state agencies come in. They go by different names, but every state has a wildlife department. Historically, these agencies concentrated on doing what hunters and fishermen wanted, and some still have that sportsman focus. But the change in name of Washington's Game Department to Fish and Wildlife Department defines the direction in which these state agencies are moving. They still enforce hunting and fishing laws, but most state laws now mandate that they manage other wildlife as well. These state agencies employ biologists with various backgrounds and do everything from investigating reported sightings of animals to chasing bears out of campgrounds.

The US Fish and Wildlife Service depends heavily on these agencies. The feds oversee, but the states have the biologists on the ground. In the North Cascades and Bitterroots evaluation areas, the feds supplied most of the funds for salaries, but the work was done primarily by state biologists. That was how Jon Almack came to be an employee of Washington's Fish and Wildlife department while heading the Cascades evaluation.

Almack lives and works at Sullivan Lake, seven miles out of Metaline Falls, Washington. He moved there from the Cascades to work on recovery of woodland caribou, another endangered species. Even though this is also in the Selkirk grizzly recovery area, he has nothing to do with bears. Sullivan Lake is the northeast outpost of Washington's Fish and Wildlife department, which is still Almack's employer. This is as far from its Olympia headquarters as you can go and still be in Washington State.

Almack's office is in the basement of his home, in a big room filled with desks, telephone, computer, and files. Maps are everywhere. Jon has the big desk in the corner. A graduate student has another desk along the side wall. Both men dress the same in their office as in the woods (step out the door and you're in the woods)—jeans, wool shirts, boots. Coats and rain gear hang in a corner. A parade of people are up and down the stairs all afternoon.

Jon Almack is describing what was involved in evaluating the Cascades as a potential grizzly recovery area. He recounts the initial dispute at the Wenatchee meeting over boundaries. After that meeting, he suggested splitting the evaluation job into three parts. The Forest Service took the lead on two; Jon handled the third while overseeing all the fieldwork.[2]

It made sense for the Forest Service to play a big role because it managed so much of the Cascades as national forests. It also made sense to commit the Forest Service directly so that it might be less of a critic. One Forest Service project was to locate all areas of heavy human activity throughout the Cascades—roads, campgrounds, garbage dumps, active grazing allotments, busy trails, and the like. It was important to know about these places because grizzlies, unlike black bears, do not adapt well to humans.

The other big Forest Service job, Almack explains, was to map vegetation in the Cascades. Because grizzlies are mostly vegetarian, a key question was whether the Cascades had enough of the right plants to feed them. How do you map vegetation over ten thousand square miles of mountains? No one had ever tried that on such a scale, Almack admits. Were it not for satellite images, botanists still would be at it for several more decades. But Almack and the Forest Service were able to find four Landsat images—photographs taken from satellites—covering the entire Cascades. The trick was to figure out how to interpret them. It turned out that different types of vegetation created different images based on the amount of light they reflected. Once you broke the code of which types matched which pixel readings, you could generate a computer map of every plant community in the Cascades!

Bill Gaines, who was hired by the Forest Service in 1987 to work on this big job, took it over when his boss left. Over the next three summers, Gaines sent teams of botanists into the hills, first to break the satellite image code and then to verify how accurately they had done it. The conclusion: their accuracy in translating the Landsat photos was better than 90 percent.[3]

This project yielded a trove of new data. It showed that vegetation in the Cascades was remarkably diverse. The wet-to-dry transition from coast to rain shadow caused this. Of 124 plants known from the Rockies to be grizzly food, 100 grew in the Cascades. Moreover, Cascades grizzlies probably enjoyed a few other delicacies unknown to the Rockies, and no one but the bears would know these other plants also were good food. The only way to find that out was to catch a grizzly.

That was part of Almack's job. With Scott Fitkin as his helper, Almack set out to trap a grizzly bear. If they succeeded, they would collar it with a radio transmitter, turn it loose, and let it lead them to other bears. Biologists call this a "Judas bear" because ultimately it betrays the presence of others. By tracking one or more bears, Almack and Fitkin could learn much about bear diet and habits, as well as something about how many grizzlies still lived in the Cascades. Besides traps, Almack and Fitkin also set trip cameras. Part of their goal was to confirm whether grizzlies still lived in the Cascades and, if so, how many, what ages, what sex ratio, and so forth.

Methow Valley residents heard of Almack's quest, and his lack of success—lots of candid camera poses by surprised animals, but no grizzly photos and no trapped bears. Folks started calling him "Jon Almost." They compared his effort to Ward Just's description of the Vietnam War: "Searching in a dark room for a black hat that wasn't there." What bothered Almack more was that game officials in his own department pointed to his lack of evidence as proof of what they claimed to know all along. "They've been driving around in their pickup with their elbow sticking out the window, and they've never seen a grizzly, so they must not be there," Almack complains with a strong hint of sarcasm.

It is clear that Jon Almack feels strongly about grizzlies. Partly that is because he is convinced they are still in the Cascades despite his five-year failure to find one. But there is also a hint of frustration about real or perceived resistance to grizzlies within his own department. Because he still works for that agency, he is circumspect.

After they finished their fieldwork in 1990 and put the final touches on their vegetative map, Almack, Bill Gaines, and Bob Naney, who had handled the assessment of human activity, were a bit unsure what to do with this mountain of data. How did it translate into an answer to the key question: could the Cascades support a viable population of grizzlies?

For starters, no one was sure of the minimum number of bears needed for such a population. As the term implies, a minimum viable population is the smallest number of animals needed to sustain a population over a long period. The notion of viability is sometimes expressed as a probability, such as "a 1 percent chance of extinction over 250 years." A probability does not provide a target number; it is simply a way of expressing the likelihood that a specific population will survive. That likelihood will vary with the population's size, makeup, and habitat, and with the threats and changes it may face.[4] At first, population experts said a minimum viable population for grizzlies in the North Cascades was seventy to ninety, but they later raised that number. Chris Servheen, the grizzly coordinator, concluded from updated research that the minimum was two hundred to four hundred bears. Population experts continue to debate what minimum population is needed to retain genetic variation in a species over the long term,[5] but for purposes of an evaluation the question became whether the Cascades could support that many bears.

This would depend on how much territory each bear needs, which turns on the quality of its habitat. With plenty of food, a bear obviously needs less space. The scientist in Almack starts to show as he launches into an explanation about "habitat coefficients." But then he stops, conceding that biologists didn't know enough about how grizzlies use Cascades habitat to apply that approach with much precision. Instead, he proceeds to a short course on grizzly territory.

Studies show that individual bears, like humans, may prefer certain habitats, but as a species, grizzlies need large areas and diverse habitats. The more diverse, the better the chances of long-term survival.[6] A female's average home range is seventy square miles; a male's is two hundred to four hundred square miles.[7] "These are based on US averages," Almack cautions. "Any variation in the Cascades would be minor. Maybe bigger than average on the east side, where habitat is more open. Range on the west side could be smaller in valleys with lots of succulent vegetation." Almack mentions a female grizzly studied on Montana's Flathead Indian Reservation. She had a summer home range of only three square miles. "She traveled straight down from her den in the Mission Mountains to this boggy area and stayed there all summer. It had food, water, and security—everything she needed." A male grizzly's range is larger because males are promiscuous. During mating season in early summer they travel far and wide searching for females.

Grizzlies differ in several important ways from other predators—maybe because they are more foragers and scavengers than predators.[8] First, they are social and gregarious—not as social as wolf packs, but certainly not loners like cougars or lynx. When drawn together by a food source, grizzlies form hierarchies. That usually means the biggest bear gets the best spot in the berry patch or beside the salmon stream, though he may tolerate other grizzlies.[9]

The biggest difference between grizzlies and other predators is that grizzlies do not defend their home range.[10] A bear will chase other bears away from food or a mating partner, and mother bears are instinctively protective of their cubs, but home ranges can overlap. Individual bears also may travel well beyond their home range, so there is a lot of mingling and mixing.

Almack's team concluded that the Cascades offered more than a hundred hypothetical home ranges. Applying habitat factors gleaned from Rocky Mountain research to the vegetative/human activity analysis Gaines and Naney had done, they also concluded that the Cascades habitat rated from average to excellent and could likely support two hundred to four hundred grizzlies.

This was the whole point of the evaluation exercise and the key biological conclusion—that the Cascades could support a minimum viable population of grizzlies. But this was such an important conclusion, with so much riding on it, that Almack wanted to be doubly sure his group had done it right. He asked Servheen for an independent technical review.

Late in 1991 Almack, Gaines, and Naney took their maps, reports, and printouts to Spokane to meet with Chris Servheen and three other senior biologists: Richard Knight from Bozeman, Anthony Hamilton from British Columbia's Wildlife Branch, and Bruce McLellan, the leading bear biologist in British Columbia's Ministry of Forestry. For several days the biologists huddled over this material. Should they be using the habitat coefficient method? Was there enough spring range? Could private landowners be taught to tolerate grizzlies when bears came looking for snow-free food in the spring? Was there enough plant food to compensate for the loss of salmon runs? In the end the technical review team agreed with Almack's group. They concluded that the Cascades met all the criteria for a grizzly recovery area. They would recommend it to the Interagency Grizzly Bear Committee.[11]

A month later they traveled to Denver to present their conclusions to the IGBC. Its members listened and agreed. In December 1991 the IGBC officially declared the North Cascades a grizzly bear recovery area, the second largest in the Lower 48. At the same meeting, after a similar presentation on the Bitterroots, the IGBC made it a recovery area too.

Adding the North Cascades and the Bitterroots boosted the number of official grizzly recovery areas to six. No more have since been added, and no more are expected. Grizzly bears still roam outside the boundaries of these six areas, but within the lower 48 states their sanctuary, if one can call it that, may never be any bigger.

Almack's description of the Cascades evaluation focused on the scientific process—assembling and analyzing the biological data. He did not dwell on the political. With federal financial support and the help of federal biologists, the North Cascades had become a grizzly recovery area under the Endangered Species Act, a federal law. But there is more to grizzly recovery than science, and in 1992 it was about to meet states' rights.

6 | A STATE OF STALLING

Jon Almack feels frustrated. Because he is still employed by the state, he is reluctant at first to reveal much about the reasons for his frustration. But the more he says, the more he wants to say. Telling becomes a catharsis. He displays a curious blend of anger and doubt. He seems unsure if he has accurately read the motives of his former superiors; he wants others to reconfirm what he says. It's as if he were begging someone to tell him he is right. In its worst light, Almack portrays what he saw as a strategy within the Washington Department of Fish and Wildlife to "deny, discount, or dismiss the evidence about Cascades grizzlies."

At first Almack thought the department's director, Curt Smitch, was supportive, but as the evaluation moved forward, the director's enthusiasm seemed to wane. By the time the IGBC declared the Cascades a recovery area, Smitch was publicly declaring his reluctance to support a recovery zone and was openly opposed to bringing in any bears. He warned Almack, "I'm not going to lock up a million acres just because you saw some tracks." Almack blames his immediate superiors for contributing to this shift from support to hostility. They filtered information passed to Smitch that might have produced a different attitude. Almack claims his superiors expressed views in meetings that were antigrizzly and unscientific.

Relations were frigid. Almack and his supervisors disagreed so much that they ordered him to add disclaimers at the beginning of his evaluation report and his oral presentation to the IGBC, saying that his views were personal and not necessarily those of his department. By distancing itself from Almack's work, the department was

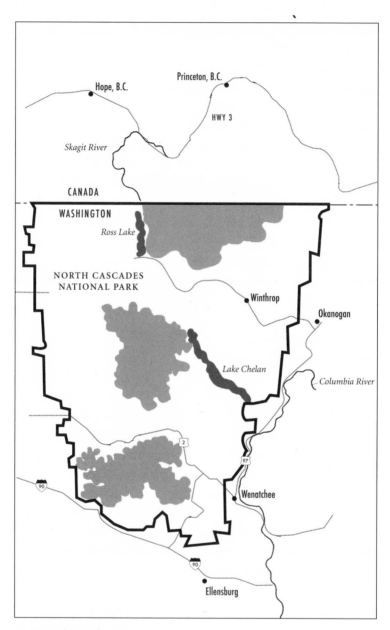

Map 3. North Cascades Ecosystem

effectively telling him to wear a scarlet "O" for "outsider." Smitch even suggested that Almack might have gathered his evidence on grizzlies in Montana and then claimed it came from Washington. Outsiders, it seems, could not be trusted. Watching the department's reaction to his evidence for grizzlies in the Cascades must have made Almack feel like Harry Truman, who said: "I never give them hell. I just tell them the truth and they think it's hell."

Almack reserved much of his criticism for the way his bosses thwarted progress after the Cascades became a recovery area. The supervisors of the three national forests and the national park, along with state agency heads, composed a North Cascades subcommittee of the IGBC. These were the local policy makers, and they would have a strong say on recovery. The biologists, including Almack, Gaines, and Naney, were members of a technical committee. Most people called it the "bear group." The bear group's first step was to draft white papers documenting the scientific basis for a recovery plan.

Almack chaired this group. After all, he had headed the evaluation they planned to document. But then his supervisors replaced him with another biologist from the department. They told Almack he could attend committee meetings by invitation only and should limit his involvement. These were slaps in the face to a professional biologist who had devoted so much to this effort.

Even while he still chaired it, the committee, according to Almack, was an instrument of delay. Discussions dragged on and on. Some attendees recall that even after they decided something, if one of the state agencies changed representatives on the committee, the new member would demand that they reopen the issue. And the committee would comply! Almack recalls leaving meetings drained from debate over insignificant points while the important issues were ignored. "It took two extra years to draft this plan because of infighting," Almack declares. It is hard to assess how much of his reaction is the result of frustration.

Almack mentions three final points. The first involved a joint effort with Canada. British Columbia had captured a grizzly near

Pemberton in the Coast Range. Bob Forbes, provincial biologist, wanted to truck it over and release it in the BC Cascades. Moving bears was routine in Canada. Almack was excited about what they might learn from a new bear. With a radio collar it could become a Judas bear or at least reveal something about grizzly habits in the Cascades. This was the next best thing to trapping a bear himself, which Almack had been unable to do. He had the funding and Forbes had the bear, so with considerable enthusiasm, they agreed to collaborate.

But then Almack's supervisors learned what he was up to. Worried about how state lawmakers might react, Almack's boss said he could not provide a radio collar or have anything to do with tracking that bear. Even though British Columbia only planned to move the bear from one part of its province to another, Washington State did not want one of its employees to cooperate with that effort. After all, there was no fence to stop that bear from entering Washington. So no state employee could do research with a non-Washington bear that might wander into Washington.

Almack's second point involves the way the state tried, in his view, to sabotage the recovery area. One disquieting discovery from the evaluation studies was that snow-free spring range in the Cascades was also heavily used by humans. That underscored the importance of a major decision by Almack's department early on.

The evaluation area embraced state as well as federal lands. The best spring range was in the state's Colockum wildlife area. It straddled the east end of the Wenatchee Mountains—ninety-five square miles of forests, open steppes, and brushy canyons rolling down to a wild stretch of the Columbia River. The Colockum was also the only place in the Cascades where you still could walk from mountaintop to riverbank without crossing a highway or railroad. The few roads that ventured into this country were so rough they would chew a passenger car to pieces within five miles. The Colockum was managed mainly for elk, but the biologists all knew it was also prime grizzly habitat, especially for that much-needed spring range.

Chris Servheen's initial promise—that the evaluation boundaries did not lock in boundaries for any recovery area—was about to be tested. In 1992, after the evaluation ended, those involved with it convened in Olympia to hear from state officials. What boundary changes did state agencies want if the North Cascades became an official recovery area?

The Department of Natural Resources (DNR), which managed state trust lands, tweaked the boundary in a few spots. It added some parcels and dropped a few. The net effect was negligible. This was significant because DNR saw its mission in terms of cutting trees to fund schools and roads. To the relief of biologists, DNR agreed to keep the big, unroaded Loomis Forest in the recovery area.

Then came the Fish and Wildlife Department. Director Curt Smitch made a few tweaks of his own. But then he dropped a bombshell. His department, Smitch declared, would exclude the entire Colockum from the recovery area! Smitch offered no explanation. From what he didn't say it was clear that this was a decision senior policy makers had made behind closed doors. Smitch was not saying who or why. He was not seeking anyone's approval; he was simply declaring his decision—the Colockum was out.

The rest of the group was stunned. Sensing this, Smitch suggested that "the way we manage the Colockum is consistent with the way we would manage for grizzly recovery anyway."

"Then why not leave it in?" someone had the audacity to ask. No one recalls Smitch's response. It was clear, however, that the state, for undisclosed reasons, did not want its big Colockum elk range in any area managed for grizzlies, no matter how important it might be.

Almack's last point related to "the bear group" of biologists. When his supervisor had him removed as chair of the bear group, he was replaced by a state biologist who specialized not in bears but in reptiles and amphibians. That in itself seemed odd. But Almack grew more suspicious when the committee's progress, already slow, slowed even more. The slow-down seemed more marked than one might expect of the transition from a chairman deeply involved with bears to one who knew more about snakes and frogs. It was as if the group's new goal was to make nothing happen very slowly. To find out why, Almack privately asked some committee members. Even though he had been told to stay out of committee affairs except when invited, he remained keenly concerned. After all, grizzlies in the Cascades had been his project.

Almack spoke with Sam Gehr, Okanogan National Forest supervisor, and Ed Gestellum, deputy supervisor of North Cascades National Park. Both were on the North Cascades subcommittee; both were concerned about the group's glacial pace. They all spoke to Chris Servheen, coordinator for the grizzly program. Servheen has never revealed what he did, but shortly afterward the state backed off its demand that it always chair the bear group. The herpetologist returned to snakes and frogs, and Anne Braaten, biologist for the North Cascades National Park, became the group's new chair.

The herpetologist bore no grudge. He seemed relieved to return to his own work. Right before he left, Almack took him aside and asked if he had been given any orders about his role as chair of the bear committee. With remarkable candor, the young man confirmed Almack's suspicions: "I was told to go as slow as I possibly could."

When wildlife issues turn political, government biologists are caught in the middle. They know what biology dictates. But they also know you can only push biology so far. Then you jeopardize the program and maybe jeopardize your career. At what point does self-preservation require good people who know better to keep their mouths shut? Or to say only what is safe?

How much did Washington State's senior scientists on grizzly bears feel such pressure? Jon Almack thinks they knuckled under. Others draw distinctions between immediate supervisors and higher-ups.

Others involved with the bear group and the North Cascades subcommittee lack Almack's personal stake, so they also lack some of his fervor. Yet they still share most of his views. The main difference is that some are more charitable toward his immediate supervisor. "I worked very closely with her, and I found that she wanted to move forward in a scientifically sound manner," says Doug

Zimmer, Fish and Wildlife official in Olympia. "But she insisted that we have the science nailed down, so that we weren't moving on somebody's emotion or 'best biological opinion' without that being backed up by scientific fact."

Bill Gaines, Wenatchee National Forest biologist, calls Almack "a very good scientist. He is careful with the details. But he gets impatient with the political side of biology." One can see how Almack may have mistaken a tough editor for a co-conspirator. If his supervisor kept asking him to rewrite his work, how was he to tell whether she was trying to make it bulletproof or simply stalling?

She probably held Almack's material to a higher standard than if he were writing a plan, say, for spotted salamanders. She knew some of her own supervisors and her agency director were grizzly skeptics. They could pounce on any weakness. And even if they didn't, politicians and interest groups would scrutinize plans for grizzly recovery far more closely than any plan to save salamanders. Grizzlies always stir strong opinions.

Zimmer recalls, "So you had the people who were actively involved, who were doing their best in good faith to move it forward, but you also had upper level management who were doing their absolute best to stall or stop the recovery."

Bill Noble, a federal biologist who coordinated his own work in the Cascades with Almack, says of the grizzly program: "The state has consistently sent mixed signals."

"The state couldn't just come out and say it was opposed to grizzly recovery," adds Bill Gaines. "Instead, it tried to subvert Almack's work."

When the federal government tells states what to do, they can be as cranky as a fossil damaged during excavation. Grizzly recovery is just another federal mandate that limits their prerogatives. As a crusty old middle manager from Washington's Department of Natural Resources put it, "We don't want your grizzly bears screwing up our ability to harvest timber."

Jon Almack was caught in a paradox of policy and politics. He was a state employee hired to evaluate the Cascades for grizzlies and then provide the scientific support for a recovery plan. Washington's wildlife department had its own endangered species program, and federal listing of any species as endangered or threatened automatically added it to the state's list. Hence, the grizzly bear was protected under state policy as well as federal law. Under the state's program, grizzly recovery was a state goal, and the state said it was cooperating with the federal government to save grizzlies. Washington's governor had joined other western state governors in signing a proclamation supporting grizzly bear recovery.

But officials charged with applying these policies may hold different private views. Sometimes their vision is stuck in the mud. The state's support for Almack's work was like wishing a runner in a race: "Good luck, but lose. Make us look good, but don't tie our hands. We want an A for effort and an F for results."

Almack may have been employed by the state, but the feds were underwriting 90 percent of his salary and he was working to meet a federal goal. Wherever his loyalties lay, they were not with Olympia. Almack may have tried to walk and talk like a state employee, but to some people he was nothing more than a wholly owned subsidiary of the federal government.

There were subtleties to state policy here that a studious and intense biologist might have missed, misread, or tried to ignore. Doug Zimmer, who attended all but one meeting of the North Cascades subcommittee and may have learned from experience to keep a sharper eye, put it this way: "I've watched bureaucratic masters at work on this. They're sitting in the meeting saying 'Grizzly bear recovery is a goal that my agency and all of us support.' But behind the scenes they have carefully dropped an invisible anchor. You can't see it. You can't prove it. You can only feel it."

7 | THE PUBLIC VOICES ITS FEARS

Mountain towns decorate their bars, cafes, and even their grocery stores with mounted bears. Invariably the bear is snarling, with fangs in full view. Snarling stuffed bears are a way for the town to declare that it is part of the rugged Wild West. You have to wonder how folks who grew up staring at bear fangs can have a balanced view of grizzlies. The truth is that often they do not. "Nobody's neutral. Some people have the same visceral reaction as to the great white shark. Pro or con, everybody has strong feelings about grizzly bears." This is the assessment of Doug Zimmer, a man who speaks from experience. He was information specialist for the US Fish and Wildlife Service in Olympia, Washington. He attends and often presides at public meetings about grizzlies. He was involved in nearly all the Cascades meetings held around the state of Washington in 1993, and he followed the public meetings held several years later in Idaho and Montana.

These were not formal hearings. Both the North Cascades and Bitterroots were in the process of drafting grizzly recovery plans. The law requires formal hearings only when the government drafts an impact statement on the eve of doing something that could affect the environment, but neither area was at that stage. These were only information meetings—a throat-clearing exercise—to tell people about the recovery plans.[1]

At these meetings the audience listened to a presentation and asked questions. The wildlife officers running these meetings were not seeking comments—just questions—but you can imagine how much difference that made. Whether they were hearings or meetings, questions or comments, this was the first chance ordinary folks had to speak up on the subject of local grizzlies. Before, the debate had been among land managers, often behind closed doors. But now, when the biologists and information officers came to town, it was open season.

Zimmer vividly recalls one such meeting in Okanogan, county seat for one of Washington's most conservative counties. Logging, ranching, and apple orchards are its mainstays. Unemployment always runs high; the brightest high school graduates leave. In recent decades the Okanogan Valley has become even more conservative.

Even before the meeting started, Zimmer knew he was in for a rough night. He was greeting people as they arrived. A little old woman promptly asked: "I suppose you're one of those people who wants to bring in grizzlies." Zimmer, who was in civilian clothes, told her he was with the Fish and Wildlife Service and "we're here to talk about that." Clearly agitated, she replied, "So you're one of those bastards in favor of grizzly bears!" She didn't wait for Zimmer to plead guilty or not guilty. Having made up her mind, she pulled her head back slowly and in a quick forward motion spat on Zimmer's chest.

"I was aghast," he recalls. "It was like having your grandmother spit on you. I just looked at her. Then she went into a rant and rave about how I was going to be responsible for the death of her grandchildren because bringing in 'those goddamn bears' was going to get her grandchildren killed and eaten while they were waiting for the school bus. She thought people like me ought to be shot."

That was how the meeting started. Zimmer was lead spokesman, so most of Okanogan County's wrath was aimed at him. Before the evening ended, he would count nine death threats. Some did not worry him; others sounded serious. Zimmer was halfway through his presentation when a man wearing a cowboy hat decided he had heard enough. He stood up, face red with rage, started jabbing his finger at Zimmer, and yelled: "You son of a bitch! I'm going to go out to my truck and get a rifle, and come back in here and shoot you!" Then he stormed out. Zimmer recalls: "We were in a motel meeting room with windows all along one side facing the parking lot. I looked at that wall of windows. I knew this guy's pickup was parked somewhere out there in the dark. I thought, 'Here I am in a well-lit room, standing up in front. I'm really obvious. If he's serious about it, I'm probably dead. But I'm not going to let these guys run me out. I'm not going to let them see me sweat.'"

No shots were fired; the outraged man in the cowboy hat did not return. When the meeting ended and the sullen audience began to leave, Zimmer breathed a sigh of relief. The wildlife folks were packing up when he had one last confrontation. As Zimmer recalls: "This guy came up to me and said he was 'of a good mind to get his lariat and take three turns around me and three turns around his trailer hitch, and three turns around town.'" Zimmer suspected the fellow was bluffing. He did not say anything, but he smiled to himself: "That guy got my award for the evening's most imaginative death threat."

All meetings were not that raw, but emotions always ran high and the room often crackled with tension, like the air just before a lightning strike. "The grizzly pushes more emotional buttons than any other endangered species that I have worked with," observes Bill Gaines, Wenatchee National Forest biologist.

Antibear sentiment came in many forms. Fear, by far, was the loudest. It was a fear that seemed to spring from primitive instincts. People were deathly afraid of grizzlies. They had heard horror stories about humans being attacked, dragged off into the brush, and half eaten. They liked their mountains because they were safe, and thought it was madness to consider bringing back these killers. They called grizzlies a "backwoods terror." Because grizzlies are so dangerous, they predicted folks would have to carry rifles whenever they ventured into the hills. Some even argued that any surviving grizzlies in the Cascades should be hunted down and shot.

In similar information meetings for the Bitterroots, some people in Idaho felt the same way. "We do not need our forests and other public lands shut down and to put people out of jobs to encourage the grizzlies to roam into our backyards and endanger our lives," said one resident. One Idaho legislator opined that bringing back grizzlies "is nothing but a polite form of genocide."[2]

Several fear-based comments probably were true. Robert DeGraw, who led outings for Parents Without Partners, warned that hikers who followed the rules still had no guarantee of safety. Bears can strike without apparent provocation, he said, and "one encounter with a grizzly is one too many." But DeGraw went farther. He claimed grizzlies were not just dangerous but downright vicious. When food is scarce, he warned, "the bears get mean."[3] "Frantic" would have been a better word for the feeding frenzy that occurs when bears are running out of time to fill their calorie quota before hibernation.

In the same vein, a resident of Salmon, Idaho, called grizzlies "a vicious monster,"[4] implying that they hated humans.

Harvey Manning, a well-known outdoor writer, also applied human emotions to bears. Trapping and drugging them, he predicted, would provoke grizzlies to "seek revenge."[5]

Such claims assume a life of their own when people are already scared. Some saw grizzlies as a symbol of big government running roughshod over local concerns. Others, who rarely articulated it this way, were troubled at the prospect of a force loose in the hills that they could not control. For people accustomed to dominating, that was just too scary.

It was evident how little many people, pro or con, really knew about grizzlies. Movies and magazines were their main sources of information. Doug Zimmer, the subject of Okanogan's death threats, says: "A lot of people base their reaction on a perception of both the bear and a western lifestyle that probably never existed outside of old western movies."

Chris Servheen, grizzly coordinator, adds: "The problem is aggravated by media images. Half the issues in some outdoor magazines show someone in the jaws of a grizzly." "This is wildlife pornography," he complains, "the exploitation and degrading of wildlife. It corrupts the views of the public."

To counter such misinformation, the Cascades IGBC subcommittee eventually published a handbook with responses to more than seven hundred public concerns.[6] In Idaho, the Fish and Wildlife Service distributed a similar brochure drafted by a coalition of wildlife and timber groups. But it was like spitting on a forest fire. People had heard a lot more about problem bears than any others. When they felt threatened, especially by something big government might do, they were not likely to believe anything it told them. And even if they did, the typical reaction reminds one of Winston Churchill, who once admitted, "I am always ready to learn, but I do not always like being taught."

Some opponents voiced more practical concerns. Ranchers feared for their livestock. Kent Lebsack, president of the Washington Cattlemen's Association, worried about bears killing cows. Ranchers would not be able to protect their stock because shooting a grizzly, he correctly observed, is illegal under the Endangered Species Act except in self-defense. Also correctly, he noted that no plan existed in the Cascades to compensate ranchers for livestock losses, like the one funded in the Rockies by Defenders of Wildlife. He had no way to know if Defenders would extend its program to the Cascades once grizzly bear recovery started.

Bob Morton, a state senator from the logging country near Kettle Falls, said he was worried for the safety of loggers, miners, and ranchers. Bears are most hungry before hibernation, Morton said, so if natural food sources disappear, "the logical choice for foraging bears would be lush apple orchards and slow-moving livestock."[7]

Eastern Washington and central Idaho, like much of the rural West, were frightened for their future. The pillars of their economy—farming, ranching, logging, and mining—were all under pressure. Urban people kept finding new ways to make rural life more complicated—growth management laws, environmental rules, and now, bringing back predators. As Chris Servheen notes: "Species recovery is not responsible for these problems, but it's happening at the same time, so it tends to be blamed."

Backcountry horsemen sounded more afraid of rules than of bears. They disliked having to set up two camps, one for food and one for humans. They thought bear-resistant boxes were too expensive and heavy, and they are. They looked at Montana's bear country rules and foresaw the same in the Cascades and Bitterroots, with more rules as time passed and people encountered more bears. Jim Murphy, executive director of the Backcountry Horsemen of Washington, complained, "Conflicts are always resolved in favor of the bear and the result is restrictions."[8] Because the Endangered Species Act "restricted recreation, threatened jobs, and reduced property values," the horsemen proclaimed, "it was a good idea gone bad."[9]

Some critics were concerned that the government would not assume liability for injuries. Others worried that grizzlies would cause road closures and reduce logging. They saw grizzlies as an economic threat. They found imaginative ways to express this. Putting roads to bed by removing culverts to protect bear habitat would add silt to streams and endanger fish, they argued. More grizzlies would eat more fish, especially endangered salmon. Other wildlife, such as deer, mountain goats, and black bears, would also suffer. Some even expressed concern for the grizzlies themselves, arguing that the trauma of being drugged and moved would be too hard on them.

Skeptics offered several suggestions. Radio-collar every grizzly and link them to satellites so people could track them on the Internet.[10] Instead of wasting tax money on bear recovery, hire more police to stop trailhead vandalism. And to make grizzlies less dangerous, why not hunt them to make them more afraid? There were also cynics who claimed biologists were promoting grizzlies simply to make jobs for themselves. They thought the whole recovery idea should be reviewed by "outside experts" who had no stake in it. Finally, some suspected a secret agenda by bear zealots to close all mountains to humans. Once those zealots succeeded in the Cascades and the Bitterroots, the argument went, they would push that lock-up throughout the Northern Rockies and down the Cascades range, eventually as far as California. Mainly this confirmed that public controversies often attract a conspiracy theory.

In the Cascades the most unexpected but potent objections came from hikers and backpackers.[11] One might have presumed they would be more sympathetic to bears. After all, they use the mountains for noneconomic reasons; they seem to appreciate and seek out wildness. Most of them respect it. Many belong to groups with strong environmental credentials.

A few hikers were concerned about losing the wilderness experience. Accustomed to moving through the woods quietly, they abhorred the prospect of needing to make noise to avoid surprise encounters. But every hiker privately wonders what he or she would do if, just around that next corner, they came face-to-face with a grizzly. Fear is real. Everyone respects grizzlies, as they should, but for some it is a question not of deference but of dread. People do not like to admit this, so they camouflage their fear with arguments about other issues. Most hikers who used the Cascades refused to acknowledge that they were already hiking in grizzly country. Even if grizzlies had been there all along, recovery would mean more bears. That was, after all, the whole idea. Some saw this as a big change and were not prepared to sacrifice their freedom and personal safety. Most outdoor groups were so deeply divided that they refused to take a stance.

To some hikers, the real fear is not safety but restrictions. Trails might be closed or not maintained. If a bear attacked someone, an area might be closed indefinitely. The Forest Service might tilt too far in favor of bears and close trails or campgrounds based on expected rather than actual grizzly presence. It was a concern similar to that of the horsemen.

Ira Spring, author of many hiking books, became a voice for these concerns. He figured that the Cascades recovery area includes two-thirds of all trails in western Washington. If 15 percent were closed due to grizzlies—the same percentage he claimed are closed in Yellowstone—that would put eight hundred miles of trails off limits. Since more people use the Cascades than Yellowstone, the closure percentage might even go up. Either way, Spring claimed, this was a clear disaster for hikers. Not only would grizzlies lock up much of the Cascades, but those closures would put extra pressure on the trails that stayed open.

Overall, Spring argued, closures were too high a price to pay, especially when grizzlies are not endangered in Canada and Alaska and the Cascades are used by so many people. Even though these mountains are one of the biggest, most remote areas in the Lower 48, Spring insisted, they are not big enough for both humans and bears.[12]

Ira Spring was a recognized and respected outdoor figure, but his views were not as influential as those of the Mountaineers, the largest and oldest outdoor recreation group in the Northwest. With its creed "to study, preserve, and enjoy the natural beauty of the Northwest," and with branches in all of western Washington's major cities, the Mountaineers spoke with considerable authority.

Don Heck, Mountaineers president, expressed the group's position in a detailed letter to the Fish and Wildlife Service. The Mountaineers supported grizzly recovery in the Cascades and felt it should move ahead promptly "while there are still resident grizzlies," Heck wrote. But his group had major concerns.

If recovery succeeded, he noted, with an ultimate population of two hundred to four hundred bears, "the total number of grizzlies in the North Cascades may increase by a factor of perhaps twentyfold. . . . This is a stunning potential increase." Yet the Cascades already hosted six million visitor use days each year. "There is much heavier backcountry use in the North Cascades than in other grizzly areas," Heck noted. "Thus, it is likely, if not inevitable, that there will be much greater potential contact between grizzlies and humans" than in any other recovery area. Focusing on this heavy backcountry use and the potential increase in the number of grizzlies, Heck criticized what he called "an inaccurate and superficial analysis of the substantial safety hazards and recreation impacts arising out of grizzly-human contact."[13]

It was hard to argue with most of what the Mountaineers said. But the Northwest Ecosystem Alliance, an environmental group that stressed wildlife more than outdoor recreation, tried. The alliance made its own study of eleven national forests and parks where grizzlies live. It concluded that the effect of closures on recreation was "virtually zero." Even in Yellowstone and Glacier national parks, which had the most trail closures due to bears, recreation opportunities were never slashed more than 4 percent, according to the alliance. Any inconvenience from temporary closures was more than offset, the alliance claimed, by the heightened sense of wilderness that comes with being on the ground in grizzly country.[14] Mitch Friedman, executive director of the alliance, wrote: "People who want to hike or horsepack without grizzly bears have plenty of options—about 98 percent of the contiguous states meet that criteria."[15] But telling hikers and backpackers to go somewhere else was not going to still critics or win converts.

Thus hikers and backpackers voiced their fears, their visions of froth and fangs, or their concerns that land managers would unload truckloads of bears at trailheads, close their mountains, or replace their freedom in the hills with tough restrictions and anxious glances over their shoulders. Grizzly recovery and outdoor recreation were on a collision course. Bill Gaines found this "dichotomy within the recreation community" unique among grizzly recovery areas. In the North Cascades, the great bear had become the hikers' spotted owl.

Saving the peregrine falcon was easy. We only had to quit using DDT. We did not even need to protect habitat; falcons can nest on office buildings and live off pigeons they snatch in city squares. The California condor needs habitat and an end to lead poisoning, but otherwise makes no demands. The wolf makes more demands because it needs both territory and fresh meat, and ranchers worry that they will be supplying the meat. But the grizzly makes the most demands of all—a huge, wild habitat, meat, and worst of all, it can and has been known to kill humans. No other animal asks so much and accumulates so many enemies because of its demands.

Among those who backed grizzly recovery despite its high demands, some were frustrated by the Cascades and Bitterroots recovery plans. They called them "toothless." They wanted to see more about closing roads, stopping development, restoring wilderness, and enforcing game laws. They wanted more specifics to reduce mortality and boost the grizzly population. They also wanted more emphasis on corridors to link the Cascades and Bitterroots with other bears. A Funds for Animals representative claimed that the Cascades plan focused more on delisting grizzlies than saving them. He dismissed it as "a prescription for extinction."[16]

Probear people also wanted bigger recovery areas. Friedman thought the Cascades zone should extend south of Interstate 90, embrace Mount Rainier National Park and the Yakima Indian Reservation, and perhaps extend to the Oregon border. Maybe that is what spawned the conspiracy theory about a lock-up.

Environmentalists criticized the Bitterroots boundaries as "socially rather than biologically defined." They sought to add parts of the St. Joe River drainage and to extend the boundaries north, closer to the Cabinet-Yaak grizzly recovery area.[17]

Regardless of which side of the issues people took, they held their views with religious zeal. Something about grizzly bears brought out this sense of certainty, leading to a view akin to that expressed by the writer Isaac Asimov: "Those people who think they know everything are a great annoyance to those of us who do."

On one point opponents and proponents agreed: both felt the feds were evasive about plans to bring in bears. Opponents wanted to ban all bear imports; proponents felt an urgency to start augmenting the Cascades population before it vanished. In the Bitterroots, they argued that putting bears back into those mountains and linking the Bitterroots to other recovery areas were critical to long-term grizzly survival throughout the Northern Rockies. But officials ducked this debate. They drew a distinction between adopting a recovery plan, which was all they had in mind for now, and resolving the tougher question of how recovery actually would work. The latter was postponed till another day. Thus, when people asked how many bears might be brought into the Cascades or Bitterroots, the stock answer was that no decision had been made to bring in bears. That sounded like a car dealer refusing to tell you the price before you took a test drive.

Wildlife management has become part biology and part socio-politics. Saving endangered species requires public support. Often that means watering down biology to what the public will accept. Social scientists have made two observations about this process.

First, attitudes expressed at public hearings are generally more extreme on both sides of an issue than are those of the general public. Special interest groups are more likely to show up and sound off. Those with the strongest views usually are the most vocal. In an effort to counterbalance opposition arguments, advocates overstate their own position. Moderate people are so intimidated by this they will not speak up. The result is polarization.[18]

Second, attitudes vary from one area to another, usually from rural to urban. A study of attitudes toward wolf reintroduction in Yellowstone found that acceptance of wolves increased with distance from the park.[19] Support for the Endangered Species Act generally is urban, while listings and recovery are usually rural.

For both reasons, social scientists stress that it is important to measure the full range of public attitudes, not just the local and vocal groups who use hearings as a soapbox.[20] State and federal wildlife officials involved with the grizzly in Washington and Idaho agreed. As one biologist said, "There was some doubt as to whether the outspoken criticism at public meetings was representative." They wanted to know what the silent majority thought.

So they commissioned several statewide polls—one in 1996 in Washington and another shortly afterward covering Idaho and Montana. Conducted by a professional pollster on a random sample basis, it showed surprising support for grizzlies. More than 70 percent of the Washington respondents favored importing more bears if that was needed to save them. An astonishing 90 percent said bringing in grizzlies would not affect their plans to use the Cascades. And 80 percent said they would derive satisfaction just from knowing grizzlies were there.[21] The Bitterroots poll showed less support, but even there a clear majority—62 percent—favored grizzly recovery.[22] Predictably, the urban side of Washington State and the urban area around Missoula gave the strongest support, but a majority in eastern Washington also favored recovery.

Commenting on the Cascades results, Bill Gaines noted, "The pollster said this was the highest level of public acceptance found at any [grizzly recovery] ecosystem."

Despite this, the Cascades lag the farthest behind other ecosystems in actual grizzly recovery, and the Bitterroots are not far behind. The reasons are numerous and complex. Some are elusive. But one of them could well be the reaction of Fish and Wildlife Service officials who personally heard the public voice its fears.

Chris Servheen, grizzly coordinator, stresses that "a successful conservation program for small bear populations must address biological, social, political, and organizational factors. Conservation programs are less effective if they focus on biological factors at the expense of [these other] factors."[23] Servheen saw the poll results. But he also attended most of the meetings. He knew antibear ranchers in eastern Washington could hurt grizzly recovery more than probear environmentalists in Seattle could help it. What would he think about public support, and how would that affect his decisions about grizzly bear recovery in the Cascades, especially when he had witnessed firsthand the hostility at meetings such as Okanogan's Night of the Nine Death Threats?

8 | ARE THEY STILL THERE?

A lot of people do not believe—some prefer not to believe—that grizzly bears still live in the Cascades. Without clear evidence that they do, some skeptics share the view of Kent Lebsack from the Washington Cattlemen's Association, who says it is not appropriate to consider bringing in more grizzlies until their presence is "confirmed."[1] The well-publicized failure by Jon Almack and Scott Fitkin to capture or photograph a grizzly did not help. If two scientists who knew what they were doing could not find a grizzly, why should anyone believe the big bears were still around? Capturing a grizzly would be fairly convincing, but short of that, proof of their existence rested on this kind of circumstantial evidence:

- A grizzly skull was found in 1987 above Cascade Pass. Biologists estimated the bear had died ten years earlier.
- Jon Almack found a deer carcass in the spring of 1989, partly buried at Hozomeen on Ross Lake. From nearby digging and some hair samples, he determined it was a grizzly's food cache.
- A year later in the same area, Almack set up a trip camera. Checking back, he found fresh grizzly tracks. Either by chance or by cunning, the bear stayed behind the camera.
- In July 1991, someone claimed they saw a grizzly along the shore of Lake Chelan. Biologists checked and found tracks and scat confirming it was a grizzly.
- That same month a hiker near Pete Lake in the Cle Elum district of the Alpine Lakes found bear tracks he thought

belonged to a grizzly. Biologists checked, made a plaster cast, and confirmed they were. This was near a valley where hunters the previous fall said they had spotted a mother grizzly with two cubs.

- Also in 1991, Forest Service biologists near Leavenworth set up a baited plate to record tracks of a pine marten. When they checked later, they were shocked to find a grizzly track that filled the entire plate.

- In June 1993 a graduate student named Stofel was conducting a bird-breeding survey for Champion International on its Kapowsin tree farm west of Mount Rainier. She found three bear tracks in the mud. She was not sure about them, so she made plaster casts and took them to bear biologists. They were grizzlies—probably a mother and one or more cubs. This surprised even the biologists, because the site was south of Interstate 90 and out in the western foothills of the Cascades, which had never been prime grizzly habitat.

- In 1994 a backpacker named Karro took a photo of a bear near the Pasayten airstrip. He thought it was a grizzly. Biologists checked tracks and agreed.

- In 2001 when the Thirtymile Creek fire was burning north of Winthrop, a helicopter pilot flying at a low altitude saw a grizzly run up the hill ahead of him. The pilot knew the difference between grizzlies and black bears.

The state classifies reports of bears based on reliability.[2] These typically start with a sighting, followed by a biologist interview with the person who saw the bear or a review of the place where they saw it. The classification is assigned by the biologist. During the 1970s the state collected fourteen class 1 and 2 (definitely or probably a grizzly) reports on the US side of the Cascades. During the 1980s, that number rose to fifty-six. In the first half of the 1990s, it rose again to sixty-one.[3]

From these rising numbers, some people conclude that the grizzly population is growing. No biologists believe this. Instead, they think more people are reporting more sightings.[4]

Forty-three of these reports from the public included photographs of bears they thought were grizzlies. Surprisingly few of these were graded as class 1 or 2. Either the bear was too far away, the light was wrong, the image was blurred, or—as any biologist will admit—a brief look at a bear is often ambiguous.

A lot of people throughout the Cascades have seen a lot of bears, and they still do. Wildlife managers complain about inadequate resources to follow up on most reports, especially with the kind of rapid response needed to check a site for tracks before they fade. Sightings leave an indelible impression on the people who see them, but skeptics are quick to add that no trained biologist has yet seen a bear confirmed on sight to be a grizzly. Until that happens, do all these class 1 and 2 incidents really prove anything?

Absolutely, the biologists reply.

Seeing may be believing, but Bill Noble, a Fish and Wildlife Service biologist who has spent years in the Cascades, warns that trained biologists themselves cannot always tell grizzlies from black bears on sight. "Sightings make better headlines than data," but as far as he is concerned, "tracks are far more conclusive."

Indeed they are. A grizzly's front foot track is so different from a black bear's that anyone who knows what to look for can tell the difference. The grizzly's signature is the alignment of its front toes. They all are ahead of its wide heel pad, while a black bear's paw is more rounded. Its toes curve around its heel. Claw marks well ahead of the toes are another grizzly giveaway, but once you see those toes out in front of the heel, the claw marks only confirm what you already know.[5] Hence, when a trained biologist follows up on a reported sighting and finds those distinctive grizzly tracks, there is nothing left to debate. Tracks do not lie. It was a grizzly.

Class 1 and 2 reports are sprinkled throughout the North Cascades. The biggest cluster is where the North Cascades highway crosses the range between Rainy and Washington passes. Many people driving through this high country see bears on the open slopes above the highway. Reports also cluster along Ross Lake, Lake Chelan, and throughout the Pasayten—all places that people frequent. The most surprising spot is along the Pacific Crest Trail northeast of

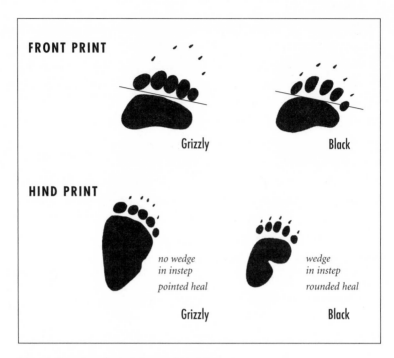

FRONT PRINT

Grizzly   Black

HIND PRINT

*no wedge
in instep
pointed heal*   *wedge
in instep
rounded heal*

Grizzly   Black

Figure 1. Pawprints of grizzly bear and black bear

Snoqualmie Pass. This area has visitors too, but no more than many other places that are equally wild. Yet it has more class 1 and 2 grizzly reports than any other part of the Cascades of comparable size.

What do all these reports tell about the number of grizzlies in the Cascades? How many different times do people see the same bear? How much do bears travel between one reported sighting and another? If they are males, they might roam for miles. Based on the number of bears seen in areas frequented by people, what does that mean about how many bears live in places where fewer people go?

Leading the Cascades evaluation team, Jon Almack studied these reports, their locations, and the size of home ranges. He found it hard to make a reliable estimate. "No scientifically valid method is available yet for censusing bears," he conceded. "We were stuck using a simple comparison of our results with other observation results from small ecosystems, like the Selkirks and Cabinet-Yaak."

Based on the number of observations in other areas compared with the reliably estimated bear population in those areas, he deduced that the Cascades still had a population of ten to twenty grizzlies.[6] Because his information on British Columbia was less complete, he hesitated to say if this was only for the US side or both. Bob Forbes, BC biologist covering the Canadian side of the Cascades, estimated ten grizzlies on his side of the border.

In 1997–98, British Columbia conducted a more thorough survey and concluded that its part of the Cascades from the border north to Fraser Canyon contained at least seventeen and maybe as many as twenty-three adult or subadult grizzlies, but only five or six of them were likely to be reproductive females.[7]

Almack is not defensive about whether his estimate includes the Canadian part of the Cascades, but he does react to other liberties taken with his estimate. He is especially riled that his state superiors in 1993 revised his original "ten to twenty" to read "ten to twenty, but no more than fifty." He felt people were playing politics with his numbers. Trying to allocate bear totals between the Washington and Canadian parts of the Cascades is futile. The border is unfenced through the wilderness. At any given moment, some Canadian animal is wandering into the United States or vice versa. So far as bears are concerned, the Cascades are all one homeland. As Chris Servheen, grizzly coordinator, says, "Many of the grizzlies seen on this side of the border hold dual citizenship."[8] But changing "ten to twenty" to "no more than fifty" implied a more robust population, which might justify doing nothing.

During a public meeting in Wenatchee, one skeptic struck a familiar theme. "I'm a mountain man," he declared. "I have prospected in the North Cascades all my life, and I have never seen a single grizzly." Apparently he meant this to mean there must not be any, but it could mean any number of things. The most likely is that grizzlies simply avoided him.

Biologists are not sure why, but they do agree that grizzlies in the Cascades are elusive. This may be because they are so scarce, or because the Cascades grizzly has become a "stealth bear"—a bear so anxious to avoid humans that it will run away. This debate is important. If the Cascades grizzly behaves like a normal grizzly, the risk to humans would rise as the number of bears rises. But if the Cascades grizzly is indeed a stealth bear, and stays that way despite recovery, such a bear would be more politically correct and easier to accept.

The stealth bear theory has its origin in the Italian Alps. At one time the brown bear—first cousin to the grizzly—roamed all of Europe. Today it survives in pockets: Scandinavia, the mountains of central Europe, the Balkans, northern Spain, and the Trentino Alps of northern Italy.[9] In the past decade, it has dispersed from Italy into Switzerland[10] and ventured temporarily into southern Germany. Following generations of persecution, the Italian bears retreated to the steep forests of Adamello-Brenta Natural Park, a remote redoubt where few people go. Today these bears are mostly nocturnal. They den well away from human activity and have lost any innate brown bear aggressiveness.[11]

This behavior is consistent with what researchers have noticed in North America. In the Canadian Rockies, studies show that in areas where human activity is high, grizzlies become nocturnal.[12] Charlie Russell and Maureen Enns noticed on Russia's Kamchatka Peninsula in the late 1990s that grizzlies who had never seen humans were neither afraid nor aggressive. Their reaction depended on the human's behavior. Only in areas where poachers had been active did bears react to people by running away.[13]

Did the shooting of aggressive grizzlies in the Cascades produce the same kind of shy survivors? Some biologists think so. Killing bears with certain traits is a powerful way to influence selection, they say. It fast-forwards normal evolution. Doug Zimmer, Fish and Wildlife information specialist, buys this theory. "We're dealing with a relatively small bear, extremely shy, that avoids any contact with humans. All the big studly bears have ended up as rugs."

Scientists have noticed a similar phenomenon in Utah, where fewer rattlesnakes now seem to rattle. When the biggest danger facing a snake was hoofed animals, rattling was a good way to avoid being trampled. But humans have taken it as a signal to unholster a gun or grab a big stick. As a result, rattling rattlesnakes die young while their nonrattling relatives live on.

If grizzlies in the Cascades really are shy, is it because of training (shy mother equals shy cub) or genes? Grizzlies in the Cascades have been persecuted by humans for about 180 years. The ancestors of Italy's bears were hunted for centuries.

Scott Fitkin, Almack's former assistant, still checks out grizzly sightings as a state district biologist for the Methow. Fitkin is unsure how much local grizzlies have already become stealth bears. He thinks elusiveness could either be taught or inherited. Over the years, however, he foresees a trend toward shyness.

Jon Almack, for his part, is convinced there is no genetic change, and he is even skeptical that local grizzlies behave any differently. "The Cascades grizzlies haven't been subjected to any more persecution than other surviving populations, such as in Yellowstone, Glacier, or Banff," he says. "Bears in those areas still behave like normal grizzlies."

Steve Carter, former Forest Service biologist in Cle Elum, agrees. "They would probably act like a normal grizzly. They weren't hunted any harder here than in the Rockies. They may be a little bit more reclusive because they have the opportunity to be. They can fulfill their seasonal needs without having to move great distances. You can change elevation in the Cascades from den to spring forage without having to travel many miles."

If grizzlies in the Cascades seem more shy than other grizzlies, Almack thinks it is because the Cascades are so "vast and wild" that local bears have had less contact with people. They have not become habituated to humans, so they retain their natural shyness. Doug Zimmer elaborates on this. "The Cascades is a clean ecosystem. You don't have a lot of the drive-through stuff as in Yellowstone, or the concentrations of people they have in Glacier. So you don't have all those established bad habits. If I were in Glacier up by Granite Park

Chalet and ran into a grizzly, I'd be real nervous. In that area the park had a dump. Those bears see thousands of tourists in a summer. They're acclimatized to people. That's why Glacier has had a number of maulings." Contrast that with the North Cascades grizzly. According to Zimmer, "The minute it catches wind or sight or hearing of me, he is going to Canada to visit relatives."

Some people argue that hunting makes grizzlies more wary. If more aggressive bears stick around when a hunter wanders through, they are certainly more likely to be shot. But the jury is still out on whether that teaches the rest of them to avoid humans. As Steve Herrero writes in *Bear Attacks*, "Death isn't an instructor—it is an eliminator."[14] Studies in both the Rockies and Europe show that bears lose their wariness when they find human-sourced food.[15] Grizzlies that have been fed come back for more and thus have more encounters with people. Garbage may affect bear behavior more than guns.

Pick whichever theory you like, but the conclusion seems to be that grizzlies in the Cascades are indeed shy. Whether they will stay that way partly depends on why they are shy now. But the fact that you have tromped around the Cascades for forty years and never seen one probably just means they heard or smelled you coming.

Supporters and skeptics alike are susceptible to believing what they want to believe, and inventing ways to ignore whatever does not fit. As Felix Cohen, Yale law professor and a pioneer in American Indian law, noted, "The theories we believe we call facts, and the facts we disbelieve we call theories."

Signpost, a Seattle hiking magazine, published comments from Joe Scott of Northwest Ecosystem Alliance about the growing evidence of grizzlies in the Cascades. This prompted Warren Guntheroth to write:

The proof that grizzlies permanently reside in the North Cascades is no better than the quality of the proof that Sasquatches are there. Scott . . . mercifully does not dredge up the plaster casts of a mother grizzly with twins allegedly found near Mount Rainier, which was probably made in Alaska or even in a zoo.

No one disputes that grizzlies were once in Washington. I am confident that if they decided to return, they would.[16]

If Almack and Fitkin had dumped the carcass of a Cascades grizzly on their director's desk, would that have changed anyone's mind? Would it have ended complaints that their evidence was no better than "some tracks"? Or would it have been dismissed as something they found "in Alaska or even in a zoo"?

If you refuse to believe that grizzlies live in the Cascades, you start by arguing there is no proof that they do. You might add that you have never seen one, therefore they must not be there. Next, you claim any evidence of them is false. Your final fallback would be that proof of grizzlies in the Cascades does not prove they live there. They are just transients, passing through. Occasionally, they wander down from Canada, look around, but then head home.

A lovesick male grizzly could do that, although the energy needed for annual treks from Canada to the Teanaway would exhaust him. But what of the females with cubs sighted in the Alpine Lakes or tracked on the tree farm west of Mount Rainier? A female's home range averages 70 square miles. Canada is 120 to 160 miles from those sites, as a crow flies. A mother bear skirting towns and farms would need to walk about 250 miles to make that journey.

The tree farm tracks were fresh when Stofel found them in June. Cubs are born in the den during winter. Typically they emerge in April or May. Would a mother bear take her newly born Canadian cubs on a two-month, 250-mile jaunt through the roughest part of the Cascades? Especially when a mother typically starts her cubs out in very small steps? Even if her cubs were a year old, why would she make such a trek? Why would she venture so far beyond her home range? What would she find so attractive about a tree farm in country that was never prime habitat for grizzlies?

Ralph Waldo Emerson noted that men value truth in proportion to its convenience. People who claim Cascade grizzlies are transients are clinging to a position because they need it. They do not care about how mother bears raise their young or the size of a grizzly's home range. The transient theory is their last stand against the inconvenient reality that grizzlies might actually still live in the Cascades.

Mitch Friedman, whose Northwest Ecosystem Alliance has been the loudest advocate for grizzlies in the Cascades, is annoyed that the area is still in limbo over this "lingering issue" of whether grizzlies are still there. "We can't get to the serious political debate over augmentation without putting this issue to rest first," he complains.

Federal law allows reintroduction of a species in suitable habitat from which it has disappeared. Hence, from a legal standpoint the presence of survivors is irrelevant, especially under the Tenth Circuit's view that "experimental" status for a reintroduced species such as wolves in Yellowstone is okay even if some of its kind were already there. But the political dynamics of trying to save an existing population are different from putting bears back in a place from which they are gone. Witness the reactions in the Bitterroots, where fearful residents had no history of living with grizzlies and bear advocates hoped to find remnant grizzlies so they could give the issue a different spin.

A study of brown bear management in Europe recounted this difference in public reactions to augmentation and reintroduction. Europeans and Americans may be different, but the study concluded: "It may be easier to recover large carnivore populations when the population has not been absent for many decades."[17]

Opponents sense this. That is why they keep raising doubts about the presence of grizzlies. So long as they can sustain this uncertainty, grizzly recovery will never move completely past this question of whether there is anything left to save.

9 | ISLANDS IN THE SKY

The North Cascades face British Columbia's Coast Range across Fraser Canyon. The juncture of these two ranges may be the only place where grizzlies can still enter or leave the Cascades on their own. The likelihood that they will has major implications for bear management in the Cascades.

Millennia ago the mountains on both sides of the canyon were a solid wall. They were making a big turn to the west when the Fraser River sliced a gash through them. That made it easier for geographers to say where one range ends and the other begins. On the east side of this canyon are the Cascades. Across the river they become the Coast Range. The question is whether grizzly bears would descend out of the Coast Range, where they still reside, cross this canyon, and climb up into the Cascades.

The heart of Fraser Canyon starts at Spuzzum, a scruffy little town that looks like a cross between a logging camp and an Indian village. Between Spuzzum and Boston Bar, the Cascades plunge down from the east and the Coast Range rises on the west. On both sides, the mountains soar taller and steeper than anywhere else along the Fraser. Dr. Walter Cheadle, a British adventurer, described this spot during his 1863 visit as a place where "the mountains on each side . . . seem almost to meet overhead" while the river "goes utterly mad, and foams and rages down the narrow and falling channel."[1] Desperate railroad builders later called this Hell's Gate because it was impassable but they had to make it passable anyway.

There are few side valleys. Streams fall out of the clouds, splashing over smooth black rock as in a Chinese painting. The easiest place for any animal to cross the canyon from one mountain range to the other is near Alexandria Bridge, just upstream from Spuzzum and the new highway bridge across the Fraser. Alexandria Bridge once carried the Trans-Canada Highway. Abandoned but still intact, it is now a bridge to nowhere.

Fraser Canyon is often wet, but it is always busy. Canadian Pacific railroad tracks parallel one side of the river; Canadian National the other. A train rumbles by on one track or the other every fifteen minutes. The highway is noisy with trucks. Since the Coquihalla toll road opened, much east-west traffic has abandoned this canyon for that faster route over the mountains. But trucks still prefer this winding water grade instead of mountain passes. The Trans-Canada Highway through Fraser Canyon still stitches Canada together.

The highway is two lanes, one each way. It has no barrier in the middle or along the sides. If traffic were quieter during the night, nothing here would stop a grizzly. The gravel pit just up the road and the campground just down it might make a bear skittish; it would depend on how much the bear wanted to cross.

Young male bears especially are explorers. Grizzlies do not defend territories, but older males may encourage adolescents to seek new country. If teenage bears are like teenage boys, they may not need much encouragement. If an adventurous bear decided to see what was on the other side of this canyon, it might well come down to this wild stretch of river. It probably would avoid Alexandria Bridge. Bears do not need bridges to cross rivers.

Bruce McLellan, one of British Columbia's leading bear biologists, says: "If the habitat is good on both sides, some bears will cross two- to three-lane undivided highways." But what if that highway is in a deep canyon that also includes a fast-moving river and two busy railroads? Obstacles usually come in bunches.

The highway up Fraser Canyon is one of three that separate British Columbia's Coast Range from the US Cascades. No single bear is likely to cross all three, but would these highways block several generations of bears from migrating between the two ranges?

The Canadian highway closest to and parallel to the US border is BC Highway 3, the Crowsnest Highway. Between Hope and Princeton, British Columbia, it crosses the Cascades through Manning Provincial Park. As highways go, Highway 3 is wildlife-friendly through this part of British Columbia. Along much of it, especially through Manning Park, virgin forest grows right to the road's shoulder. Depending on passing lanes, Highway 3 varies from two to four lanes. Busy in summer, it is quiet at night.[2]

By contrast, the Coquihalla toll road, BC Highway 5, is the high-speed link between Vancouver and eastern British Columbia. It is a limited-access four-lane highway built for freeway speeds, slicing diagonally across the Cascades north of Manning Park and east of Fraser Canyon. It is not free, but it looks like a freeway and is busy like most freeways. Before the Coquihalla toll road starts up the mountain on the west side, a grassy median strip separates the lanes. It offers no cover for an animal daring to cross, but at least it is not a barrier. But higher up, where this freeway look-alike crosses Coquihalla summit, a 2.5-foot-tall concrete barricade called a Jersey barrier divides the east and west lanes. At places there are similar barriers along each side. East of the summit, in addition to Jersey barriers, a tall wire fence borders the highway. All that is missing are guard posts with searchlights and machine guns. The best, and perhaps only, animal crossings are not over but under the Coquihalla highway at places like Ladner Creek, where the road soars high on a bridge above the stream.

Imagine walking across an active runway at Los Angeles International Airport. That is what grizzlies would think of the Coquihalla toll road.

This is a big problem wherever busy roads cut through wildlife habitat. Between Banff and Lake Louise, a region famous for its wildlife, the Trans-Canada Highway follows the Bow River. At one time, animals were killed so often on this stretch of highway that

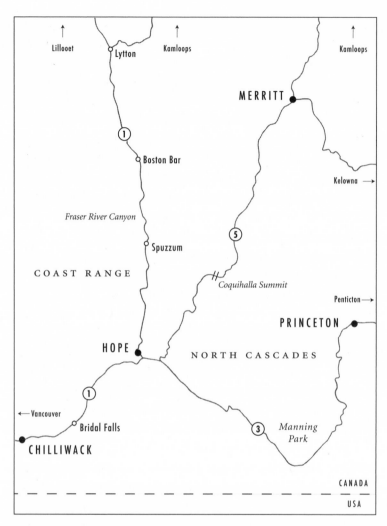

Map 4. British Columbia's Fraser Canyon and vicinity

locals called it "the Meatmaker." Parks Canada built twenty-one underpasses and two wildlife overpasses, added soil, planted native shrubs, and built a fence to herd animals toward them.[3] Since then, elk, black bears, pine marten, and cougars have used these under- and overpasses, but no wolves or grizzly bears.[4]

In 1993 Stephen Herrero, bear biologist from Calgary, helped radio-collar twenty-five Banff bears, fifteen of them females. Since then, not one of those females has crossed that road. "As far as female bears are concerned," Herrero concludes, "the Trans-Canada Highway might as well be a fence."[5] Brian Horejsi, another Calgary-based bear biologist, says the only way to reverse this is to bury the highway in tunnels at least a kilometer long with natural vegetation on top. "Sinking the road," he says, "is the only way to go."[6]

A Montana study on grizzly crossings of US Highway 2 between Glacier National Park and the Bob Marshall Wilderness found that bears mostly cross at night or early in the morning, when traffic is lightest.[7]

Land trusts and agencies are buying conservation easements from ranchers to preserve wildlife corridors across private land,[8] but highways remain one of the biggest obstacles for an animal as big, wild, and wary as the grizzly. Wildlife crossings are under study or being built over or under several highways in the Rockies and Cascades, but it remains to be seen how effective they will be for bears. The Banff experience is not encouraging, but planners still hope they may work on other roads.

Dennis Pemble, British Columbia's wildlife control officer for the lower Fraser, adds a point based on his own years of experience with bears. It is not just a question of whether a grizzly could cross Fraser Canyon or one of British Columbia's three highways, but why it would want to. "The only incentives to cross are a need for food or pressure from other bears," says Pemble. "Neither is a problem in this area." The best overpass or underpass in the world may not matter if no bear has a reason to reach the other side.

Bob Forbes, British Columbia's counterpart to Almack, is also pessimistic. "A viable population of grizzlies lives in the Pemberton area [west of Fraser Canyon]. A healthy population lives in the Coast Range. But there is probably no natural migration from the west. Highways bring many people to Fraser Canyon. Two million people from the Vancouver area recreate on both sides of the Fraser. They are not prepared to put up with grizzlies. Any bear trying to cross is likely to be shot."

A 2004 study refers to this area as the "Fraser-Coquihalla Fracture Zone," and it underscores Forbes's prediction. Defining "fracture zones" on the basis of road and human population densities, land cover, and topography, it rates this area as poor for "permeability," the ability of grizzly bears to cross it.[9]

East of the Cascades on the US side of the border is a region variously known as the Okanogan Highlands, Columbia Highlands, or the Okanogan-Kettle fracture zone. Once every few years someone reports a grizzly in the Tonasket ranger district east of the Okanogan River. In 2003 a grizzly sighting was confirmed on a ranch near Chesaw. Farther east the sightings increase. Ferry County's Kettle River Range is due south of a grizzly population in British Columbia's Granby. Even farther east, across the Columbia River, grizzlies become more common nearer the Selkirks, the closest grizzly recovery area to the Cascades. Could grizzlies move between the Cascades and these other bear habitats to the east?

After Northwest Ecosystem Alliance changed its name to Conservation Northwest, it launched a fundraising campaign for the twofold purpose of buying land in this area and launching a wilderness initiative designed, in its words, to restore "the land bridge" between the Selkirks and the Cascades.

Bears in this region find it easier to travel north-south than east-west. The hills and valleys run north-south. Staying in the hills is reasonably safe, but trying to cross a valley is downright dangerous. The valleys, especially the Okanogan, are full of towns, ranches, highways, and people with a low tolerance for grizzlies. East-west movement would mean crossing these minefields.

The study that rated the Fraser-Coquihalla "poor" claims that the BC Okanogan south of Penticton may offer "the best linkage between the North Cascades and the Columbia Mountains." But it would also require bears to make long swims across one of several lakes that make the BC Okanogan popular, as well as cross two busy highways.

Whether it is Okanogan's deadly valleys or British Columbia's lakes, railroads, and highways, the conclusion seems to be the same: natural migration of grizzlies into the Cascades would be tough. Most biologists are skeptical of migration across the Fraser, and none believe grizzlies could safely arrive from the east. The last word comes from Matt Austin, large carnivore specialist in British Columbia's Ministry of Environment, Lands, and Parks. Austin oversaw grizzly management for the province, represented British Columbia on the IGBC, and led plans for grizzly recovery in British Columbia's Cascades. What does he think of the prospect of grizzlies naturally entering the Cascades? "Reluctantly," Austin concedes, "I'm leaning towards the resignation that the Cascades must be managed as an island."

Bill Gaines, US Forest Service wildlife biologist for the entire east slope of the Washington Cascades, shares this concern. "Grizzlies in the US and BC North Cascades are very likely isolated from any other grizzly bear populations and should be managed as such."

All grizzly recovery areas are islands. Change the names of the roads and valleys and the conclusion is the same everywhere—grizzly recovery areas are isolated remnants of bear habitat, cut off from each other by barriers that range from formidable to impossible. As a Canadian bear biologist concluded, "Genetic groups are bounded by highways."[10] The Fish and Wildlife Service now claims that the Selkirks are linked to the Cabinet-Yaak recovery area through Canada. Even if they are, the Greater Selkirks-Cabinet-Yaak is still an island separate from other grizzly recovery areas. The only relevant question is the size of the island.

The Bitterroots come the closest of any in offering a way to reconnect grizzly bear "islands" in the Northern Rockies, but highways and populated valleys mark even the boundaries of the Bitterroots.

The Cascades are simply the most isolated of them all. Unless expensive steps with dubious chances of success are taken to improve bear access over or under British Columbia's highways and the multiple obstacles in Fraser Canyon and the Okanogan, the Cascades will always be an island—a big, wild island, for sure, but still only a refuge in the sky, surrounded by a sea of hostile habitat.

10 | CAN THEY SURVIVE ON THEIR OWN?

During the public meetings about a Cascades recovery plan in 1993, some people told wildlife managers that they could tolerate those grizzlies already living in the Cascades but not more. Some things, like cod liver oil, are acceptable only in small doses.

State senator Bob Morton said: "I respect and appreciate the native population of bears already in the Northern Cascades and believe they should be allowed to live and prosper. But I do not feel it would be wise to import large numbers of additional bears."[1]

Norma Gellert, a hiker from Mercer Island, took a different tack. Writing to a local hiking magazine, she voiced concern for the surviving bears: "The existing grizzlies most likely have all they can do to sustain themselves in their diminished habitat; the artificial introduction of new ones would only add to the congestion and increase the possibility of attack."[2] A number of people questioned why it was necessary to boost a bear population that currently was not bothering anyone. Why not leave well enough alone?

Biologists felt a need to evaluate the assumptions behind these claims, to know if a population of ten to twenty grizzlies really could "sustain themselves" or "live and prosper." Without natural links to other bears, could this island population survive? Could it grow? Could it ever reach a level where anyone could say it had recovered?

Wildlife specialists know that grizzlies and musk ox are the slowest reproducing land mammals in North America. Whatever the musk ox's reasons, several things work against grizzlies. A female grizzly does not breed until she is four to seven years old. The better her habitat, the sooner she matures sexually. She only has cubs every three years.[3] The number depends on her weight when she starts hibernation, which again depends on habitat. She can have up to five cubs, but one or two is normal. Cubs stay with her through their second and into their third year while she teaches them survival skills. Then she weans them, chases them off, and tries to mate again. Black bear mothers send their cubs off a year sooner, so they are ready to mate again in two years rather than three.

The oldest known grizzly reached the ripe old age of thirty-five, but biologists suspect few live past twenty or twenty-five years. Since bears reach sexual maturity slowly (males actually take a bit longer than females),[4] a female has a chance to breed only five or six times in her life. Her breeding chances decline with age, so a total of three or four litters of cubs is more typical. On average, it takes her a decade to replace herself with another breeding-age female.[5]

Cub mortality is high—30 to 40 percent in the first two years. The main cause seems to be adult males. In the cat family, toms kill kittens to induce a female to breed again. Some biologists suspect male bears do the same thing: they try to kill cubs they did not sire so that their own genes perpetuate the species.[6] Others suggest this infanticide helps keep grizzly populations dispersed in densities the habitat will support.[7] Whatever the reason, this aggression goes a long way toward explaining why mother grizzlies are so fiercely protective of their young.

After the mother abandons her two- to three-year-old cubs, those subadults are vulnerable. If the habitat is marginal or their mother did not teach them well, they may starve. Young females create a home range that at least partly overlaps their mother's, but adolescent males go farther and encounter more hazards. Like teenage boys, they are prone to trouble—campground raids, visits to ranches, or highway crossings. As a result they are more vulnerable. Jon Almack estimates that half of all adolescent males never make it to maturity.

The net effect is low survival and glacial growth for the species. Population growth rates range from flat or negative in the Kananaskis region south of Banff to about 5 percent within Yellowstone to 8.5 percent in Montana's Flathead Valley—considered some of the best grizzly habitat anywhere.[8] Even at that phenomenal rate, a Cascades population of ten to twenty bears would add only one or two bears a year.

Would other dynamics affect survival in a small population? How many breeding females are actually in the Cascades? If these grizzlies are cut off from others, what about inbreeding? Vulnerability to disease or natural disasters? Faced with public calls during and after the 1993 meetings to leave Cascade grizzlies alone and let them recover naturally, Almack and his team felt they needed better answers.

Bill Gaines became the population guru on Almack's team. Bear biologists have developed a number of models for projecting populations. They all build on the basics of breeding age, litter size, breeding frequency, survival rates, and so forth.[9] Gaines turned to a 1986 population study by bear biologist Mark Shaffer in Yellowstone. Shaffer had developed a simulation to estimate how long a grizzly population of a given size could survive.[10]

Unfortunately, Gaines lacked data on the age or sex of Cascades grizzlies, so he made best-case assumptions about the ratio of males to females, made no downward adjustment for any inbreeding problems, and fed these numbers into his computer. He concluded that ten to twenty bears could not survive on their own. Even under the most optimistic assumptions, a population that small would continue a slow tailspin until the last one died. If there were only ten bears now, they would be gone in about fifty years. A population that small simply could not sustain itself. In increments of ten, Gaines kept raising his assumption about the number of grizzlies still living in the Cascades. It made no difference which side of the international border they called home. Forty would die off, so would fifty, so would sixty. These populations were just too small to breed themselves back from the brink. Not until he assumed seventy bears did this downward trend stop.

So much for "natural recovery." If the model Gaines used is right, in a population of less than seventy grizzlies, so-called natural recovery will not work. "It was not a pretty picture," Gaines recalls. "Five bears added in the next five years would introduce some genetic freshness," he says, "but that probably would not be enough in the long run to reverse the population decline."

Jon Almack agrees. Genetic freshness is important, he says, but alone it is not enough to save so small a population. "The smallness of the population makes it very vulnerable. A natural catastrophe, such as a late frost that kills the huckleberry crop or a major wild-fire that kills bears, could have a devastating effect," Almack cautions.[11] "Such a small population could simply stop reproducing." Biologists often talk of ten new bears over ten years to ward off extinction in the Cascades. Whether it is five in five years or ten in ten, they all agree that the remaining survivors have no chance of making it on their own.

Science, unfortunately, drives a hard bargain. It has a certain insistence that sometimes seems downright unreasonable. To many people, the idea of leaving grizzlies alone and letting them recover naturally sounds like a fair balance between the needs of bears and the needs of people. But now the scientists say it will take five or ten more bears just for the sake of "genetic freshness." Some people may not like that, but if five or ten is what it takes, spread over several years and ten thousand square miles of mountains, they might tolerate it. But science keeps upping the ante. Warding off short-term extinction via genetic freshness is not the same as what biologists call a "viable population." Short-term survival, it turns out, is not the same as long-term survival. For the latter, five to ten more bears will not even come close.

African cheetahs and Kodiak bears illustrate the problem. Over the years both have lost genetic diversity. In the case of the cheetah, ten thousand years ago something nearly wiped it out. Cheetahs today are clonelike, descended from the few survivors. That population bottleneck left them with little genetic variety, even though their range is not islandlike. Kodiak bears reached the same condition by living on real islands isolated from mainland Alaska twelve thousand years ago. In the short term, scientists are more worried about the cheetah than the Kodiak bear. The cheetah does a poor job of defending its kills from hyenas and lions.[12] Less than a quarter of all Serengeti cheetahs produce offspring that survive, and the ones that do tend to be from the same bloodlines, thus shrinking genetic diversity even more.[13] The biggest short-term concern for the Kodiak bear is human encroachment on its habitat,[14] but the habitat is so good that the bear still grows to monster proportions.

Nature provides a safety valve against loss of genetic diversity. A certain amount of mutation occurs naturally, and this helps offset the harmful effects of isolation. A population of any species has stable and healthy DNA when the effects of genetic isolation are in equilibrium with natural mutation and migration.[15] If migration is cut off, as in the case of island populations, mutation alone carries the full burden of counteracting the dangers of isolation. In small populations, that may be too much to ask.

Populations that lack genetic diversity sometimes experience what is called inbreeding depression—reproduction slows or stops. Professor Lisette Waits, who specializes in genetic biology at the University of Idaho, warns that "long-term population viability and evolutionary potential will decrease as genetic diversity decreases."[16] Put another way, genetic diversity improves a population's ability to adapt and thus evolve in the face of a changing environment.[17] Whether the challenge is climate change or disease, survival of the fittest does not work well when everyone has the same genes.

When populations are chopped up into genetic islands, they face all these risks. Small or isolated populations lose genetic diversity.[18] Today, half a million black bears roam North America. They are far more tolerant than grizzlies are of humans and the changes humans bring. North America has fifty thousand brown bears, including grizzlies. Over the entire Arctic, only twenty-five thousand polar bears remain. Black bears are genetically the most diverse group, followed by brown bears, followed by polar bears. As population shrinks, so does genetic diversity.[19]

Small or isolated populations also undergo what is called genetic drift. Without the moderating effect of a large gene pool, these populations develop quirks. As the population shrinks, genetic gaps grow.[20] Hence, the panther in Florida's Everglades, cut off for generations from other cougars, has a distinctive whorl of hair on its back and a kink in its tail.

The longer a grizzly population is isolated, the more it loses diversity and the farther it drifts from the genes of other grizzlies. Some studies suggest that Yellowstone's grizzlies already have lost 10 percent of their genetic variety since they were cut off from populations farther north.[21] If grizzlies still survive in Colorado's San Juans, they certainly have lost more genetic diversity and may have drifted genetically even farther from other grizzlies.

Distance alone can cause genetic differences by impeding the flow of genes. Even within what seems to be the same species, the genetic difference can reach between-species values. A University of Alberta study compared grizzlies from Alaska's Brooks Range with grizzlies from the east slope of the Canadian Rockies. You could hardly call them kissing cousins. They had a genetic difference measure of 0.50, almost as much as the 0.64 difference between Brooks Range grizzlies and east slope Canadian black bears![22]

Other studies suggest that human impacts reduce genetic diversity in grizzlies even more.[23] Besides isolating populations into separate islands, human persecution of aggressive bears changes bear behavior and, eventually, bear genes. The stealth bears of Italy's Trentino Alps are the living proof.

Genetics is only part of the equation. In a given population, such as grizzlies in the Cascades, survival is also influenced by the population's makeup—how many breeding females, the ratio of males to females, whether a few males dominate the breeding, and so forth. In an isolated population, these demographics can dramatically influence size requirements.

Finally, there are environmental unknowns, such as the effects of global warming on vegetative changes and hibernation patterns, and the growing human population along the western edge of the Cascades.

When you consider all these variables—genetic isolation and drift, population demographics, climate change, and so forth, you end up needing a much bigger number to ensure survival. To adapt to changes over the long haul and still survive—what biologists call a minimum viable population—an isolated population like that in the Cascades requires two hundred to four hundred grizzlies. That is a far cry from the ten to twenty that live there now, or the seventy needed to halt short-term die-out.

For now, biologists say the Cascades can support a minimum viable population of two hundred to four hundred bears. But nearly every time scientists review what is needed for a population to stay viable, they raise the minimum. "A viable population can be a moving target," warns Bill Gaines. "It depends on how long you hope to keep the population alive. You need more to sustain it for a longer period."

To the scientist it is a question of risks, but to Gaines it eventually becomes a debate about angels dancing on the tip of a pin. At some point it no longer matters, and the Cascades, in his view, have already passed this point. "We don't use minimum viable population anymore," he explains. "Our ability to augment is limited by the availability of bears, not by how many we need."

Ponder the implications of this. If there are not enough bears available to bring the Cascades population up to a minimum needed to ensure long-term survival, it becomes a matter of bringing in just enough bears to stave off extinction and waiting for that tiny population, at an annual growth rate of perhaps 1 percent, to stage its own comeback—assuming that over the centuries this might take no big threat comes along and wipes them out. This brings new meaning to the concept of "long range." "Don't expect any eighteen-wheelers to back up to a trailhead and unload a bunch of bears," adds British Columbia's Matt Austin. "The speed of recovery will be very slow."

But just in case those aren't enough hurdles, Bill Gaines adds one more. Even if we had an unlimited supply of bears, he theorizes, if experts decide that a viable population means more than the current upper limit of four hundred, which is the most the US portion of the Cascades could support, the Cascades could actually be too small! In other words, if population wizards keep raising the goalposts, an area as vast as the Cascades, now cut off from other bears by highways, railroads, and ranches, may not be big enough by itself to ensure the grizzly's long-term survival.[24] The same problem faces the Selkirk, Cabinet-Yaak, and Bitterroots grizzly recovery areas. If they remain isolated from each other, they may not be big enough by themselves to support bear populations large enough for long-term survival.

You have to start thinking about "metapopulations," Gaines warns. That means concepts such as Yukon-to-Yellowstone ("Y2Y"), the proposal to preserve or restore wildlife corridors down the backbone of the Continental Divide in an effort to stitch isolated populations back together.[25] Whether that concept can work across Manning Park's highway, the Coquihalla toll road, and Fraser Canyon's Trans-Canada Highway and railroads is a question managers eventually will have to confront.

But grizzlies in the Cascades face a more immediate crisis. Minimum population debates are like wondering what color to paint a sinking ship. Without new blood, these bears are functionally extinct; they are the walking dead. It may have been times like this that prompted Theodore Roosevelt to advise, "In any moment of decision the best thing you can do is the right thing, the next best thing is the wrong thing, and the worst thing you can do is nothing."

British Columbia's Bob Forbes, always a straight shooter, sees the choices clearly: "We are working under a deadline in the Cascades," he says. "Without transplants, that population will wink out. They'll die out within my lifetime. We are obligated to recognize and redress this problem. This is not rocket science—you either do something or they're going to go."

11 | NEW BLOOD

Once there was a grizzly bear known as Winston. His home was in the hills around Pemberton Meadows in the Coast Range of British Columbia. For generations his family had lived in these hills and dined on the lush shrubs that sprout each spring and summer in Pemberton Meadows. But then people came and fenced off the meadows for livestock and to grow crops of carrots and rutabagas. Most bears did not like this, but Winston acquired a taste for such exotic vegetables, and that led him to become British Columbia's best-traveled bear.

He took his first trip in October 1991 after a farmer in Pemberton Meadows rang Dennis Pemble, wildlife control officer, to complain that a bear had killed one of his four-hundred-pound heifers. Pemble set live traps attached to logs and snared two grizzlies— Winston and a female. Winston dragged his log half a mile before Pemble shot him full of tranquilizers and loaded him into a cage.

Pemble had no way to know if he had caught the heifer killer, but he ear-tagged both bears and called in a helicopter to move them far away from Pemberton Meadows. It was and still is the policy of British Columbia's Wildlife Branch to relocate problem grizzlies. Black bears, because they are so plentiful and the government can only afford to spend so much time on each incident, usually face summary execution.

Winston and his possible partner in crime were airlifted to an inlet off the Strait of Georgia. They were released with the hope that they would adapt to this wild new home in coastal British Columbia and stay out of trouble. Other bears exiled to Toba and Bute inlets did just that. But not Winston. He and the female spent the winter somewhere in the mountains west of Whistler ski resort and by the next summer they both were back at Pemberton Meadows. As a crow flies, they had walked 80 miles. As a bear walks, it was probably more like 120.

Pemble does not recall why someone called him the second time, but he thinks it was because a grizzly was digging up carrots. After a boring diet of glacier lily roots, carrots are like candy to some bears. Exactly a year after his first capture, Winston met Dennis Pemble again and ended up in another cage, this time on the back of Pemble's truck. As before, Pemble could not be sure if Winston was the culprit or was just in the wrong place at the wrong time.

This time Bob Forbes, senior biologist for the BC Cascades, saw Winston as an opportunity. Forbes was concerned that the little group of grizzlies that still lived in the Cascades was too small to survive on its own. He wanted to augment them. BC wildlife managers can move bears without the environmental impact statements or public hearings required by US law. Winston, who was about fifteen years old, was in good breeding condition and had no history of aggression. "He seems to have a real aversion to humans," Forbes told a Vancouver reporter.[1]

Besides, Forbes and Jon Almack both wanted to learn more about bears in the Cascades. Almack told Forbes about his lack of success in trapping one. They both saw the value of radio-collaring and tracking a grizzly. No one had ever done that in the Cascades. Almack had a radio collar, Pemble had Winston, and Forbes and Pemble worked for the same agency.

The plan hit two snags. First, Almack's boss ordered him to stay away from it. Politically it was too hot for a Washington State employee to help British Columbia move a grizzly into the Cascades when that bear could end up in Washington (which it briefly did). Second, Forbes discovered that some folks on his own side of the border were nervous too. Ranchers around Princeton wanted no grizzly within miles of their cattle, and rangers at Manning Park wanted no grizzly within miles of their park. Forbes managed, Houdini-like, to thread his way between all these problems. Instead of using Almack's radio collar, he somehow acquired one from Chris Servheen, the US grizzly coordinator. The fewer questions asked, the better. Just east of Manning Park, Forbes drove Winston up a rough road that paralleled the Pasayten River. Where the road ended just short of the US border, east of Manning Park and well south of Princeton's cattle, Forbes turned Winston loose.

It was sometime around then, late in 1992, that people became interested in this bear. With his new radio collar, his travels became a matter of public record. The *Vancouver Sun* soon was carrying regular accounts, and everyone was reading about him. That is when Winston got his name. Winston crossed the US border into the Pasayten Wilderness. A Washington State biologist who had taken some personal time to go hunting found Winston's tracks in fresh snow. He followed them back to the border. Winston then reentered Canada and walked past Lightning Lakes, one of the most popular spots in Manning Park. No one saw him. By then it was clear that Winston was heading west. Still in Canada, he crossed the Skagit River, left Manning Park, and was next discovered in the Chilliwack River valley. Hound hunters found his tracks in snow, claimed they thought he was a black bear—a dubious claim—and let their hounds loose. They chased Winston over the mountains until he evaded them near Bridal Falls next to the Trans-Canada Highway.

It was now winter. Winston had not hibernated. He had lost weight. He crossed the four-lane Trans-Canada Highway and the railroad tracks next to it. Fishermen saw him on the bank of the Fraser River. The bear was feeding on salmon near a fish hatchery. Pemble suspected Winston was weak and hungry. He worried that the bear was too close to farms and people around Chilliwack and might attack someone. He considered shooting it with real bullets instead of tranquilizers. Then Winston vanished. He probably hibernated somewhere above Bridal Falls. It was spring before biologists picked up his signal again. He had swum the broad Fraser River, crossed more roads and railroads, and was headed up the east side of Harrison Lake. There was no doubt now where he was going—straight back to Pemberton Meadows. In what may be a record, Winston had walked two hundred miles to go home once again.

Months later, Winston's collar signaled an alert that it had stopped moving. That usually means a dead bear. But the collar was never found; Pemble thinks it may have slipped off because Winston was so thin. This may be the end of Winston's story, but Pemble is not sure. After trapping this bear twice and never being sure if he really was a problem bear, Pemble had developed a keen interest in Winston.

Seven years later a big male grizzly was captured near Pemberton and released up the Anderson River east of Fraser Canyon. Like Winston, it walked back. A farmer near Pemberton then caught it raiding his chickens and killed it. Killing grizzlies to protect property is still legal in British Columbia but not in the United States. This bear had a notch in his ear where there may have been an ear tag. Pemble wonders if he might have been Winston. If it was, by the end of his life Winston had been captured and relocated three times—each time to a different place—crossed six highways, four sets of railroad tracks, swum the Fraser River twice, and visited two countries.

In a statement announcing Winston's relocation to the Cascades, Forbes explained: "We regularly move grizzly bears from core grizzly population areas to peripheral areas with fewer bears as part of our ongoing grizzly bear management program."[2] In unprepared remarks, he added, "We were just doing what we could on an interim basis. We moved whatever bears were available. The sex of the bear was just the luck of the draw. A real recovery program would concentrate on subadult females." Winston was one of four grizzlies moved into the BC Cascades that year; Forbes asked Dennis Pemble to put the other three north of the Coquihalla.

Dennis Pemble sees more bears that anyone else in British Columbia's lower mainland. As wildlife control officer for that region, he is the man who comes when frightened people call about a bear or cougar. In the past ten years Pemble has caught six or seven grizzlies in the Pemberton area, driven them up Fraser

Canyon, and turned them loose on the Cascades side of the river. Winston was the only one released near the US border. Several bears were dropped off between Spuzzum and Boston Bar, but most were released up Anderson River east of Boston Bar.

BC Wildlife does not have much money for radio collars. Thanks to the United States, Winston had a collar. British Columbia collared one other bear. Like Winston, this other grizzly did not stay put. He ended up in Agassiz, where he was recaptured and released again. The other grizzlies, including several females just past puberty, were only ear-tagged. If someone finds a dead grizzly with an ear tag, they are supposed to call Pemble's agency. Except for the old male who lost his ear tag as well as his life for raiding a Pemberton chicken coop, no one has reported the other bears. That either means that they are dead and unreported or that four or five released grizzlies are still living in the British Columbia Cascades.

Winston is a case study in how *not* to augment a bear population.[3] Mature males have the lowest transplant success of any bears. They are too headstrong about heading home. In one case, a male brown bear was transplanted by boat to an island in Alaska's Prince William Sound. Depending on which way the tide was flowing, he swam either six or nine miles to go home.[4] Winston had already shown this trait when he returned to Pemberton Meadows the first time. By the time he walked home the second time, he had become a world traveler.

The attempt to relocate Winston in the Cascades and Pemble's relocation of grizzlies up Fraser Canyon suffer from the same flaw. They were made not primarily to augment the Cascades population but to find some place to relocate problem bears. It is the same approach park rangers use in deciding what to do with bears that get into trouble at campgrounds. Instead of shooting them, rangers pack the bears off to far corners of the park and hope they stay there. You could call it reactive relocation.

If the main aim is to augment a frail population, what you might call proactive relocation, you would come at it the other way around. Instead of trapping problem bears, you would try to catch nonproblem bears, especially subadult females. They are the best transplant candidates. "The first transplant should be a collared female," explains Jon Almack. "Then watch to see what happens and decide based on that whether the next transplants should be male or female. The first bear would tell us about others. In the Selkirks, for instance, the first transplant revealed the presence of nine other bears, even though many people thought there were none."

The homing instinct is weakest in pregnant females, Almack explains. Their interest is in finding a suitable place to raise cubs. Once they do, they start looking for a den. Late summer or fall is the best time to transplant, because bears are less likely to start trips late in the season. No one apparently told Winston.

Where should bears come from? The donor and transplant areas should be as much alike as possible. Grizzlies are adept, but the chance of success improves if they are relocated into similar habitat. We all do better in familiar surroundings.

That poses a problem. The Cascades are drier than British Columbia's Coast Range. The grizzly population in parts of the Coast Range most like the Cascades—directly across Fraser Canyon—is also threatened. Using it as donor area is like robbing Peter to pay Paul. Grizzly populations farther west in the Coast Range are in better shape, but that country is also wetter and warmer. Bears from farther west eat different plants and more salmon. David Dunbar, who has replaced Bob Forbes as area biologist in the BC Cascades, concedes, "It is not a super fit."

British Columbia thus has its own problems in finding a good source for bears to move into its part of the Cascades. It has gone through this same analysis and decided to focus on the Wells Grey area northwest of Kamloops as the best donor site. Wells Grey contains a healthy grizzly population and reasonably similar habitat.

If the United States ever decides to augment grizzlies on its side of the Cascades, where would they come from? Could we count on British Columbia to donate bears when its own are already in short supply? Forbes thinks the American side is a better place to put bears because North Cascades National Park and the wilderness around it are bigger and wilder than anything on the British Columbia side. If his view prevailed, British Columbia would donate bears to the United States on the theory that what is good for the US side of the Cascades is ultimately good for both sides. But everyone in British Columbia may not agree.[5]

Some Washington State biologists think grizzlies from the Rockies could adapt to the Cascades. No one knows if they would use the Cascades the same way they use the Rockies, but at least the climate and habitat along the east slope of the Cascades is much like the Rockies.[6] They have many of the same foods, and grizzlies in both have adapted to the loss of salmon. Yellowstone grizzlies have come off the threatened species list, and some grizzlies around Glacier National Park have already been moved into the Cabinet-Yaak, so bears might be available.

But politics starts where biology ends. Skeptical state officials are suspicious that Montana or Wyoming might use Washington's Cascades as a dumping ground for problem bears. And environmentalists in the Rockies insist that they have no surplus bears.

Ironically, those people who still have grizzlies may grow more protective and possessive, while those who want more bears look on with envy. A spokesman for British Columbia's East Kootenay Environmental Society has publicly admitted to "a lot of reticence" about seeing "his" grizzlies exported to the United States. Whether it is water in the desert or grizzlies in the Northwest, this is what happens when resources grow scarce.

Augmenting an existing population is not the only way to recover a threatened or endangered species. For small island populations, however, scientists claim it is the only way to reverse inbreeding depression and short-term extinction risk. In a transborder study of grizzly bear populations in the Northern Rockies and southeastern

British Columbia, scientists found that augmenting was the critical first step, followed over the longer term by reducing the causes of initial population loss and, finally, by reconnecting populations through linkage zones—building bridges, so to speak, between the islands. The authors were clear, however, that augmenting is the critical first step.[7] Biologists feel an urgency to get on with it. Bill Gaines says the remnant Cascades grizzlies are "in serious trouble." Bob Forbes warns that without help, they will "wink out."

If they do wink out, that means several things. Anything special about the genes of those grizzlies now in the Cascades will be forever lost. Reintroduced grizzlies might do fine. But that ancient and mystic link to the land would be severed. Part of that land's unique spirit would be silenced. As the bumper sticker warns, extinction is forever. The newcomers would be just that—newcomers, emigrants, just like us. Something about that seems manipulated and artificial.

In a reintroduction program, everything rides on the genetics of the new bears. Instead of supplementing a resident gene pool, reintroduced bears start a new one. They would need to come from one or more donor populations that are themselves genetically diverse. Otherwise, it would be a population with a built-in bottleneck—the same problem that now faces cheetahs. Ideally, a reintroduced population should also replicate a natural population, which means bringing in different sexes and age classes. Thus, from a biological standpoint alone, reintroduction is more complicated than augmenting.[8]

If the survivors die out before any transplants, it will also take more bears to reach anything near viable population levels. The sooner the current population is augmented, the fewer bears are needed. Perhaps there are only ten to twenty bears in the Cascades now, but that is ten to twenty more than there will be if managers do nothing.

Finally, public resistance to reintroduction could be stronger than resistance to augmenting. As one study warns: "Although the biological issues are complex, it appears they can be overcome for most bear species. Perhaps more daunting are the social aspects of bear reintroduction."[9]

Witness the two decades' effort required to return wolves to Idaho and Yellowstone. Witness the hostility toward grizzlies at Okanogan's Night of the Nine Death Threats. Managers are keenly aware of this. So long as bears are still in the Cascades, some part of the public will support saving them, even if that means bringing in more. When those survivors go, so does the urgency. The pressure is off; there is nothing left to save. Organized support for bears would fade. People would grow accustomed to their "safe" mountains and think twice about bringing bears back. Who, for instance, is pushing to restore grizzlies to California's Sierra Nevada?

"The tacit understanding among bear managers is that if we ever lose this population, the chances of reintroduction are nonexistent," warns Doug Zimmer, Fish and Wildlife information specialist. "That makes the issue far more urgent. If we lose this population, grizzly bears are gone from the North Cascades forever."[10]

12 | IMPORT BANS

Any plan to bring more grizzly bears into the US side of the North Cascades will require a formal decision by the US Fish and Wildlife Service, an environmental impact statement, and public hearings. So far, none of these has happened.

The Cascades recovery plan sets the goal of recovery but does not specify ways and means. During public meetings about this plan, many people complained about this lack of specificity. They accused officials of ducking the real issues, and arguably those officials did. The Interagency Grizzly Bear Committee knew that augmentation would be a charged issue, and they deferred any decision about it.

That did not stop people from asking, nor did it stop some officials from talking about augmentation, at least hypothetically. It quickly became obvious that talk about bringing in bears, even hypothetical talk, set off alarms. When Chris Servheen told a Wenatchee public meeting that, hypothetically, augmentation in the Cascades might mean bringing in four to six bears over two or three years, Tim Waters from the state Department of Fish and Wildlife told reporters, "That was, in our opinion, stepping a little bit out of line."[1]

WADFW
Public Comments

Servheen's hypothetical prediction made many people nervous, especially the state agency that was working with the feds on the recovery program. Curt Smitch, the department's director, told a Spokane audience: "At this point, as far as I'm concerned, augmentation is off the table."[2] His department seemed bent on keeping it off. In Almack's evaluation report, his superiors boosted Jon's esti-

118

mate of ten to twenty grizzlies currently living in the Cascades to read "but no more than fifty." A larger population might suggest that bears could survive on their own, and then augmenting could be taken "off the table."

State senator Bob Morton seized on what he sensed was a surge in anti-augmenting sentiment. In 1993 he introduced a bill in the state legislature to ban importing bears into Washington except for research, zoos, or circuses. Representatives from cattle ranchers, backcountry horsemen, and muzzle loaders rallied around the bill. The first two groups had already voiced concerns about grizzlies in the Cascades. Mitch Friedman from the Northwest Ecosystem Alliance spoke in opposition. He warned a legislative committee that the bill violated the federal Endangered Species Act, which it probably did if it sought to tie the federal government's hands. Friedman also claimed that the bill wrongly assumed that any bears brought into Washington would be nuisance bears. Finally, in what was probably an overstatement, Friedman predicted that the bill would bring the extinction of grizzlies in Washington.

Senator Morton's proposal failed, but it made him the hero of the movement to ban imports. He told local reporters: "It is one thing for native bears to cross into our state as part of their natural range, but it would be foolish and dangerous to introduce bears with prior conflicts with people into our natural areas from other states or countries."[3]

Senator Morton [handwritten marginalia]

Morton revised and reintroduced his bill in the next legislative session. With support from the same groups as before, this time it passed. In 1995 it become law as section 77.12.035 of the Revised Code of Washington. It says: "The department [Fish and Wildlife] shall protect grizzly bears and develop management programs on publicly owned lands that will encourage the natural regeneration of grizzly bears in areas of suitable habitat. Grizzly bears shall not be transplanted or introduced into the state. Only grizzly bears that are native to Washington State may be utilized by the department for management purposes. The department is directed to fully participate in all discussions and negotiations with federal and state agencies relating to grizzly bear management and shall fully communicate, support, and implement the policies of this section."

Morton's law made some questionable assumptions. If population projections by the biologists were right, encouraging "natural regeneration of grizzly bears" without augmenting was mission impossible. It is not clear if Senator Morton knew this. His law did not prohibit moving grizzlies from the Selkirks in the northeast corner of Washington to the Cascades; it only banned bringing in bears from out of state. Yet there was no reason to assume that Selkirk grizzlies would be better or worse than Idaho, Montana, or British Columbia grizzlies. Idaho's Department of Fish and Game had expressed a similar sentiment in 1986, saying it was acceptable to move grizzlies from one Idaho ecosystem to another, but not from out of state.[4] A ban on out-of-state bears has a nice ring to it, but by and large grizzlies are grizzlies. Senator Morton's expressed fear was that Washington's bear imports would be someone's problem exports. That was an understandable concern; hence the preference for "good" local grizzlies over "bad" bears from elsewhere. Yet the import ban did not say that. It was broad and unconditional.

The final sentence of this law directed the state Department of Fish and Wildlife "to fully participate in all discussions and negotiations with federal and state agencies relating to grizzly bear management." Morton wanted Washington State to stay in the game, but it seemed naive to assume that the state would have much of a voice in grizzly bear management when everyone knew it could not participate in any bear transplants. That was akin to the state staying in a poker game without paying its ante.

Some biologists dismissed the law as an ineffective gesture. Despite its unqualified language, it only applied to state agencies. Washington's legislature had no power to tie the hands of federal wildlife managers implementing the federal Endangered Species Act. Moreover, if the state was directed by this law to stay in the discussions and negotiations about grizzly bear management, the law seemed to acknowledge that augmentation might go ahead even if the state was not involved.

Others feared the law would still slow grizzly recovery—not because of the ban itself, but because it barred the state from helping recovery if it included moving bears. "The state's ban makes US Fish and Wildlife cooperation with the state more difficult," a federal biologist explains. "Fish and Wildlife doesn't have the staff to do the work itself. It typically acts as an advisor and relies on states to do the work."

A state biologist who asked not to be named echoes this concern. "The ban could slow things down. The more partners the better. Wildlife management is always looking for extra people." But others think the state may have shot itself in the foot. As one wildlife manager privately concedes, "The state doesn't want to be left in the dark. It wants to be a part of the decision-making team. The law effectively says that. But the ban forfeits all control to the feds. That was a big mistake. Generally, the same people who support the ban are also anti–big government. From that standpoint the ban is counterproductive." Adds yet another: "I think it was poor judgment by the state. It effectively excluded itself as a player from the augmentation process."

Chris Servheen notes: "Idaho did the same thing. Its legislature barred the Fish and Game Department from participating in wolf recovery. They reasoned that if the state didn't assist, wolf recovery wouldn't happen. As a result, guess who is managing wolves in Idaho? The Nez Perce Indian tribe! Idaho disenfranchised itself, wolf recovery went ahead without it, and the state now sees the error of its ways."

The US Fish and Wildlife Service released Canadian lynx into the Colorado Rockies under a recovery program. Colorado ranchers had no cause to worry—unless they raised rabbits. But ranchers saw the lynx as a precedent for reintroducing other carnivores, such as wolves, which might be less livestock-friendly. There are no plans to reintroduce wolves in Colorado, but worried ranchers and hunters nonetheless worked themselves into a lather. They convinced state legislators that the federal government should be limited in what wild animals it could turn loose in their state. The result was a state law requiring approval by the state legislature before any more wildlife reintroductions took place in Colorado.[5]

Colorado's law is almost certainly illegal. The federal Endangered Species Act preempts conflicting state law. The state has no power to require that federal agencies obtain its approval before they implement a federal law. Yet Colorado's statute reflects local sympathies, the same sympathies that Montana and Wyoming voiced over federal plans to return wolves to Yellowstone. State officials stymied that effort for fifteen years. Nor are these attitudes limited to the West. Word that the US Fish and Wildlife Service might restore wolves to New England prompted New Hampshire's legislature, again despite dubious legality, to pass a preemptive ban.[6]

Montanans claim federal wildlife policies tread on states' rights. In the early days of grizzly recovery, when Montana came under pressure to stop grizzly hunting, the director of its Fish, Wildlife, and Parks Agency told a *New York Times* reporter, "It's Montana's bear. America is trying to tell us how to manage it from Washington DC, and they don't know how."[7]

Custer County, Idaho, passed an ordinance declaring itself "grizzly-free" and urging that any grizzly be shot, even though that would be a federal crime.[8] Wyoming's Fremont County declared grizzlies "socially and economically unacceptable and therefore unwanted."[9] Idaho tried to ban imported grizzlies, arguing that it was all right to move grizzlies from one Idaho ecosystem to another but not to bring in out-of-state bears. As one wildlife manager notes, "These state bans are the product of political hacks in the legislature. They work themselves into a states' rights frenzy. It's a disservice to their people."

⁂

Invisible anchors are one way to frustrate wildlife recovery, but elected politicians do not have the same need to be subtle. They survive by staying attuned to what their voters want to hear. Ed Marston, publisher of *High Country News*, sometimes compares Western politicians to their Deep South counterparts during Civil Rights days. "They hate the federal government, they practice the politics of resentment, and they have no vision of the future other than to continue to run for office by being for guns and against environmental protection."[10] So state legislators in the West have become inventive at finding ways of obstructing wildlife policies. Washington State's legislators are no exception.

The biggest effect of Washington's import ban is probably symbolic. Like a big flashing sign on a hilltop, it declares Washington's opposition to augmenting the isolated grizzly population in Washington's Cascades.

Chris Servheen offers the broader view: "Whether it's the red wolf, black-faced ferret, prairie dog, or Mexican wolf, no states want any of these things to happen. If we only moved ahead in states that were accepting, we wouldn't move anywhere.

"State fish and game departments generally have been superb in assisting our implementation work. The professional biologists have been crucial to the success of our program. But the states themselves haven't been forthcoming on recovery of endangered species.

"There's a conflict here between local and national goals," Servheen notes. "Recovery takes some level of pain."

Yet Servheen also concedes, "The primary factor determining the future of the grizzly is public acceptance and support."[11]

Opinion polls in Washington State may tell a different story, but one measure of public acceptance and support certainly is what elected officials do. RCW 77.12.035 is a powerful declaration that Washington State was not ready to do what it takes to save grizzlies. In the choices Servheen was about to face in 1995, that reluctance would play a crucial role.

13 | A TOUGH CHOICE

Tiffany Mountain is the tallest peak on the divide between Washington's Methow and Okanogan valleys. From its tundra-cloaked summit, well above the tree line, the vista is panoramic.

In a sweeping westward arc you can see nearly a quarter of the US North Cascades. Looking to the east across the Okanogan Valley desert, wooded hills rise, the ends of ranges that roll down out of Canada. Mount Bonaparte, monarch of the Tonasket country, is one of the last hurrahs of the Monashee Mountains. In the hazy distance is the Kettle River Range east of Republic. It too marks the southern end of mountains pressing down out of Canada.

Head north into British Columbia and those ranges rise. The Monashee, Selkirk, and Purcell ranges all reach a crescendo in the ten- and eleven-thousand-foot peaks near Revelstoke. Only a deep trench separates those summits from the main spine of the Rocky Mountains. Tiffany, one of the tallest and easternmost points of the Cascades, offers a high and windy vista to the westernmost foothills of the Rockies. Somewhere out there in the haze is an invisible line that has big implications for grizzly recovery.

Few boundaries in this part of the world make much sense. They were drawn for political reasons by people who knew little and cared less about the topography. The farther east you go in Washington, the louder people complain about this. Spokane, on the eastern edge of the state, is the economic capital of a region that boosters call the Inland Empire. Roughly it embraces eastern Washington, northern Idaho, and the northwest corner of Montana, an area halfway between the Rockies and the Columbia basin. Residents in all these places grumble that they are in forgotten corners of states that pay them scant attention. They feel remote geographically, economically, culturally, and politically. If lines were being drawn today, they would redraw them to make Spokane a real capital.

Montana's western boundary is the only one in this region that follows the ground. It traces the crest of the Bitterroots for most of its length, but then becomes a straight line for the last seventy-five miles to Canada. The US Fish and Wildlife Service split its regions along Montana's western border, putting everything west of that in the Pacific region, headquartered in Portland, and land to the east in its Mountain-Prairie region based in Denver.

Everyone agrees that somewhere between the crest of the Bitterroots and the crest of the Cascades, perspectives change. The Forest Service itself waffles. For years, its regional dividing line was on the Okanogan-Ferry county border. West of that line was the Pacific Northwest region, with its headquarters in Portland, Oregon. East of it was Colville National Forest, part of the Northern region administered out of Missoula. For government foresters, the other side of that line was like another country. The Forest Service has since changed its mind and moved its regional boundary east to the Washington-Idaho border. Shifting the line underscores that no one is quite sure where the Rockies end and the Pacific Northwest begins. Yet everybody knows they are different.

This is especially true of wildlife people. Biologists on the Pacific Northwest side complain about what they call Rocky Mountain syndrome, and claim they are victims of it. Rocky Mountain syndrome, they say, is a superiority attitude held by wildlife people in the Rockies. Those Rocky Mountain folks think they have all the megafauna associated with the American West—bison, wolves, moose, wolverines, elk, lynx, and, yes, grizzly bears. Not only do they have them but they ignore the possibility that anyone else could have them too. So far as they are concerned, research and management of these big animals begins and ends in the Rockies.

Wildlife folks in Colorado and the Southwest would probably add that the correct name for this affliction is *Northern* Rocky Mountain syndrome, because they too feel ignored for much the same reasons. They live in the Rockies too, just the wrong part.

On the question of grizzly bear management, one must pay the Northern Rockies region its due. It hosts more than 90 percent of all grizzlies still living in the lower 48 states. The ecosystems around Yellowstone and Glacier national parks alone support perhaps 1,200 grizzlies. Fewer than 200 bears live everywhere else south of Canada. Put another way, only about 120 US grizzly bears out of a total of some 1,200 do *not* live in the Rockies. And more than a hundred of those are in the Selkirks, which the Fish and Wildlife Service now says are linked through Canada to grizzlies in Montana's Cabinet-Yaak, thus making the boundary between the Rockies and the Pacific Northwest even more blurred.

Grizzly recovery started with four recovery areas in the Rockies. Most of the United States–based research and management of grizzlies has been in the Rockies. Chris Servheen, coordinator for all US grizzly recovery, is based in Missoula. Montana is headquarters for most of the nongovernmental bear advocate groups, ranging from the Great Bear Foundation, Alliance for the Wild Rockies, and Craighead Environmental Research Institute, to the Rocky Mountain offices of Defenders of Wildlife, Natural Resources Defense Council, and the Sierra Club's Grizzly Bear Ecosystems Project. Doug Peacock, the spiritual guru for many grizzly lovers, lives in Montana. There are plenty of reasons for bear managers to have Rocky Mountain syndrome.

Budgeting for bear recovery between two Fish and Wildlife Service regions has always been tricky. Servheen coordinates all grizzly work from his office in FWS Region 1, but the Cascades and Selkirks are in FWS Region 6. Until the mid-1990s, each region had its own budget for grizzlies, even though the Pacific regional director deferred to Servheen on fieldwork.

When the Pacific region concluded in 1995 that all future funding for large carnivore work should go to Region 6 instead of splitting it between the two regions, some Pacific Northwest folks were suspicious. One theory was that FWS Pacific regional director Mike Spear, having suffered through the northern spotted owl furor, wanted nothing more to do with controversial animals, so he washed his hands of grizzlies.

Several other theories imagined behind-the-scenes maneuvers. One implicated Washington's congressman Norm Dicks for switching grizzly money to wolves so he could fund his pet project of putting wolves back in the Olympics. Another was that Dicks and Curt Smitch, director of Washington's Fish and Wildlife Department, conspired to shift the money as a way to kill grizzly recovery. Yet another blamed environmental groups for pushing their own pet causes so loudly that grizzly money was diverted to placate them.

All these theories sold Mike Spear short. He had a long and impressive record, first with the Forest Service and then with the Fish and Wildlife Service—assistant director for Fish and Wildlife ecological services, Southwest regional director, and assistant director for planning and budget. Spear was no stranger to cutting-edge endangered species issues.

Most people had their own ideas about how to prioritize Fish and Wildlife's budget. There is never enough money to go around, which inevitably pits one worthy cause against another. As one Fish and Wildlife biologist laments, "The culprit is inadequate funding." Regional director Spear was mostly looking for ways to use money better. He decided to transfer responsibility for large carnivores to Region 6 because the expertise was there. Serveen was grizzly coordinator for the whole United States and had the authority to direct recovery work regardless of region boundaries.

Maybe that was the Rocky Mountain syndrome in action, or at least one version of it. But the issue had other dimensions. Spear faced many dilemmas. His region included California and Hawaii, where a number of species face imminent extinction. Island species, which may be more vulnerable because of limited range and small populations, tend to be overlooked in funding.[1] The Fish and Wildlife Service reasoned it might raise visibility and focus more attention on those seriously endangered species if it split the Pacific region so that California and Hawaii were not in the same region with the Northwest.

Congress rejected the idea. With limited funds, Spear faced one crisis after another. He chose to put more money into saving species on the brink of extinction than trying to prevent extirpation of the grizzly in the Cascades. Not only did it seem as if he were managing a hospital emergency room, but he felt doubly justified when local opposition to grizzlies appeared so strong that money spent in Washington State might accomplish nothing.

Here was an example of the chilling effect of the state's ban on grizzly imports.

The Cascades and the Bitterroots marched lockstep through the recovery area process. They were nominated at the same time, evaluated at the same time, presented simultaneously to the IGBC, and both designated as grizzly recovery areas in the same IGBC order. Work then proceeded simultaneously to document the evaluation in each area and to write the recovery plan chapter for each area.

And then the lockstep suddenly stopped.

Jon Almack remembers that day in late 1995. Servheen called and told him, "I've had to make a command decision." As Almack recalls, Servheen explained that the Bitterroots study was already done, the Cascades were dragging on, and Servheen only had enough money to implement recovery in one area. So he was shifting all grizzly work to the Bitterroots. That meant Fish and Wildlife would no longer contribute 90 percent of Almack's salary in Washington State. Almack's work on grizzly recovery in the Cascades would have to stop. Biologists from other agencies who had their own funding could keep working, but Almack had been both the point man and the lightning rod. He was the only biologist who focused exclusively on grizzly recovery in the Cascades. Without him the program was sure to stall.

Servheen's need to chose between the Cascades and Bitterroots is undisputed. He lacked the funds or prospect of funds to move ahead with both. Implementing a recovery plan is a major federal action requiring an environmental impact statement, public hearings, and all the procedural hoops of the National Environmental Policy Act. It is time-consuming and expensive.

But why did Servheen pick the Bitterroots over the Cascades? On the one hand, it looked like a bad case of Rocky Mountain syndrome. The Cascades had a remnant population of resident grizzlies. The Bitterroots, according to the best evidence, did not. Given the greater political obstacles to reintroduction compared to augmentation, would it not make sense to proceed in the Cascades first?

Biologists in the Northwest could also make a strong argument for saving the Cascades grizzlies before bringing new bears back into the Bitterroots. The Cascades are the last grizzly holdout in the Pacific coastal ranges of the United States. The coastal mountains of British Columbia are similar, but grizzlies there face intense pressures. The Cascades may be their last, best refuge in North America's coastal ranges.

Biologists cannot say if grizzlies in the Cascades differ genetically from grizzlies of the Rockies, but the likelihood is great enough to worry about extinction of the few that are left. Augmenting this westernmost population would dilute it, of course, but the alternative is to lose forever whatever might be unique to these bears. As the local US Fish and Wildlife Service office recognized in an unsuccessful budget request: "Prompt action could ensure that elements of the genetic material that evolved in this ecosystem will be present in a future grizzly bear population."[2]

The genetic differences between Yellowstone's grizzlies and bears farther north shows what isolation can do.[3] Grizzlies in the Cascades have been cut off from their cousins in the Rockies for at least a century, leading to the real prospect that genetic drift has already started. It may not be enough yet to call the Cascades bear a subspecies, but that variation could become critical to the survival of grizzlies everywhere. It could be what biologists call an "evolutionary significant unit."[4] Genetic variation is key to the adaptability and long-term survival of any species.[5] If grizzlies in the Cascades were left to die out, the new blood they could have offered grizzlies in the Rockies in a pinch would be gone, and the great bear as a species would take one more step toward the brink.

The Cascades offered a hedge. Those grizzlies still in the Cascades, living in isolation from other grizzlies, could provide a backup. If something worse than the West Nile virus, which has hit two hundred species and devastated wildlife across North America,[6] felled grizzlies in the Rockies, the Washington State and British Columbia Cascades bears might provide the gene pool to save the species. For the same reasons that financial advisors preach the virtue of diversifying, it made sense to protect grizzlies in the Cascades as a kind of insurance policy.

But wildlife policy rests on politics as well as biology. During the public meetings around the Bitterroots—the same process as occurred around the Cascades—the leaders of Idaho's timber industry sensed early on that grizzly recovery was going to happen whether they liked it or not. Strategizing among themselves, they concluded that they could oppose it from the outside and probably lose or become involved and try to influence the outcome. Remembering how they had been run over after taking a hard line on the spotted owl, they opted to cooperate.

Two national wildlife groups, Defenders of Wildlife and the National Wildlife Federation, had made grizzly recovery in the Bitterroots a priority. Learning from the polarized battle over wolf reintroduction in Yellowstone, they too were seeking ways to build bridges. Cautiously, they set up some meetings starting in 1993 with representatives of Idaho's timber industry, labor unions for sawmill workers, other small businesses, and Native American tribes.[7]

Not surprisingly, those initial meetings were full of distrust, but gradually people came to know each other and understand their differences. Over time, a coalition emerged.[8] Ultimately they all agreed that bringing grizzlies back to the Bitterroots was the right thing to do if locals had a voice in the process and local impacts were minimized. Once they moved past the suspicion phase, these unlikely allies worked together to produce a bear information booklet that they distributed widely in Idaho. They held public meetings in rural communities, drafted a recovery plan proposal, pressured the Fish and Wildlife Service in Washington DC to give the Bitterroots priority, and jointly lobbied Congress in 1994 to fund the environmental impact process.

Politically, the Bitterroots were miles ahead of the Cascades. Aside from Mitch Friedman's Northwest Ecosystem Alliance, most environmental groups in Washington State were still arguing about whether to support grizzly recovery. No one around the Cascades had even started to think about building bridges.

To be sure, bridge building was easier in the Bitterroots. Most of the recovery area was already in three large wilderness areas. Available timber was generally marginal, so the timber industry had less to lose than in the Cascades. There was almost no grazing in the Bitterroots, so ranchers had less reason to resist. Outdoor recreationists in the Missoula area were already accustomed to hiking in grizzly country, so there was no panic in their ranks. And the Bitterroots had little potential for mining or oil and gas. In short, the Bitterroots lacked many of the conflicts that bedeviled the Cascades.

The national wildlife groups and the Fish and Wildlife Service might be criticized for deciding to back the Bitterroots when the Cascades had a more urgent biological need. Abandoning the Cascades because of its challenges could mean sentencing to death as many Cascades grizzlies as they might reintroduce in the Bitterroots. However, the Bitterroots had a biological argument of their own. They could form a key link between the Yellowstone, Northern Continental Divide, and Cabinet-Yaak recovery areas. Connecting those island populations could do wonders for grizzlies.[9] Howie Wolke, cofounder of Earth First! and a vocal grizzly advocate, told *Sierra* magazine, "If we connect the ecosystems, the Northern Rockies can probably support two thousand grizzly bears."[10] Recovery in the Cascades, on the other hand, could not directly help bears anywhere else, either in the United States or in Canada.

In the end, however, biological arguments made no difference. The key was that Congress came up with the money and Fish and Wildlife's Washington office agreed that it could be used for a Bitterroots environmental impact process. Nobody had even asked for funding in the Cascades. The final choice was driven not by biology but by money.

The effect in the Cascades was devastating. In 1995 Jon Almack left, moved to the Selkirks, and switched from grizzly recovery to woodland caribou. Scott Fitkin, Almack's assistant, became a regional biologist. With that team dismantled, grizzly work in the Cascades lost momentum.

The Forest Service and Park Service still had wildlife budgets, but the local Fish and Wildlife Service office had no more grizzly money. Not only did that put them out of business, but it also wiped out funding for grizzly work by the state's Fish and Wildlife Department, which had relied on the feds for 90 percent of its grizzly dollars. Hence there was no money for fieldwork by the two agencies who had done most of the earlier work.

Once work stopped, even those agencies that still had money lost interest. Bill Gaines, who retained his Forest Service funding, admits, "It was hard to work up much enthusiasm when nothing was going on." The Cascades technical committee of biologists stopped meeting. Agencies stopped forwarding reports of grizzly sightings to the state's endangered species database. Out of sight, out of mind. One biologist who lost his funding noted, "Since the project folded, public awareness has dropped. Nobody is pushing to report or record sightings. The griz is not on most people's radar screen anymore." A Fish and Wildlife Service biologist complained: "Before, we were looking for a needle in a haystack; now we're just waiting for someone to stumble on a needle in a hayfield."

The lack of funds did not reduce the need for knowledge. Matt Austin, who headed grizzly recovery for British Columbia, complained, "We don't know enough about how these bears live in the Cascades—we don't know their population makeup, their habits, or their diet." With a touch of irony, Doug Zimmer noted: "There's a pattern here. If you can't get the money to do the research, you can't find where the bears are, you can't show what you could do to recover them. If you can't show that the bears are there, then one of these days they won't be."

"One of the best lessons children learn through video games," say Jinx Milea and Pauline Lyttle in *Why Jenny Can't Lead*, "is that standing still will get them killed quicker than anything else."

Standing still in the Cascades had several effects.

First, state fish and wildlife commissioners refused to ban baiting and hound hunting of black bears within the grizzly recovery area. It took a lawsuit by three environmental groups to stop it. Federal Judge John Coughenour found that "continued use of hounds and bait in the NCE [North Cascades Ecosystem] is highly likely to result in the taking of grizzlies." He permanently banned such hunting. Two years later, Washington voters approved an initiative extending that ban statewide.

Second, the state Department of Natural Resources decided to log Loomis Forest, approving a plan to punch over three hundred miles of roads into a thirty-thousand-acre area north of Tiffany Mountain. Mitch Friedman complained, "The state is arguing that there aren't any bears up there and that Almack's study was poorly done. The state is really attacking grizzly bears in general."

When Northwest Ecosystem Alliance and others filed suit to stop the Loomis logging, attorneys for the state quietly contacted biologists to see if anyone would discredit Almack's grizzly findings. No biologist would, but in argument before the court, the state's attorney still compared grizzly sightings in the Cascades to the legendary Sasquatch or "Big Foot." Environmentalists raised more than $16 million to buy the timber rights and save the Loomis from logging.

At best, state agencies always had a very shaky commitment to grizzlies. When forward progress stopped, they were the most likely to start backsliding, and they did. Grizzly recovery is like flying a plane. You go forward or fall.

≈ ≈

Six years after Servheen's "command decision," the Bitterroots environmental impact statement finally was finished, and the Fish and Wildlife Service decided to proceed with grizzly recovery. It had been a long, expensive, and emotion-draining process. But the Bitterroots decision did not mean the Cascades automatically moved up in priority. Moving up requires money—at least $600,000, if the Bitterroots are any measure. It could cost even more in the Cascades. Moreover, if the Fish and Wildlife Service ever implements the decision that its final environmental impact statement supports, it will want to put what money it has into a program of moving bears into the Bitterroots. After all, that is what the $600,000 invested in that process was designed to do. "It could take millions to implement recovery in the Bitterroots," Chris Servheen warns.

The Fish and Wildlife Service has little interest in diverting funds to the Cascades when it still has so much unfinished business in the Bitterroots, and the two biggest and most effective wildlife advocates in the United States—Defenders of Wildlife and National Wildlife Federation—would hesitate to lobby Congress for Cascades funding when they have invested so much of their resources and reputations in the Bitterroots. They would have little reason to ask for Cascades money when that same money could be spent on actual recovery work in the Bitterroots. As Bill Paleck, North Cascades National Park supervisor, observed to the IGBC's Cascades subcommittee: "The North Cascades need for EIS funding is in competition with other trains that have already left the station."

Nor is it just an issue about where to spend money earmarked for grizzlies. Grizzlies compete for funding with a host of other species, and one could make a compelling case that the same number of dollars would save a lot more species quicker than it will save bears.[11] As long as the funding pie is small, all the major players view it as a zero-sum game. What you give grizzlies you take away from other plants and animals that face imminent extinction. What you give the Cascades, you take away from the Bitterroots. If these are the rules of grizzly recovery, it will not even start in the Cascades until it ends in the Bitterroots.

14 | HOLDING PATTERN

The funding cutback of 1995 coincided with a changing of the guard in the Cascades. Without funding, changing the guard was only marginally more significant than changing pilots in a plane parked on the tarmac with no fuel. Yet the changes advanced the cause of grizzly recovery by paving the way for it to run more smoothly if money became available. In this sense it was more like completing the preflight checklist on a plane that was waiting for fuel.

In part, the funding cutbacks and the personnel changes were coincidental. New faces in management posts around the North Cascades were coming regardless of budgets. This was natural turnover that had nothing to do with wildlife policy. But the new forest supervisors, the new park supervisor, and the new directors of state agencies were different from their predecessors, who had stonewalled Jon Almack or developed the art of invisible anchors. These new people were not necessarily bear lovers, but the status quo had changed. As any student of government affairs can explain, bureaucracies have an institutional inertia. Whatever direction they are going, they tend to keep going, even if they initially fought it. These new people, instead of having grizzly recovery imposed on them in the same way as their predecessors, accepted with little question the policy that was now set. The old-timers had been fighting change. When their replacements arrived, the change on this issue was already history. For these managers, grizzly bear recovery was just another part of their job description.

Sonny O'Neal, supervisor of the consolidated Wenatchee and Okanogan national forests in the late 1990s, typified this new breed.

He was a professional. He had no personal agenda. If he had a personal opinion about grizzly bears, he never revealed it. So far as O'Neal was concerned, the law required grizzly recovery and the Cascades were a grizzly recovery area, so the Okanogan and Wenatchee national forests, which he supervised, would do whatever they were supposed to do to support it.

Doug Zimmer, information specialist for the Fish and Wildlife Service, watched this change evolve. Zimmer had attended every meeting of the IGBC's Cascades subcommittee, save one when a snowstorm kept him away. Over the years he had seen people come and go, and he had seen a big shift in attitudes. Zimmer believed that personnel changes accounted for some of this, but public land management had also evolved. "The Forest Service has moved away from timber," Zimmer observed. "Thanks to the spotted owl, the forests now recognize that their biggest role is in recreation."

He might have added bull trout, salmon, and a host of other wildlife concerns that had become issues of a new day. "People used to use various pretexts to stall," Zimmer recalls. "I see none of that now. Everyone in the room seems to be on the same page."

Ironically, the funding cutback actually accelerated other changes in the Cascades. If necessity is the mother of invention, a funding cut by one government agency can spur another agency to take more action.

Bill Gaines, Wenatchee-Okanogan National Forest biologist, recalls when the Cascades entered hibernation because of Servheen's "command decision" to favor the Bitterroots. For a while nothing happened on grizzly recovery in the Cascades, but then several things rekindled that work. First was the Loomis lawsuit filed in 1997 by Northwest Ecosystem Alliance and other environmental groups against the state of Washington. That lawsuit focused on the effect of roads on grizzly and lynx habitat in the Loomis Forest, in the northeast corner of Washington's Cascades.[1] The case attracted broad attention. Then, in 1998, the IGBC updated its standards for human access in all grizzly recovery areas.[2] These guidelines explained how to analyze the effects of roads and trails on bear habitat. What worried land managers was that the guidelines provided specific ways to measure their agency's compliance with the requirements for protecting bear habitat. Suddenly the accountability meter rose from 1 to 10. New forest policies based on growing recreation use also favored bears. Emphasis on roads and logging waned, as issues such as access and wilderness overuse gained attention. Subtly the ground was shifting.

Then came a big timber sale that the Okanogan National Forest had planned near Loomis Forest. Wildlife activists appealed. As land managers had feared, appellants figured out how to use the new access standards like a sword. Recognizing its vulnerability, the forest dropped its proposed sale.

The final event, Gaines recalls, was a 1998 petition by Northwest Ecosystem Alliance to upgrade the Cascades grizzly listing under the Endangered Species Act from threatened to endangered. The petition was well supported and there was little the Fish and Wildlife Service could do to dispute its merits. Taking advantage of a provision in the Endangered Species Act, FWS dodged the bullet by conceding that such a move was "warranted but precluded."[3] This gave the agency a temporary reprieve, but the FWS also knew that environmentalists were still on the offensive.

Grizzly coordinator Chris Servheen felt the government needed to show more progress. Even if the Fish and Wildlife Service had no funds for grizzly recovery in the Cascades, the Forest Service and Park Service had their own wildlife budgets; perhaps it would be wise for them to start looking at this growing issue of access.

That prompted an enthusiastic Bill Gaines, biologist Anne Braaten of the North Cascades National Park, and other federal biologists to roll up their sleeves. In 1998, four years after Jon Almack had retired from the Cascades to the Selkirks, work on behalf of grizzlies was about to restart.

As a first step, the biologists subdivided the North Cascades recovery area into "bear management units" (BMUs). Then they arranged the BMUs based on how accessible they were. From a bear's viewpoint, the best BMUs were the so-called core areas—areas without roads, campgrounds, even trails. Core areas represent the wildest of the wild.

The Cascades subcommittee was concerned that the national forests and national park had no formal process for managing human access. They had not even adopted the IGBC's guidelines. Gaines recalls that the federal agencies felt they were vulnerable to a lawsuit over this. As a result, the forest supervisors and Bill Paleck, superintendent of North Cascades National Park—the three new men overseeing federal land in the Cascades—signed an agreement to protect the status quo in all core areas until the biologists learned more about how to manage them. The key point, they agreed, was to ensure no net loss of core areas.

Observers soon had a chance to witness this agreement in action. At an IGBC Cascades subcommittee meeting, Anne Braaten explained the need to relocate part of a trail in the Ross Lake National Recreation Area. The trail crossed the mouth of a stream that flooded every spring. The Park Service kept replacing footbridges, and the stream kept washing them away. To avoid this, they needed to relocate the trail into a core area. To compensate, they planned to close the area where the old trail crossed the stream. The result: no net loss in core area. Relocating a trail was not itself that significant, hardly an agenda item for senior federal managers, but the discussion showed how accountable these managers felt about their commitment to preserve core areas. Protecting grizzly habitat had become important and decisions about it transparent. The old days of invisible anchors were over.

"In the last few years, we have gained momentum in cleaning up campgrounds and installing bear-resistant containers," says Gaines. "This has been prompted by black bears, but are needed for griz too. And we are now managing human access, which has positive conservation implications for a whole host of wildlife species. So we're doing some things that will be important when we do get some bears."

Instead of dragging their feet, by the late 1990s federal land managers around the Cascades seemed focused on facilitating the recovery of grizzlies. As part of this momentum shift, fieldwork resumed in the Cascades for the first time in years. In 1998 two biologists undertook a survey of army cutworm moths. A graduate student at Montana State University had discovered that such moths congregate in talus slopes, and grizzlies find and eat them in large quantities. The student determined that a grizzly could gobble up to forty thousand plump moths in twenty-four hours, and if it ate that many for a month it would have consumed up to a third of the calories it needed for a whole year.[4] The search to locate cutworm moths in the Cascades was modest, but it marked a revival of fieldwork.

Close on its heels came three other projects, all designed to address questions of whether and how many grizzlies still lived in the Cascades. None of these efforts found any grizzlies, but the wildlife managers concluded that this only proved how elusive grizzlies can be. One of these projects was a joint effort headed by Scott Fitkin from the state Fish and Wildlife Department with volunteers from Northwest Ecosystem Alliance. Starting in the summer of 2000, they installed trip cameras in likely parts of the North Cascades in hopes of snapping a photo of a grizzly. It was a repeat of the project Almack and Fitkin had tried years before.

Like Almack and Fitkin's work, the new photos included cows, black bears, cougars, and lynx, but still no grizzlies. That effort continues.

A second project was more ambitious. Kim Romain, a graduate student from Washington State University, set out scent stations in the summers of 1999 and 2000 to snag bear hairs and analyze their DNA. Several agencies pooled funds for her project.

Hair snagging has been a biologist trick for years. In the early days, they used something smelly like a rotting horse head to attract bears. Now they have chemical scents in a bottle that supposedly are just as attractive. Researchers circle the scent with a wire that snags a few hairs when a bear comes to investigate, and then collect and send those hairs to a laboratory for DNA analysis. Just as scents have evolved from horse heads to bottled products, DNA work has grown in sophistication. Not only can a lab now tell the difference between a black bear and a grizzly, but under the right conditions, they can assess even its age, sex, and genealogy.

Romain collected hundreds of bear hairs. One hair she picked up in the Freezeout Creek drainage east of Ross Lake was significant. The first two DNA tests showed it to be from a grizzly, but she could not reconfirm that in three later tests. Does that mean there is only one, if any, grizzlies in the North Cascades? Hardly. British Columbia biologists had set scent stations in their part of the Cascades a year earlier. Their grizzly hair score was only one, but they spotted four grizzlies on the helicopter ride into their snag sites.

Romain and her female assistants, soon nicknamed "the Grizzly Gals," were back in the hills the next summer, but again they found no hairs they could confirm in the lab as grizzly. One thing Romain discovered from comparing results in the Cascades with a parallel scent study in the Selkirks, which host a known grizzly population, was that detecting members of a small population becomes harder when there are fewer bears. She concluded that home range size grew as the number of bears shrank. With fewer bears around, they simply spread out, which makes them even harder to find, no matter what method you use.

The third project sought similar information a different way. Sam Wasser, a University of Washington professor, had used dogs to locate bear scat.[5] Collected samples of the scat were sent to a lab for analysis, similar to that used for hairs. Wasser claimed his dogs could smell bear poo a half a mile away when conditions were right. Scat samples allow a technician to measure hormone concentrations as well as DNA. But this is still such a young science that biologists are not sure what it implies when, for example, they find increased levels of a particular hormone.

Lab detectives can tell a lot more from hair samples than from scat, because scat contains less of the DNA type that holds the best clues. For similar reasons, species identification is easier than sex or genealogy. The scat's age, how much it has weathered, what the bear was eating, and other variables can influence DNA analysis. Sex is especially tricky, because the marker for gender is the same in all mammals. So if a female bear gulps down a male mouse, the mouse's Y chromosome could make her scat seem to be from a male. This is still an inexact science.

Wasser tested his technique on a project for the province of Alberta, where he gathered scat in an effort to assess the effect on grizzlies of oil drilling and logging near Jasper National Park. He ran transects through disturbed and undisturbed areas, took his dogs along those lines, collected scat, and compared the results. The project yielded important facts about grizzly and black bear behavior in areas disturbed by humans.

Wasser claims that scent stations and scat-sniffing dogs work best together. Scent stations, he warns, do not attract bears as well when natural food is abundant. The type of scent also biases the study, he claims. Essence of cow blood, for instance, attracts male bears more than females. In Alberta he found that grizzlies visited scent stations more often than black bears. As Romain's study had shown, grizzlies could be as picky about what they would sniff as a child eating peas.

North Cascades National Park decided to use Wasser with his dogs on a sample test in 2000. It was designed to determine how well the technique worked rather than to find grizzlies. Over three small areas in the North Cascades, Wasser's dogs found about 175 piles of bear scat. Lots of bears! But the lab work did not confirm any grizzlies.

Anne Braaten, the Park Service biologist who oversaw this study, insisted that she was not disappointed. This was "like separating out a wheelbarrow of hay from the very big haystack, and looking only through that," she explains. The project was "in no way" designed to determine the presence or absence of grizzly bears. Finding any grizzly bear scat among the samples would simply "have been a bonus."

All these efforts support grizzly recovery by helping us to understand the ecosystem better and adopt bear management practices, but the key is more bears. This effectively means importing them—

a federal action with significant environmental effects. This in turn triggers the requirement under the National Environmental Policy Act for an environmental impact statement. An EIS, which must include various assessments and public hearings, is a big, expensive project.

Bill Gaines is right that the efforts he has helped advance will be important—indeed, critical—"when we do get some bears." Until the Fish and Wildlife Service finds the funds for an EIS, however, they are mainly exercises in completing the checklist while waiting for fuel. Chris Servheen realizes that everything depends on funds. "If someone gave me the money to do the EIS in the Cascades," he says, "we would start tomorrow."

He lists "multiple reasons" for moving ahead in the Cascades:

- a remaining US bear population,
- it adjoins a British Columbia population,
- the BC population is the most endangered in British Columbia, and
- British Columbia has given grizzly recovery in the Cascades its top priority.

Would completion of the Bitterroots EIS move the Cascades up in priority? "No," Servheen warns. "We have no funding for the Cascades. Besides, it would take millions to implement recovery in the Bitterroots, and we'll be lucky to get that money. That decision must be made at the DC level."

Despite changes in the North Cascades, it remained the largest grizzly recovery area with the fewest grizzly bears. And still there was no plan "at the DC level" to do anything about it. The question of when and if grizzly recovery would start in the North Cascades had moved from the local to the national stage.

PART 3
THE NATIONAL SCENE

15 | RESISTANCE GROWS

The Endangered Species Act, on which recovery of all threatened and endangered species in the United States depends, has always rested on a fragile detente between wildlife supporters and skeptics. Applied too vigorously, it has the potential to disrupt local economies and lifestyles. Applied too cautiously, it could mean extinction for more animals and plants. Critics have argued since before its adoption that the law lacks "balance"—that it allows science to trump common sense with no regard for the common good.

In the act's early days, euphoria was widespread about America's new commitment to save wild species. It was a "feel good" subject. But as people learned what was required to meet this lofty goal, and how the sacrifices to get there were not evenly spread, some came to wonder if the Endangered Species Act, in the words of the Backcountry Horsemen of Washington, "was a good idea gone bad."

Deep fissures grew in public opinion between urban and rural, liberal and conservative, east and west. In the nation's capital, where politics always reflect these divisions, resistance to the Endangered Species Act grew. This became especially evident after voters in 1994 installed a conservative "Contract-with-America" Congress led by Newt Gingrich.

The following year, the Clinton administration successfully launched one last big wildlife initiative, when it overcame two decades of contention and finally reintroduced wolves in Yellowstone and Idaho. A majority of the American people loved it. Rodger Schlickeisen, president of Defenders of Wildlife, praised it as "a fresh stimulus to the saving of endangered species generally."[1]

But that was the high-water mark for endangered wildlife recovery. Josef Hebert, Associated Press writer, described the Endangered Species Act as "the noblest and most powerful of environmental laws, and also the most despised and feared." Critics started flexing their new muscle in Congress, and those in charge of the Endangered Species Act were forced into defensive mode.

The conservative offense was soon under way. The new Congress came within two votes of enacting the Risk Assessment and Cost-Benefit Act of 1995, which would have allowed any industry to challenge any federal regulation and have it voided unless the government promptly provided cost-benefit proof to justify the rule.

This was one of many proposals. This one would have applied to any regulation, but other bills aimed squarely at the Endangered Species Act. One favorite target was the law's process for listing threatened or endangered species solely on the basis of biology. Several bills proposed to add economic and social concerns to that equation. Other bills would have softened the rules on wildlife habitat protection. Still others would have allowed local officials to veto Fish and Wildlife Service actions. One of these bills passed, but Congress fell short of the votes needed to override President Clinton's veto.

Interior secretary Bruce Babbitt watched Capitol Hill like a rancher watches the weather. He noticed how the likely votes to weaken the Endangered Species Act went up or down as the Fish and Wildlife Service made particular moves. He became more accurate than a weatherman at predicting the political risks of any proposed action.

The directors of Fish and Wildlife—several people held that post while Babbitt was secretary—may not have had his political forecasting savvy, but they certainly shared Babbitt's desire to protect the Endangered Species Act. It only took a few phone calls between the secretary, who oversees the Fish and Wildlife Service, and the director of that agency, before senior officers at the Fish and Wildlife Service had internalized Babbitt's political weathervane.

Two other things were less subject to Babbitt's control or prediction: riders (amendments added from the floor of the House or

Senate) to appropriation bills, and lawsuits by environmentalists. Both gave the interior secretary heartburn. He could not stop them and he could not placate those who authored them. Compared to conventional warfare, rider sponsors and environmental plaintiffs were guerrillas. They fought by rules outside his control.

The riders started after Republicans took over Congress in 1995. They scrapped Senate Rule 16, which had limited riders to nonpolicy matters germane to an appropriations bill. Historians may label the ensuing four years as the Rider Era.

Riders have always been around Washington, but never like they were in the Clinton years. Before that era, maybe one or two passed each year. In 1998 an unprecedented thirty riders were attached to three appropriations bills. All thirty addressed environmental or land use issues, mostly in the West. Washington observer Jon Margolis described them: "It would be an exaggeration to say that all the riders together are an attempt to accomplish piecemeal the broader weakening of environmental laws the Republicans tried and failed to do in 1995. [But] it would not be a gross exaggeration."[2]

Most of these riders could never have survived the light of public hearings or a straight up-or-down vote on their merits. They passed because their sponsors attached them to critical appropriations that had to pass and the president had to sign. The more urgent the bill, the more brazen the rider. Maybe the skeptics lacked the votes to tackle the Endangered Species Act head-on, but they could use riders to punch holes in it. As Carl Pope, executive director of the Sierra Club, complained, "Such backdoor tactics have become the norm because a straightforward approach no longer works."[3]

Thus, Senator Conrad Burns (R-MT) attached a rider to an Interior Department appropriations bill in 1997 to block any reintroduction of grizzlies in the Bitterroots during the next fiscal year. Because a veto would have shut down the whole Department of Interior, President Clinton reluctantly signed it. It worked so well that the following year Burns attached the same rider again and blocked grizzly reintroduction in the Bitterroots for another year.

Washington State's Slade Gorton chaired the Senate Interior Appropriations Committee. This put him in command of the purse strings for national parks, reclamation, oil and gas, Indian affairs, and wildlife—all big issues in the West. Gorton became a rider specialist, exempting mining companies from federal laws, overriding a grazing ban in Lake Roosevelt National Recreation Area, freezing funds to study wolf reintroduction in Washington's Olympics. Because he chaired the appropriations committee for environmental issues, no one was going to challenge his right to slap riders on environmental appropriations. He was a power unto himself.

Democrats, who had far less power, learned to play the game too, and fears that they might use riders to their own advantage finally prompted senators late in 1999 to reinstate Senate Rule 16. As a result, four riders to that year's Interior appropriations were ruled out of order. One would have given the governors of Montana and Idaho a veto over reintroduction of grizzly bears.

After the revival of Senate Rule 16, riders became harder to pass. Most had to go through committees, where they often bogged down. The political winds also started to shift, and moderate Republicans, anxious to distance themselves from more strident colleagues, joined Democrats to resist some riders. Finally, President Clinton took a harder stance and threatened to blame the GOP if unacceptable riders forced him to veto appropriations and shut down the government. As a result, Republicans dropped the worst of their 1999 riders, including the one that had blocked grizzlies in the Bitterroots for two successive years.

The Rider Era highlighted the sensitivity of wildlife politics. Riders identified the hot spots with the precision of heat-sensing radar. Judging by the number of them, grizzly reintroduction in the Bitterroots was one of the hottest.

Even though the threat of riders receded, the only way Babbitt and the Fish and Wildlife Service could end such ad hoc attacks was to stop administering the Endangered Species Act. They were not ready to go that far, but managers throughout the agency became well aware of the dangers of moving faster than public opinion, especially on controversial projects. The motto might have been borrowed from James Pike, the controversial bishop from California, who advised: "In our changes we should move like a caterpillar, part of which is stationary in every advance, not like the toad."

Dave Parsons, head of the agency's reintroduction program for Mexican gray wolves in the Southwest, learned this the hard way. His regional director, Nancy Kaufman, thought he was moving too fast. She resisted efforts to expand wolf release areas and demanded that she personally approve the release of each wolf. When it came time to renew his job in 2000, Parsons was the only applicant, but she refused to rehire him.

The sensitivity scale measured about the same for wolves and grizzlies. Chris Servheen wryly notes that no other species in America puts agency personnel on a plane back to Washington DC faster. If he took any initiative on grizzly recovery, he might as well book his flight because he knew he would be called back to Washington to explain himself.

Lawsuits by environmentalists were the other cause of Babbitt's heartburn. He saw the turmoil created in the Pacific Northwest after a federal court backed the Fish and Wildlife Service into a corner and caused it to list the northern spotted owl as an endangered species. That shut down Forest Service timber sales in the Northwest and thrust the spotted owl onto the cover of *Time* magazine and into presidential politics. Babbitt called it a "national trainwreck."[4]

Lawsuits shifted control over the pace of species listings from Fish and Wildlife Service managers to federal judges. In Babbitt's view, environmentalists did not bother with the big picture. They did not worry about stepping on toes. Babbitt was convinced they did not care that pushing too hard or fast could endanger the Endangered Species Act. Plaintiffs only cared about the Canadian lynx, northern goshawk, or whatever other species they sued to protect. Babbitt was determined to avoid a repeat of the spotted owl train wreck. He had to regain control over the listing process. He could not stop lawsuits or tell judges what to do, but he could control the Fish and Wildlife Service's response to both.

A court can reject the agency's reasons for not listing a species but cannot order a listing. A judge can only require the Fish and Wildlife Service to reconsider its decision. Aside from other acceptable reasons for not acting, the Endangered Species Act allows the agency to declare that a particular action is "warranted but precluded" by other priorities. The Fish and Wildlife Service may so declare when it finds that there is a substantial basis for acting, such as listing a species, but its backlog exceeds its resources so much that it cannot act in a timely way.[5] Once it calls something "warranted but precluded" and publishes a finding in the Federal Register to that effect, its decision is effectively unreviewable for a year. For that year, the hands of those who seek action are tied. At the end of twelve months, the agency must revisit its decision, but nothing stops it from making the same declaration again. So long as it repeats this annual mantra, the Fish and Wildlife Service can delay a listing or other action forever.

Thus began the process of limiting the Fish and Wildlife budget for endangered species. No matter what a court ordered, the agency could do nothing if it had no money. Without funding, the agency could say with a straight face that a listing or other action was "warranted but precluded." And if it did nothing, or carefully regulated how much it did, the conservative objections to the Endangered Species Act would never grow completely out of hand.

Thus Babbitt discovered how to control the uncontrollable. "Warranted but precluded" was his trump card. Limiting the budget allowed him to wrest control from the courts and put it back in his administration. Despite the Endangered Species Act's declared aim to ensure that wildlife decisions are based "solely on scientific considerations" rather than politics, in the end they were based solely on politics.[6]

In 1999 Fish and Wildlife Service director Jamie Rappaport Clark asked Congress to cap her agency's funds for listing and designating critical habitat for endangered species. Later that year Secretary Babbitt asked Senator Slade Gorton to sponsor a rider to restrict critical habitat funding to only $1 million. Babbitt's apparent reasoning was that short-sheeting the budget would allow the agency to avoid compliance with court orders that might rub important people the wrong way. Thus, a secretary of the interior appointed by a Democratic president asked a Republican senator to sponsor a rider to restrict the secretary's budget!

The Fish and Wildlife Service also consciously chose to spend its limited funds in ways that may have saved more species and stepped on fewer toes. Mark Van Putten, president of the National Wildlife Federation, experienced this firsthand. He expressed his frustration in trying to deal with the director of the Fish and Wildlife Service:

> I have seen director Jamie Clark several times to ask for $148,000, so the Fish and Wildlife Service regional office can complete a reintroduction plan for grizzlies in the Selway-Bitterroots. But every time she says she doesn't want to see a return to the old days when Fish and Wildlife spent all its money on the charismatic megafauna like wolves and bears at the expense of a lot of less obvious species that are also endangered. She feels she can do more for the overall benefit of biodiversity by spreading the funds around to smaller but equally deserving projects. That's why you see so much money going into the Great Lakes region, for example, to save species like the plover.[7]
>
> Clark tells me that if we can convince Congress to come up with more money for the Bitterroots that would be great, but she is not going to use her existing funds "by going back to the old way of doing things."

Yet when the Northwest Ecosystem Alliance asked Congressman Norm Dicks, Washington's senior Democrat and a member of the key House appropriations committee, for a $300,000 appropriation so that Fish and Wildlife could start the environmental impact process for grizzly recovery in the Cascades—the same process already under way in the Bitterroots—Dicks rebuffed it. His aide explained that the agency "wasn't pushing for more money because it was just used up defending lawsuits."

Babbitt also used his self-inflicted funding shortage as a reason to restrict petitions and lawsuits. In defending a proposed rule in 2000 that would ban public challenges to the timing of agency action on species identified as "candidates" for listing, Babbitt admitted that the rule was designed to protect the agency's discretion over which species to list first. "What we are trying to do in a case of woefully inadequate resources is to use them in areas needed most."

Was Babbitt trying to sabotage the Endangered Species Act? Jeffrey Ruch, executive director of Public Employees for Environmental Responsibility, was convinced of it. In a paper entitled "War of Attrition: Sabotage of the Endangered Species Act by the Department of Interior," he showed that Clinton, in his first presidential budget, sought $1.6 million more for endangered species listings than in the last year of George Bush's administration. For the next several years, Clinton's requests stayed at this same level. But they began to drop in 1996, and by 1998, budgets had fallen nearly 40 percent. Ruch's paper documented a self-imposed moratorium on listings and repeated efforts by the Department of Interior to cap endangered species funding. It concluded: "As a consequence, today, the greatest barrier to implementation of the Endangered Species Act is Bruce Babbitt."

Pablo Picasso once claimed: "The world doesn't make sense, so why should I paint pictures that do?"

Washington veterans themselves had a hard time making sense of wildlife politics. Even though frustrated groups on the left disagreed, the truth was that Babbitt was seeking a very delicate balance between protecting wildlife and a conservative Congress that thought wildlife protection had gone too far. He was convinced that rigorous enforcement of the Endangered Species Act would provoke its repeal. President Clinton had vetoed one bill designed to do that, but there was no assurance he had the votes to sustain a veto the next time. Babbitt blamed the spotted owl train wreck on his predecessor's failure to seek a balance between resource use and endangered species. Babbitt championed the idea of habitat protection plans, which gave landowners more flexibility over the way they managed privately owned habitat of protected species. If the Fish and Wildlife Service pushed too hard, Babbitt warned, "the [Endangered Species] act would have been repealed, and rightly so."[8]

Historians may debate whether Babbitt's strategy was right, but the Endangered Species Act did survive, and because of that, at least in principle, so did the possibility of grizzly bear recovery.

≈ ≈

The North Cascades subcommittee of the Interagency Grizzly Bear Committee was tired of waiting. Its members had seen the shift in Fish and Wildlife Service funding from the Cascades to the Bitterroots. They had seen the environmental impact process move ahead in the Bitterroots while the Cascades languished. Besides, Northwest Ecosystem Alliance kept suing Fish and Wildlife for doing nothing, and agency officials kept saying that action in the Cascades was "warranted but precluded."

The subcommittee decided it was time to draft a budget to fund the same process in the Cascades as in the Bitterroots. It was time, they concluded, to stop relying on nongovernmental requests such as the one Congressman Dicks had rebuffed, and to start an official appropriation request on behalf of the Cascades. Dave Frederick, who chaired the subcommittee and supervised the western Washington office of the Fish and Wildlife Service, came up with a draft budget of $500,000 to $600,000. With inflation, that was identical to the $500,000 earmarked earlier for the Bitterroots. When the subcommittee met to review the draft in November 2000, the national election was over, but the country still did not know if its next president would be Al Gore or George W. Bush.

16 | "W" DOES NOT STAND FOR "WILDLIFE"

Other elections have been closer, but never in American politics has a presidential election brought more profound change on the basis of such a slim and disputed margin.[1] Bush's win in 2000 was part of a continuing swing in political sentiment that had started during the Clinton years, when conservatives swept to power and began to turn America in a new direction. *Washington Post* columnist George F. Will called George W. Bush the most conservative president since Calvin Coolidge. The Republicans did not always control Congress, but during Bush's eight years as US president, his conservative instincts remained consistent. He saw free-market capitalism and environmental protection as adversaries, and he was determined throughout his tenure to shift that balance to the right.

President Bush wrought a watershed change in environmental policy. By the end of his first year in office, the Natural Resources Defense Council cited what it claimed were over a hundred antienvironmental actions by the Bush administration.[2] In the area of wildlife, they included:

- withdrawing biological opinions by the Fish and Wildlife Service that called for protecting nine endangered species of fish in the Columbia and Snake rivers.
- refusing to remove cattle from parts of the Mojave Desert that were critical habitat for an endangered desert tortoise.
- abandoning a plan to change stream flow in the Missouri River to protect endangered fish and birds.

- blocking the Fish and Wildlife Service from submitting negative comments to the Corps of Engineers about a proposed relaxation of wetlands protection rules.

None of these alone had earth-shaking consequences beyond the species directly affected. But the cumulative effect of a series of similar actions began to roll back wildlife protections across a broad spectrum. Pull enough threads out of a tapestry and eventually it will unravel.

These initial moves were not the work of an overzealous rookie. Each change became a snapshot of a broad determination to change directions. Agencies rescinded millions of acres of critical habitat for endangered wildlife. Interior Secretary Norton shelved a wilderness study program in national wildlife refuges. The White House intended to weaken or shelve many environmental programs, including the right of citizens to sue over endangered species listings.

Rodger Schlickeisen, president of Defenders of Wildlife, warned: "One must admire the consistency in the Bush administration's antienvironmental proposals. Very businesslike. No nonsense. Get right to the heart of the matter—and cut it out."[3]

Mitch Friedman, executive director of Northwest Ecosystem Alliance, summarized the view of many environmentalists: "A more aggressive assault on our conservation laws and lands could hardly be imagined."[4]

After President Bush's second year in office, the Natural Resources Defense Council warned: "America's environmental laws face a fundamental threat more sweeping and dangerous than any since the dawn of the modern environmental movement in 1970. Environmental protections have been challenged before, most notably in the James Watt era and in the Newt Gingrich Congress, but never through a campaign as far-reaching and destructive as the threat posed today by the Bush administration and the 108th Congress."[5]

Others took a different view. They expressed relief that the "overzealous" bureaucracies of the Clinton era had changed. The new chief of the Forest Service claimed that regulations had brought his agency to a state of "analysis paralysis."[6] Business leaders spoke of bringing rationality to government oversight that had often been irrational.

Regardless of which view of reality was right, few disagreed that President Bush, by the end of his second year, "had done more to change the way federal environmental laws are defined and implemented than any other president in the last three decades, leaving his mark on virtually every aspect of national environmental policy."[7]

How President Bush did this provides a textbook lesson in how to concentrate executive power. He started by appointing industry officials and former industry lobbyists to key environmental posts. When they took office, many were already well up the learning curve and brought agendas of their own.

He encouraged the White House Office of Management and Budget to launch a quiet but profound revolution in government operations. OMB began to centralize control and diminish the power of agencies that oversee the environment. One step in this process was the reincarnation of a rule conservatives had almost enacted during Clinton's presidency. It allowed OMB, at anyone's request, to suspend a proposed regulation until an agency provided a cost-benefit justification. This gave complaining parties a way to freeze proposed regulations without formal review. OMB also had its own ideas about how to measure cost-benefit, and those sometimes varied from the criteria statutes required an agency to follow. Critics claimed this allowed the White House to usurp the statutory roles of agencies without replicating their expertise. Because this process was internal, it also escaped public scrutiny or judicial review. Federal agencies had always been subject to presidential oversight, but never before in such a systematic and secretive way.

Beyond reining in the independence of agencies, the administration drew up an agenda of its own. Soon after John Graham took over at OMB's Office of Information and Regulatory Affairs, he met with the American Petroleum Institute, the American Gas Association, and the National Association of Manufacturers, to compile a list of what they called "ill-advised" regulations. The Mercatus Center, a conservative think tank supported by industry, also nominated regulations for review. From this, OMB prepared a "hit list." Distributed to White House staff and agency heads, it identified twenty-three rules and policies as targets for change. Thirteen of them related to the environment.

Contrast this focused approach to President Clinton's. In his appointments, Clinton sought to placate every supporting interest group from labor unions to Latinos. As a result, his appointees showed more diversity than experience. Bush preferred insiders; they knew the subjects they were asked to regulate. Early in his first term, Clinton proposed tougher rules and higher fees for grazing on public lands. After western senators kicked up a fuss, the Clinton White House simply abandoned the idea. Much the same happened after Clinton proposed to amend the laws that allow mining on public lands: proposal-resistance-retreat. The contrast in Bush's approach was like the difference between a playful puppy and a trained Doberman.

Paradoxically, President Bush never had a mandate to change America's environmental policy. Opinion polls consistently showed public support for the environment. A November 2002 *New York Times*/CBS News poll found that 62 percent of Americans believed the federal government "should be doing more to protect our environment" while only 7 percent felt it "should be doing less."

After the terrorist attacks of September 11, 2001, antienvironmental policies became more aggressive. Ten days after planes crashed into the World Trade Center and Pentagon, the Corps of Engineers was directing its staff to expedite wetland development permits as a way of spurring "economic development and moving money into the economy."[8] The EPA's inspector general has since conceded that his agency, under White House pressure, played down air quality warnings on lower Manhattan because of "national security concerns and the desire to reopen Wall Street."[9]

Justified on the grounds of war or America's need for self-sufficiency, this trend grew, prompting a National Wildlife Federation official to complain that the government was cloaking environmental rollbacks in "patriotic slogans."[10]

Budgets also took a new direction. Bush's first budget chopped all natural resource and environmental programs 11 percent in the first year, cut the Fish and Wildlife Service budget 9 percent, trimmed spending on endangered species by 8 percent, and shifted funds from federal to state programs. It included no funds to implement court orders brought by citizen suits under the Endangered Species Act.

The combined effect of Bush's first budget was a $2.3 billion hit for environmental and natural resource agencies, and a $100 million annual loss for wildlife. After that, the environmental cutbacks deepened and spread. By the end of his first term, the Bush administration had listed only twenty-five endangered species, less than half as many as in the last year of Clinton's presidency, and only a tenth as many as under Bush's father.[11]

The White House also diverted appropriations. President Bush pledged better maintenance for the decaying infrastructure in national parks, then moved funds from wildlife and wildlands preservation to pay for it. After 9/11, funds from the Park Service repair budget were shifted again, this time to added security at such high profile sites as the Statue of Liberty. Park Service and Forest Service rangers were transferred from their posts in the West to guard duty around public buildings in the East. Guards may have been needed, but it is curious that rangers and foresters seemed more available than staff from other federal agencies.

The administration also pressed ahead with plans to privatize more federal posts, especially those involving natural resources. Instead of career biologists in national parks, for instance, the White House claimed contractors could do the same work for less. Critics suspected that replacing experienced professionals with potentially compliant contractors was driven by more than budgets.

Because President Bush never had a mandate for environmental change, his strategy concentrated on moves that avoided public attention. Control of federal agencies through budget caps and internal oversight were ideal for this, but the government also perfected another technique: the use of lawsuits to change environmental rules. Pro-industry groups would file lawsuits to challenge existing rules. The Justice Department would defend on behalf of the government, but critics claimed it did not always defend with much vigor. If the court ruled against a challenged rule, the government sometimes chose not to appeal. In this way, critics claim that the Bush administration abandoned key water rights for a wildlife refuge on Idaho's Snake River and rolled back Clinton's initiative for national forest roadless areas.

The government settled other lawsuits on terms that critics saw as eviscerating the rules it was supposed to defend. In a lawsuit brought by snowmobilers, for instance, the settlement reversed a rule designed to limit the impact of snowmobiles on wildlife in Yellowstone and Grand Teton national parks. These settlements lacked public notice or scrutiny, leading inevitably to charges about "backdoor" and "stealth attacks" on wildlife protection.[12] This followed the broader charge that "unlike Watt and Gingrich, the Bush administration has done most of its [environmental] work behind closed doors."[13]

When they gained Republican majorities in Congress, Bush's allies were emboldened to try changing national policy more openly by rewriting the laws. They largely failed. The legislative process was more transparent and gave the public more chances to have its say. At least a half dozen times, bills were offered to open the Arctic National Wildlife Refuge to oil and gas drilling. To the embarrassment and consternation of the White House, they failed every time. Congressman Richard Pombo's bill to emasculate the Endangered Species Act passed the House but died in the Senate because Lincoln Chafee, Republican chairman of the Senate Fisheries, Wildlife, and Water Subcommittee, thought it went too far. Elected congressmen proved to be a lot more independent than agency directors.

Bush's reelection in 2004 demonstrated how much he had changed America's agenda. The campaign resulting in his reelection was openly contested on such issues as terrorism and national security, and quietly contested on such issues as abortion and gay rights. The environment was barely mentioned.

The effects on grizzly recovery were predictable. After the Bush administration had set its new course, Ken Berg, Fish and Wildlife Service director for Washington State, told the IGBC Cascades sub-committee, "[Augmentation] is not something we see happening in the next couple of years." He did not say why, but every committee member already knew.

Funding sank below the low levels of Clinton-Babbitt. Sonny O'Neal, Wenatchee Forest supervisor, complained to the Cascades subcommittee that staff limits were crippling education programs needed to address public concerns about bears and cougars. He and other committee members knew that without education, public prejudices could persist. Lack of budget equals ignorance equals opposition to bears.

Two times may not make a trend, but it was interesting that two Cascades budget requests started on election eves. The first reached the Fish and Wildlife Service's regional office right after Bush's first election had been confirmed. It was dead on arrival. A second Cascades budget request started up the line after the full IGBC committee encouraged the Cascades subcommittee to submit it. No one said so, but the thinking seemed to be that Senator Kerry might beat Bush, so it might be timely to have a funding proposal ready. The bet lost, and the second proposal went no further than the first.

"Funding inertia is catching up with us," warned the Cascades subcommittee after its members pointed out that budgets were tight not only for the Fish and Wildlife Service but also for the Park Service and Forest Service. These two agencies had picked up much of the slack after Servheen shifted Fish and Wildlife funds to the Bitterroots.

The situation was no better in the Rockies. As unlikely as it seemed after he blocked grizzly reintroduction in the Bitterroots with two successive riders, Republican Senator Burns from Montana managed to add funds to two appropriation bills for wildlife work in the Northern Rockies. But then the White House

OMB stripped them out and Burns stopped trying. With no funding in sight, a frustrated Doug Zimmer, the Fish and Wildlife spokesman, warned the IGBC: "The pace of recovery in the North Cascades is a national policy issue. It does not just affect the North Cascades, and not just grizzlies, but the entire endangered species program."

The changes wrought by the Bush administration affected grizzly recovery in other major ways. Just as the Forest Service and Park Service had stepped up when Fish and Wildlife funding was cut in the Cascades, now, as all federal agencies were crippled by a lack of funding, state resource agencies stepped up, especially in Montana, and nongovernmental groups like Defenders of Wildlife took more initiative in filling the vacuum. Both trends bode well for the longer-term future of grizzly recovery, not because these groups could fill the federal government's shoes but because the feds need a supporting cast.

The effect of other decisions was less certain. In Yellowstone, the Bush administration provided a receptive climate to push ahead with delisting grizzly bears—removing bears in the Yellowstone recovery area from the list of threatened species. Some claim this strengthened the Endangered Species Act by proving it could work. Critics claim that Yellowstone represented a shift in emphasis from actual progress to an appearance of progress, from actual recovery work to a declaration of recovery. The question of who is right about the impact of Yellowstone on grizzly recovery and how much of that is due to George W. Bush is a debate that could rumble on for years. But there is little doubt that the biggest setback for grizzly recovery was a direct result of the Bush years—the shelving of an approved plan for grizzly recovery in the Bitterroots.

17 | BACK TO GO IN THE BITTERROOTS

On November 16, 2000, the Fish and Wildlife Service adopted a final plan to reintroduce grizzly bears into the Bitterroot Mountains of Idaho and Montana. Why it picked that date is intriguing. The presidential election was over, but the outcome was still in dispute. Ralph Morgenweck, regional director for the Fish and Wildlife Service, wryly noted that the future of grizzly bears in Idaho would depend on what happened in Florida,[1] where recounts and court cases were still trying to settle whether Florida's electoral votes would go to Al Gore or George W. Bush. The most likely reason for the timing of its Bitterroots decision was that the Fish and Wildlife Service concluded it should release it immediately rather than await the election outcome. If it waited, its authority to act might be questioned, if not legally, at least politically.

How the agency had managed to get itself into this bind is another matter. The important point, however, is that after a contentious process spanning more than six years, the Fish and Wildlife Service had adopted a grizzly recovery plan for the Bitterroots. That plan called for the reintroduction of five bears a year for five years starting in 2002. They would be the seed for a new grizzly bear population that could eventually reach 280 in the next fifty to a hundred years. For those who supported grizzly bear recovery, this was a huge step.

Regional director Morgenweck described the process leading to this plan as "exhaustive."[2] "Six years of hard work" was how Mark Shaffer, senior official at Defenders of Wildlife, recalled the effort. He and others had formed a coalition of timber, labor, and wildlife groups, who developed a "consensus plan" that the Fish and Wildlife Service, with minor changes, finally adopted.[3] Counting the time spent by this unusual coalition holding their own meetings around Idaho and Montana and drafting their consensus plan, plus the formal public hearings conducted by the Fish and Wildlife Service, the Bitterroots process really took over seven years.

It had been exhausting and exhaustive—hundreds of live witnesses, thousands of written comments, hundreds of thousands of hours, hearings in towns like Salmon, Idaho, that turned into shouting matches. But passions aside, the public comments had been remarkably balanced. The consensus plan won wide support, despite railing against it from environmentalists on the left and frightened residents on the right. Staking out one's position in the center—when you can find it—is always a winning strategy.

The final Bitterroots plan looked much like the plan proposed by the coalition. No bears with any history of conflict would be used. All would be released in remote locations. All would be radio-collared and monitored. All would be designated members of a nonessential, experimental population, which allows more flexibility in relocating or even killing a bear that causes trouble.

The plan feature that caused the most debate—because local residents and officials insisted on it and conservationists were equally suspicious of it—was the fifteen-member Citizen Management Committee. This committee was to be a cross-section of local citizens and delegates from federal and state agencies and the Nez Perce Tribe. The US secretary of the interior would appoint all of them, but most members would be recommended by the governors of Idaho and Montana. The committee would have a strong say in grizzly recovery. "This is the first time a reintroduction effort will be overseen by a citizens' group," said Morgenweck. "The Service believes the involvement of local residents is crucial to a successful reintroduction effort."[4] Defenders of Wildlife called it "a grassroots plan that earned broad popular support."[5]

Broad does not mean unanimous, however, as critics continued to show. On the left, Alliance for the Wild Rockies and Friends of the Bitterroots argued for a bigger area and for downgrading the

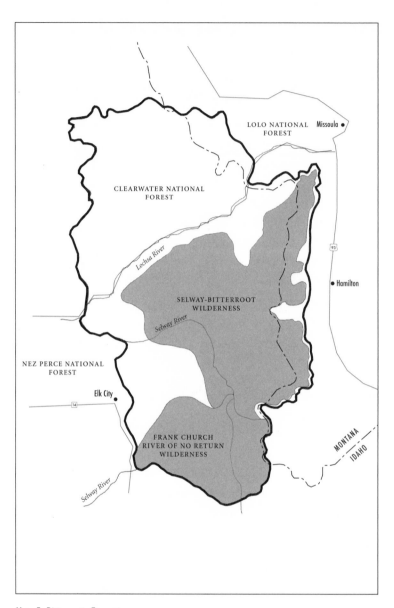

Map 5. Bitterroots Ecosystem

citizen committee to an advisory group. Great Bear Foundation called the plan a victory of politics over science.

The right also continued to thunder. Retired Congresswoman Helen Chenoweth (R-ID) likened the plan to "introducing sharks at the beach." A retired Forest Service supervisor said backpackers would "rather reintroduce rattlesnakes." Idaho's Republican governor Dirk Kempthorne snarled that grizzlies were simply "massive, flesh-eating carnivores," and any plan to reintroduce them "could be the first land management action in history likely to result in injury or death of members of the public."[6]

At Governor Kempthorne's direction, on January 19, 2001, the state of Idaho filed a lawsuit to block the Bitterroots plan. The next day George W. Bush was inaugurated president.

🐾 🐾

As a target for the new Bush administration, the Bitterroots plan was too easy. Adopted at the eleventh hour, controversial, opposed by the governor of the most affected state, not yet funded—it offered the White House an easy way to demonstrate the direction it would take on wildlife policy.

And it did. Newly appointed interior secretary Gail Norton announced on June 20, 2001, in the fifth month of the Bush administration, that she was suspending the Bitterroots recovery plan. She declared that the Fish and Wildlife Service was proposing a "no action" alternative. The public would have sixty days to comment before she made a final decision. If she picked the "no action" alternative, no grizzlies would be brought into the Bitterroots.

This should have caused little surprise, although Norton had indeed promised during her Senate confirmation to enforce the Endangered Species Act, which was federal law. And it was not as if the Bitterroots plan had run roughshod over the locals. Despite Governor Kempthorne's complaints, the plan had considered and addressed most local concerns. Indeed, Montana's Republican governor Marc Racicot, who was no fan of the federal government, was optimistic about the Bitterroots plan. One of the things he liked best was that it was the first federal reintroduction plan, in his words, to recognize the concerns of states and local residents.

Yet Norton had also stressed during her confirmation the importance of paying heed to local concerns, and nothing in the Endangered Species Act said she could not. Bush's first budget had shifted wildlife funds from federal to state programs. The extent of his prolocal strategy was not yet fully known, but there was already a philosophical tilt in that direction.

Idaho's lawsuit challenging the Bitterroots plan claimed that it violated the Constitution's Tenth Amendment, which reserves unenumerated powers to the states. Few lawyers could imagine a court giving much credence to this argument in light of earlier rulings that found authority at several places in the Constitution for Congress to adopt the Endangered Species Act.[7] Because the Bitterroots plan was adopted under and in compliance with that act, by definition it did not trample on any rights reserved to the state of Idaho. The lawsuit was more a political statement than a legal theory with any traction. But Secretary Norton was disturbed more by the fact of the lawsuit than by its merits. "Building support from state leaders is an important element to any potential partnership of this size and scope," she said. She spoke about the need for support from "the states, local communities, and all interested stakeholders."

This did not mean she would proceed only on projects where a state agreed. That was clear from a decision she had made five days earlier. On June 5 she declared that the federal government would proceed with oil and gas drilling on the Outer Continental Shelf off the coasts of Florida and California, despite loud protests from the governors of both states. Norton was willing to forgo state acquiescence on petroleum projects but not on wildlife. She later stressed that consensus was essential under the Endangered Species Act, especially when it involved predators.[8] This was a higher standard than she applied elsewhere.

No one would quarrel with the value of consensus, especially on wildlife issues that need cooperation from large numbers of people, often with diverse interests, and could span large chunks of public and private lands. But the flip side of consensus is that, rigidly applied, it gives anyone who chooses not to consent a veto. If twelve jurors are required to convict and one juror holds out, the defendant goes free.

This worried wildlife advocates. Saving endangered species was a national goal. The reason they were endangered in the first place was that locals often put their own interests ahead of plants and animals. If these locals could veto a recovery plan, overriding the national goal for endangered species, the people of Massachusetts, for instance, would have no say in whether grizzlies should survive in one of the few places where they could. Republican senators in 1999 had offered an appropriations bill rider that would have given the governors of Montana and Idaho a formal veto over grizzly reintroductions in their states. The rider was rejected. Did Norton's decision in 2001 effectively do the same thing?

Beyond the question of a veto, Secretary Norton was concerned about the need for more partnership with state and local officials. She stressed this in many decisions. Pushing ahead with a plan while the governor was suing to stop it was not a good way to show cooperation. Grizzly coordinator Chris Servheen saw Norton's decision in these terms. "This whole ordeal wasn't even about grizzly bears," he said. "It was state versus federal control, about a struggle to keep the states in control."[9]

Less is sometimes better than more. Norton would have been better off had she justified her Bitterroots decision solely by this need for more recognition of local concerns, especially on such a controversial subject as grizzly bears. The question of how much to bend federal goals to placate local worries was certainly an issue that reasonable people could debate. However, the balance of her decision detracted from what she had already said.

"The grizzlies deserve the best opportunities for their populations to thrive and prosper and I am fully committed to the recovery of grizzly bears in the lower 48 states," Norton announced. The Fish and Wildlife Service, she declared, would concentrate recovery efforts and resources on existing grizzly bear populations in the Lower 48 while withdrawing its plan to reintroduce bears into the Bitterroots. "Concentrating" on existing grizzly populations, Norton explained, meant that the agency would "continue to focus on recovery efforts and methods to preserve and increase populations in the Selkirk, Cabinet-Yaak, Northern Cascade ecosystems."

To anyone familiar with grizzly recovery, this was all hyperbole. The Fish and Wildlife Service was doing little or nothing in the Selkirk and Cabinet-Yaak recovery areas to "preserve and increase populations." In the North Cascades, which Norton misnamed, it was doing nothing. If the secretary's decision was a promise of things to come, it would have been welcome. But it was not. Instead, as *Los Angeles Times* columnist John Balzar said, it was just another in an "endless string of one-sided decisions . . . dripping [with] condescension."[10]

In the public comment period that followed, Norton's "no action" proposal to shelve the recovery plan was overwhelmingly opposed: 98 percent of the 3,130 comments from Idaho and 93 percent of the 2,964 comments from Montana supported going ahead with recovery in the Bitterroots. Of the 28,000 nationwide comments, 97 percent opposed Norton's decision. All eight of the scientific groups who commented, including the prestigious International Association for Bear Research and Management, championed the recovery plan. No scientist or scientific organization supported Norton's proposal to shelve it.[11]

Mark Pfeifle, Norton's spokesman, said the reintroduction plan was "never a public opinion contest," but the overwhelming opposition gave Interior Department lawyers some pause. If the secretary went ahead and entered a final decision, which could then be appealed to the courts, where would she find support in the record for her decision to shelve the plan? The record was awash with opposing comments, with the entire scientific community lined up against her. A decision maker is not limited to evidence contained in comments, but what could Norton use to rebut that mountain of critical evidence?

Rather than run the risk of being reversed, Secretary Norton took a calculated risk: she made *no* decision. She never entered a decision adopting the "no action" alternative. No final decision meant no judicial review, and no review meant no risk of reversal. She preferred to leave the Bitterroots in limbo rather than subject a decision to the scrutiny of an independent court. As we have seen in related contexts, this typified the Bush administration's aversion to processes it could not control.

It also left the Bitterroots in an interesting legal posture. The only final decision of record was the Fish and Wildlife Service decision of November 16, 2000, adopting a grizzly recovery plan for the Bitterroots. If a future director of that agency chose to proceed with recovery under that plan, no one knew if the lapse of eight or so years between adopting and implementing the plan might pose a legal barrier. Does the decision, as some claim, only have "a limited shelf life"?[12]

Leaving such issues for another day, the reality in the Bitterroots was that grizzly recovery was shelved, perhaps temporarily and unofficially, but at least until the political climate became more receptive to bringing in bears. The effect in the Bitterroots was clear, but less clear elsewhere.

Unanimously, bear biologists supported reintroduction of grizzlies in the Bitterroots as a bridge between isolated bear populations to the south in Yellowstone, to the north in the Cabinet-Yaak, and to the northeast in the Northern Continental Divide grizzly recovery areas. Fragmented populations are vulnerable. Genetic drift and loss of gene variability pose serious threats to small, isolated populations. The Bitterroots offered the best promise of stitching back together all the islands of bear population in the Northern Rockies.[13]

Indeed, only seven months before Norton's nondecision, Ralph Morgenweck, Fish and Wildlife regional director, had described the Bitterroots this way:

> Of all remaining unoccupied grizzly bear habitat in the lower 48 states, the Bitterroot Mountains wilderness area has the best potential for grizzly bear recovery.
>
> The grizzly bear is a native species of the Bitterroot Ecosystem and was once common there. . . . This area has high-quality grizzly bear habitat, and the largest block of wilderness habitat in the Rocky Mountains south of Canada. As such, the Bitterroot Ecosystem offers excellent potential to recover a healthy population of grizzly bears and to boost long-term survival and recovery prospects for this species in the contiguous United States.[14]

Viewed in terms of what the Bitterroots could have done for grizzlies throughout the Northern Rockies, Secretary Norton's notion of "moving forward" on grizzly recovery in other areas by abandoning the Bitterroots had really shifted grizzly recovery into reverse.

The one recovery area not potentially connected to the Bitterroots was the North Cascades. After Norton's decision, the question naturally arose about whether the Cascades, which had been in lockstep with the Bitterroots before Servheen's "command decision," could somehow leapfrog the stalled Bitterroots.

There were plenty of reasons to support this "leapfrog" idea. An existing population of grizzlies with its own gene pool, perhaps different from those in the Rockies, was perilously close to extinction in the Cascades. British Columbia had given its part of the Cascades top priority for grizzly recovery, and had urged the United States to help because the Cascades grizzly was truly an international species. And because of the bigger and better habitat south of the border, recovery on the US side might do more for BC bears than anything

British Columbia could do on its own. Even from a political stand-point, the Cascades were a good prospect. Washington State did not have a governor like Idaho's Kempthorne. Interior Secretary Norton might find Washington more supportive, and if recovery depends on a receptive state government, she might make some real progress in Washington.

But the list of negatives was long and daunting. Foremost, they included a lack of Fish and Wildlife Service funds for grizzly recovery anywhere, plus an administration with no interest in providing those funds, a state statute that purported to ban bear imports, a dearth of effective local advocates, a potential for strong opposition from hikers, horsemen, and backpackers, loud if less effective opposition from all the other usual opponents, and a national political environment that did not encourage wildlife initiatives.

Secretary Norton's decision in the Bitterroots also contributed to an attitude noted by the IGBC Cascades subcommittee. Just before his retirement as Wenatchee National Forest supervisor, Sonny O'Neal remarked during a discussion about adding more subcommittee members: "Many people don't accept that there's a requirement for grizzly bear recovery. They think somehow there's a way to turn this whole thing off." That prompted Bill Gaines, forest wildlife manager, to reply, "What happened in the Bitterroots has probably fueled that feeling."

Secretary of Interior Gail Norton abruptly resigned in 2006, citing her desire to leave government and return to the West. "Good riddance" was the Defenders of Wildlife's reaction, citing a long list of adverse decisions and her persistent but unsuccessful campaign to open the Arctic National Wildlife Area to oil drilling. Others were more charitable, recalling Norton's success with "cooperative conservation" programs that emphasized partnerships with landowners instead of regulations.

Whatever Gail Norton's legacy, it seemed unlikely that much about grizzly bear recovery would change after she left. This was especially so when her successor as new secretary of the interior was Idaho governor Dirk Kempthorne. By then, it was already clear that despite the promises Norton made in her Bitterroots decision "to focus recovery efforts . . . and increase populations," the first and arguably only priority for grizzly bear recovery was to take them off the threatened species list in Yellowstone.

18 | YELLOWSTONE: HOW SHOULD WE MEASURE SUCCESS?

Americans have long equated Yellowstone with bears. A June 1940 *National Geographic* article shows a photo of tourists watching grizzlies feed at a garbage dump, with the caption: "Nowhere else in the world can you see wild grizzly bears both in safety and in numbers." The article explained that "every night in summer some 1,500 persons sit on logs behind strong wire fences and watch." It described the twenty or more bears in the photo as eating "'combination salad,' table scraps, while from time to time a late arrival shambles down from the woods."[1] After Old Faithful and the Grand Tetons, the Yellowstone plateau's wildlife—especially its bears—were the highlight of any family vacation.

Americans also came to equate Frank and John Craighead with Yellowstone's grizzlies when the two biologists started in the 1960s to publicize their bear research and efforts to census the region's grizzlies. By then it was evident both to park officials and the Craighead brothers that bear management needed to change. Feeding grizzlies at dumps while crowds of tourists gawked taught the bears to equate humans with food and conditioned them to lose their natural wariness of people. The number of human-bear encounters was high. Most human injuries occurred along roadsides or in developed areas and involved bears attracted to human food and garbage.[2]

Park officials and the Craigheads concluded that the dumps should be closed, but they disagreed over how to do it. The Craigheads argued for weaning the bears slowly. They feared that a cold-turkey cutoff from an abundant food source that bears had relied on for nearly a hundred years could produce problems, perhaps even starvation. Other biologists were split. Following the publicized killing in Glacier National Park of two women by two different grizzlies on the night of August 13, 1967,[3] the Park Service declared the debate over and shut the dumps.

The result was much as the Craigheads had warned. At least 158 grizzlies died, roughly half the population.[4] Mortality was highest within two years after the dumps were closed. One hundred forty-seven bears were relocated, with dubious results. Thirty-nine incorrigibles were shot. By 1975, when grizzlies were listed under the Endangered Species Act, the Greater Yellowstone Ecosystem, comprising Yellowstone and Grand Teton national parks and surrounding national forests, contained perhaps as few as 136 grizzlies. In less than a decade after shutting the dumps, most of the bears that had depended on human food were dead.[5] John Craighead described the dump closures as "catastrophic."[6]

Almost everything about grizzly bears in Yellowstone is disputed, yet there is a begrudging consensus that over the next thirty years the bears made a remarkable comeback. Their numbers more than tripled, from roughly 140 in 1975 to about 580 in 2005. Such a recovery showed what can happen when a grizzly population has sufficient numbers to start with, mortality is controlled, and the bears enjoy enough protected habitat. Some also saw this as proof of the great bear's resilience—its ability to adapt, as it must have many times before, to major changes in its environment. This point of view would become significant.

As the bear population grew, so did the clamor from the surrounding states—Wyoming, Montana, and Idaho—to stop treating the grizzly as a threatened species. These states had resisted the federal takeover in the first place, and they wanted to regain control of the bears. If grizzlies had recovered, the feds no longer had any excuse to deprive the states of what was rightfully theirs.

As early as 1998, Senator Craig Thomas (R-WY) warned the Fish and Wildlife Service director that any delay in delisting the Yellowstone grizzly would only "strengthen the fears of folks who believe the Fish and Wildlife Service never intended to remove these

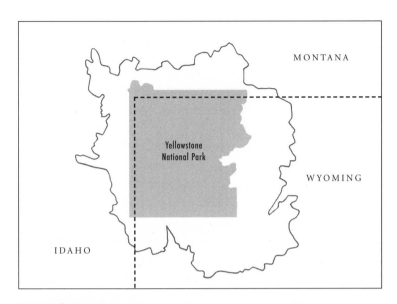

Map 6. Yellowstone Ecosystem

animals from the endangered list." Tensions began to rise within the IGBC. Committee members from state agencies, especially in Wyoming, were showing their frustration with federal officials who wanted to study the Yellowstone grizzlies more before making any moves.

Wyoming's Senator Thomas kept pushing. After Gail Norton replaced Bruce Babbitt as secretary of the interior, Thomas telephoned Norton demanding answers about the government's delisting plans. "Interior has been sitting on this proposal and Wyoming deserves to know about the timing," Thomas said. "I told [Norton] that Interior's credibility hangs on this action."[7]

Wyoming's other US senator, Mike Enzi, decided to work in tandem with Thomas. Senator Enzi wrote Secretary Norton: "I have been told many times that we will move forward with grizzly bear delisting, and I am disappointed that this effort has not moved forward. It is time to make delisting the grizzly bear a reality."[8] Wyoming governor Dave Freudenthal chimed in: "I'm not gonna fund the Wyoming side of bear management much longer. We're spending a couple million bucks a year managing a species that's not ours."[9] Freudenthal said he was at least the third Wyoming governor to whom the federal government had made promises about delisting the grizzly. Wyoming officials were the loudest of the three affected states, perhaps because most of the Yellowstone recovery area was in Wyoming.

Throughout 2005, grizzly coordinator Chris Servheen kept predicting that a delisting decision was imminent. Hurricane Katrina delayed the announcement, but on November 17, 2005, the Fish and Wildlife Service unveiled its draft decision to delist the Yellowstone grizzly. It reported that the bear population had grown 4 to 7 percent per year, which is like a wildfire for such a slow-breeding species, and that bears had expanded their range by 48 percent since the 1970s. "Grizzly bears in the Yellowstone area now occupy habitats they have been absent from for decades," the agency said. It estimated that "more than 580" grizzlies called the Yellowstone region home. Fish and Wildlife said this population was "viable," meaning that there was "a high likelihood that [it] will continue to exist and be well distributed throughout its range for the foreseeable future."[10]

In fact, federal biologists were not relying on these population totals as their grounds for declaring Yellowstone's grizzlies recovered. They based their conclusion on more precise goals set in the grizzly recovery plan. These covered three key points: the number of breeding animals, their distribution within the habitat, and mortality levels. The numbers differ for each grizzly recovery area, but these are the ways that the Fish and Wildlife Service measures success in all areas. In Yellowstone, this required at least fifteen mothers with cubs, dispersed over 89 percent of the habitat, with known human-caused mortality not exceeding 4 percent of the total estimated population, and no more than 30 percent of those deaths could be female.[11] If the population was 580 bears, this meant that no more than twenty-three could die from human causes, and no more than seven of those could be females. These were not one-shot requirements where you could ring the bell once and win the prize. The number of breeding females and the mortality caps had to satisfy six-year averages, and the dispersal rule required a three-year average. In addition, the mortality limits could not be exceeded in any two consecutive years, regardless of the six-year average. The Fish and Wildlife Service said Yellowstone's grizzlies met all these requirements.

Some claimed these criteria conflicted with the Endangered Species Act[12]—one of several issues courts will likely have to resolve. Others questioned the criteria from a biological rather than a legal standpoint.[13] Yet others questioned the reliability of any conclusions about mortality,[14] while Earthjustice questioned everything about the criteria and sued to require the Fish and Wildlife Service to divulge its data. The agency called this "preposterous," while Chris Servheen insisted that the Yellowstone story represented "the greatest success in the Endangered Species Act."[15]

This was typical of most discussions about grizzlies in Yellowstone.

The recovery plan required, in addition to its demographic goals, that a "conservation strategy" be in place to manage the bear population and its habitat once it had recovered. For the Yellowstone Ecosystem, this meant management plans by the three states and surrounding national forests that would take control of grizzlies. For many environmentalists, handing management of grizzlies over to the states, especially to outspoken Wyoming, was like a nightmare at noon. They envisioned ranchers and hunters already licking their chops at the prospect of putting grizzly bears literally in their sights.

The states insisted on drafting their own plans, but these were subject to federal review. If the Fish and Wildlife Service was not satisfied with a state plan, it could say no and there would be no recovery until that state presented something acceptable. In reality, there was a lot more give-and-take about the state plans, and in the end all of them were approved.

The one that raised the most concerns, as expected, was Wyoming's. The local Game and Fish Commission found itself in the middle, trying to satisfy the feds on the one hand and rebellious county commissioners on the other. Cutting through all the rhetoric about bear attacks, local control, and who could you trust, it came down to the question of whether and where to draw lines through the Wind River Range, which points southeast from the Grand Tetons. All of this high and lonely country, which included a major wilderness area, was good grizzly bear habitat. But Sublette, Lander, and Fremont counties saw these mountains as a juggernaut thrusting down into ranch land and toward towns, potentially delivering grizzlies into these areas for the first time in generations. The local commissioners passed resolutions declaring grizzlies in their counties to be "socially and economically unacceptable."

The final Wyoming plan split the Wind River Range in two. In the north half, grizzlies would be fully protected, but in the south half, along with two smaller ranges nearby,[16] they would be "discouraged." This meant limited hunting, with the number of permits dependent on mortality from other causes. If the state was up against its limits on acceptable mortality, problem bears would be trapped and relocated without a hunting season.

Environmentalists saw this splitting of a mountain range as reminiscent of the Bitterroots on a smaller scale—the exclusion of bears from suitable habitat because of local objections, effectively giving the locals a veto. Meredith Taylor, from the Wyoming Outdoor Council, accused the state of retreating under political pressure from an earlier plan that drew no boundaries but allowed bears to expand into any suitable habitat, coupled with educating the public to avoid bear conflicts and a plan to deal with problem bears. "With less habitat, you're guaranteed more conflict, and that's a recipe for relisting," Taylor warned.[17]

Aside from this Wind River Range retreat, Wyoming's plan called for a stable grizzly population but no encouragement for bears to spread any farther.

The Fish and Wildlife Service found all the state plans acceptable, and proceeded toward delisting grizzlies in the Yellowstone Ecosystem.

A single public hearing on February 8, 2006, and 213,000 written comments followed. Unofficially, 983 of those comments supported delisting, about 100 took no position, and the remaining 212,000 were all opposed. This was a disapproval rating of 99.5 percent. Two environmental groups—National Parks Conservation Association and National Wildlife Federation—did support delisting. The comments raised some two hundred separate issues. The main ones concerned genetic isolation and habitat, arguing either that the Yellowstone Ecosystem was already too small—and thanks to Wyoming, likely to shrink more due to human encroachment—or that the habitat was changing in ways that posed new threats.

The evidence of changing habitat was compelling. Beetles were attacking the whitebark pine, which was an important food source for bears. Scientists noted that when the pine nut crop was good, grizzlies stayed in the high country and avoided humans. When the crop was poor, the bears came down, ran into more people and thus into more trouble, with the result that more bears died.[18] What would happen if beetles, which first became an epidemic in 2003, killed all the whitebark pine? Dan Reinhart, a resource management specialist in Yellowstone, warned, "If we lost whitebark pine on a major scale, that would be a big hit."[19]

Cutthroat trout, another major food source for grizzlies, were being squeezed out or eaten by transplanted nonnative lake trout. Army cutworm moths, a third important food, were declining. Milder winters allowed the whitebark pine beetles to multiply and were reducing a fourth major food source: the winter kill of ungulates that grizzlies fed on in early spring.[20] With so many key foods at risk or in decline, wildlife advocates and nongovernmental biologists argued that delisting was premature.

They also worried about how good the management plans would be on the ground, citing budget concerns by both the federal and state governments. The much-touted conservation strategy was only funded for the next several years. The IGBC had been warned that "long-term funding . . . remains an issue."[21]

Adequate habitat was a major concern. Because the Wind River Range was so high and cold, scientists predicted that whitebark pine would survive there after the pines were gone from everywhere else in the ecosystem.[22] Yet Wyoming had drawn a line through these mountains and declared half of them off-limits to grizzlies. In every direction, bears trying to disperse out of Yellowstone ran into a crossfire of deadly enemies—trophy homes, ranchers, off-road vehicles, and hunters. Human-caused grizzly mortality around the fringe was high.

A national change in Forest Service rules also meant that plans to protect bears and bear habitat in the national forests surrounding Yellowstone were less predictable or enforceable. Little or nothing would stop the Forest Service, for example, from opening national forest lands to oil and gas leasing. Chris Servheen himself complained that these Forest Service changes were "not acceptable. We need standards."[23]

Despite the avalanche of antidelisting comments, the Fish and Wildlife Service made its final ruling to delist in the spring of 2007. It analyzed and responded to the comments, as the law required, but nothing changed its mind. Senator Larry Craig praised the decision for restoring the Endangered Species Act's credibility. Opponents declared their intent to challenge it in Congress and the courts. As Mitch King, regional director for the Fish and Wildlife Service, predicted: "We know we're going to get litigated."[24] Wyoming county commissioners talked of challenging the plan for going too far, but most of the challenges were expected from environmentalists and wildlife advocates who opposed delisting. On cue, seven environmental groups represented by Earthjustice challenged the delisting in federal court in Idaho. They claimed the decision was unlawful, for many of the same reasons raised in earlier comments.

Judicial review does not allow a court to substitute its judgment for that of a government agency. A court can only decide whether the agency followed the law in reaching its decision. That meant a judge had no power to reconsider most of the issues raised in the public comments. It is less clear, however, whether a court could consider the agency's reliance exclusively on what opponents call its "surrogate criteria" for recovery—the demographic goalposts—while appearing to ignore substantial evidence that

Yellowstone's bear habitat was changing in ways that could threaten the bears.

Yet that appeared to be exactly the Fish and Wildlife Service's position. "If we waited for stability in the system, we would never delist anything," said Chris Servheen. "It's not surprising that there are going to be changes in the system, whether there are changes due to bugs, disease, or global warming."[25] Grizzlies have lived in North America since before the last Ice Age, Servheen stressed, and they have shown a remarkable ability to adapt. Look at how they recovered after Yellowstone closed its dumps. More recently, their numbers have kept growing despite Yellowstone's major wildfires.[26] "We're not saying things will always be stable," he said, but the best measures of how well grizzly bears are doing are the demographic parameters—the number of breeding females, dispersal throughout the habitat, and sustainable levels of mortality. Like taking someone's temperature, these are the ways grizzlies tell us if they are sick. To Servheen, these numbers are "the vital rates."[27]

In the Numbers versus Habitat Debate, there was no question which side Servheen was on.

Before its delisting decision, the Fish and Wildlife Service took another action: it issued a rule declaring that grizzlies in the Yellowstone Ecosystem were a "distinct population segment" under the Endangered Species Act. This raised other issues about grizzly recovery everywhere. The act recognizes that a species may exist in distinct population segments, and different segments may justify different treatment. The wolves of Minnesota, for instance, may need different management from those in the Northern Rockies. Before the Yellowstone delisting, the Fish and Wildlife Service's position had varied on treating grizzlies in different recovery zones as distinct populations. Its recovery plan said that each remaining bear population should be delisted when it met its recovery goals. That meant they would be treated separately. However, for reasons explained below, Servheen had opposed petitions in several recovery areas to uplist bear populations from "threatened" to "endangered." This raised more than an academic question, because the Fish and Wildlife Service is required by law to do different things depending on how a species was listed. If it is "endangered," the agency must identify and protect its critical habitat, which is more than it must do if a species is only "threatened." Since its initial listing in 1975, the grizzly bear had been ranked as "threatened" throughout its range in the lower 48 states. This became a point of contention. Bear advocates argued that the grizzly's status was more precarious in the Cascades and Selkirks and should, in those two areas, be listed as "endangered." The government refused, claiming that the grizzly should not have separate listings in separate parts of its range. Separate listings might complicate overall recovery, it reasoned. If the grizzly were listed as "endangered" in one area and only "threatened" in another, Servheen might have to shift funding to areas where the grizzly was endangered but had a poorer chance of recovery. But, as Yellowstone showed, this opposition to uplisting apparently did not extend to delisting. The agency's apparent position was that grizzly bears should have the same listing or rank throughout their fractured range until the bear population in a given area recovered. Then that population could be treated differently. Put another way, resistance to changing the listing only ran one way.

Delisting in one recovery zone when grizzlies still struggled in others raised other policy questions. Historically, grizzlies in the Rockies were one continuous population. Biologists agreed that all these fragmented groups needed each other. Daunting as it might be, wildlife corridors could still stitch those areas back together, especially if bears repopulated the Bitterroots. Servheen himself was a frequent advocate of these corridors.[28] Wildlife supporters believed links to other areas could do wonders for the tenuous bear populations in the Cabinet-Yaak and Selkirks. According to some, treating the Yellowstone population as if it were on a separate planet failed to leverage its arguable success into a benefit for troubled bears elsewhere. And even in the Yellowstone Ecosystem, it effectively capped population size at a level that may not, over the long run, be sustainable.[29] Nonetheless, delisting area by area had its political upside. It gave state and local officials an incentive to cooperate in recovery, so that they could reclaim control over "their" bears.

Professor Lisette Waits, a respected bear geneticist, had warned several years before delisting started that Yellowstone's grizzlies had the lowest genetic diversity of any in North America except those on Kodiak Island. One had to wonder if a genetic bottleneck had been created after closing the dumps, but she believed it was mainly because Yellowstone grizzlies had been cut off from other populations longer than any other, and their genetic diversity had continued to decline.[30] Such was life on Yellowstone Island. Doug Peacock, the grizzly guru from Bozeman, wrote in the *Los Angeles Times*: "[Yellowstone] is an island surrounded by an inhospitable human landscape of highways and towns. Without linkage to other grizzly bears, it is genetically doomed. . . . The gene pool doesn't get any bigger."[31]

The Fish and Wildlife Service knew it had a problem and provided in its recovery plan to augment the Yellowstone grizzly population. Unless it found other bears sneaking in from outside—like immigrants seeking the promised land—it would import from somewhere else at least one grizzly bear every decade. This, it concluded, should be enough to ensure genetic freshness.

So Yellowstone bears had been classified as a distinct population segment for delisting, even though the government opposed segmenting other bear populations that had not recovered. And even if they had, they would still need genetic imports from elsewhere. This policy of treating Yellowstone's population as distinct may have been pragmatic, but it certainly was not symmetrical.[32]

🐾 🐾

If history is prologue, delisting in Yellowstone set the model for grizzly recovery in other areas. From Yellowstone, several key points emerged about how the Fish and Wildlife Service would approach recovery elsewhere:

1. It would place primary reliance on the demographic goals set in its recovery plan.
2. It would be willing to assume that ecosystem health and stability were reflected in those demographics, rather than speculate about the effects of less measurable factors.
3. It would give considerable deference to states in the plans they developed to take over bear management after recovery.
4. It would treat each recovery area as a distinct population for purposes of measuring success.

Critics claimed that the Yellowstone delisting was based more on politics than science. Inevitably, that led to the question "whose science?" The recovery plan's demographic goals were themselves based on science. They might be disputed, but they did not change with who was in the White House. The government's exclusive reliance on demographic numbers in the face of other evidence might have been politically motivated, or it simply might have reflected a desire to rely on objective criteria rather than softer, less measurable warnings of habitat instability. The pressure from local politicians to delist had come during both the Clinton and Bush administrations. Delisting may have happened during the Bush administration, but that proved nothing about political motives.

Nonetheless, the pressure to delist, whether it came from the states or the White House or both, produced a shift in emphasis that was unfortunate for grizzly recovery generally. It was a shift away from actual recovery work to a declaration of recovery. Before Yellowstone, the Fish and Wildlife Service had been on the offense—seeking ways to expand grizzly range, to link individual recovery areas, and thereby build a basis for a healthy population across the entire range of the great bear's suitable habitat. But along the way the process retreated into exactly what it had meant to avoid. The emphasis switched to declaring victory in individual areas. The effort to recover grizzlies across their entire range had faded. Instead of moving toward recovery in areas where grizzly populations were endangered or extinct, resources were directed to taking the grizzly off the threatened species list in areas where populations were relatively healthy. The program seemed to have moved from offense to defense.

Is it a coincidence that this happened at the same time as America's watershed change in wildlife policy and politics? In the closing days of the Bush administration, it is time to ask where grizzly recovery is headed from here.

19 | GLACIER IS NEXT

The US Rockies reach their crescendo in the Northern Continental Divide Ecosystem, known in bear circles as "Glacier" or "the NCDE." Within this spectacular region, Montana's Front Range culminates in the high peaks of Glacier National Park, while the Mission Mountains on the west edge of the area soar into the sky from Flathead Valley with a majesty all their own.

Together, Yellowstone and the NCDE account for half the acreage in the lower 48 states devoted to grizzly recovery, and they host about 88 percent of the grizzly bears. The two areas are roughly the same size, but the NCDE also shares some eighty-five miles of border with Canada. Contiguous grizzly range extends north from Glacier into Canada's Waterton National Park and Akamina-Kishinena Provincial Park in the southeast corner of British Columbia. The latter is part of Canada's proposed Flathead National Park.[1] From there, grizzly range continues north up the spine of the Canadian Rockies. In the Castle-Crown and Crowsnest areas along the British Columbia–Alberta border, habitat is less secure,[2] but still the Canadian Rockies give the NCDE more contiguous bear habitat than Yellowstone and less genetic isolation. If the other recovery areas are islands, the NCDE comes closest to being the mainland.[3]

Land ownership in the NCDE differs from Yellowstone. Both areas include national parks, but national parks take up less than a quarter of the NCDE, compared to nearly three quarters of Yellowstone. The NCDE also contains more private land, especially in the Swan Valley, which separates the Mission Mountains from the big Bob Marshall Wilderness and the Front Range. As in Yellowstone, the rest of the recovery area is national forest.

Along its eastern edge, the NCDE includes part of the Blackfeet Indian Reservation, where bears are generally respected. It also abuts high plains east of the Front Range—a splendid landscape of tawny foothills with willow- and aspen-lined streams, all against a backdrop of snowy peaks. Grizzlies, which once were common on the high plains, have started recolonizing this country, which raises special concerns for ranchers[4] and teachers, especially when a grizzly wanders across the school playground. On such an occasion, Choteau Elementary School did not close—people in these parts are accustomed to bears—but it did cancel recess.[5]

Even before its final Yellowstone decision, the federal government was already starting an ambitious census of bears in the NCDE. If the Fish and Wildlife Service planned to base recovery decisions on demographics, it would need reliable numbers. Chris Servheen, grizzly coordinator for the agency, also hoped he might have more time to focus on other recovery areas once Yellowstone was finished. This led some to wonder if delisting in the NCDE might start as soon as the bear census was over and analyzed in 2006, well before the end of President Bush's second term. Servheen had already expressed his view that the bear population "is pretty robust,"[6] and the political climate might well be more favorable at that point rather than later.

But Servheen dispelled such notions, downplaying any suggestion that a delisting in the NCDE was imminent. Comparing the studies that had been done on Yellowstone's grizzlies with those in the NCDE, he said: "We are where we are in Yellowstone because the investment [in research] was made. In the Northern Continental Divide Ecosystem, we are years away from delisting."[7]

A research biologist with the Montana Fish, Wildlife and Parks Department estimated that Yellowstone research had a thirty-year head start on the NCDE. No one was suggesting it would be thirty more years before grizzlies in the NCDE were ready for delisting, but they still had a lot of catching up to do. As the biologist pointed out, "We have no large-scale ecosystem habitat or population studies in the NCDE."[8]

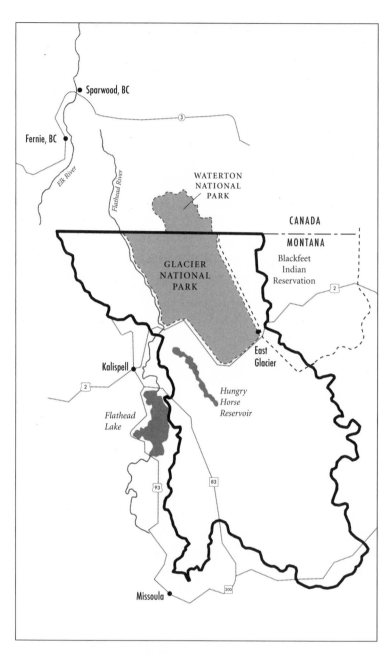

Map 7. Northern Continental Divide Ecosystem

Servheen was almost apologetic about why the NCDE lagged so far behind. His office had been crippled by a chronic lack of money, he said, and that was why they knew so little about bears in the NCDE. "It's frustrating for those of us who could get the job done," he complained.[9] Ironically, the census under way at that time was funded not by the Fish and Wildlife Service but through the US Geological Survey.

Wayne Kasworm, Fish and Wildlife Service bear biologist and Servheen's assistant on grizzly recovery, reminded the North Cascades IGBC subcommittee: "The Fish and Wildlife Service will have significant ongoing obligations in Yellowstone, so no big bunch of money will be freed up as a result of delisting."

The Cascades subcommittee hoped that completing Yellowstone might breathe new life into other recovery efforts. "Servheen has been quoted as saying that the Fish and Wildlife Service will have more time to work on other recovery areas," Kasworm told subcommittee members. "That's the hope, but it's based on the assumption that Congress might appropriate more based on the Yellowstone success story."[10]

But the NCDE was not waiting entirely on Yellowstone.

US Highway 2 and the main line of the Burlington Northern Sante Fe Railroad cross the Rockies by slicing straight through the NCDE, separating Glacier National Park to the north from the Bob Marshall Wilderness on the south. Because the highway and railroad parallel each other, together they pose a fairly formidable barrier for bears. One of the first studies was designed to find out how formidable.

For his doctoral thesis, John Waller studied grizzly crossings in this corridor over three years, from 1998 to 2001. He found that bears did cross, but mostly at night when road traffic was lightest. Ironically, that was also when train traffic was heaviest. Between 1980 and 2002, trains killed twenty-nine grizzlies in the sixty-mile stretch of track from West Glacier to Browning. In the same period, motor vehicles hit only two bears.

About half the bears captured and released in Waller's study did not try to cross. Those that did tended to be subadults of both sexes. Older bears crossed less, and mothers with new cubs steered clear of both the road and the railroad.[11] This study proved that the corridor was something of a barrier, but biologists still did not know how serious.

The ambitious bear census conducted by the US Geological Survey came next. It offered the first real insight into grizzlies in the NCDE. As early as the 1970s, scientists had estimated a grizzly population of about two hundred, but that was based only on sightings. Over the years, bear sightings had increased within the national park, but scientists did not regard them as a reliable indicator of population trends.[12] More sightings could mean more bears or just more people seeing bears.

Beginning in 1998, Kate Kendall, a USGS researcher, launched a study to estimate the bear population within the NCDE. She used the scent station–hair snag technique that had become standard among bear biologists. For the next several years, she and a group of rangers and volunteers crisscrossed the backcountry collecting nearly thirty-four thousand samples of bear hair from snag stations and rub trees. They sent these hairs off to a wildlife genetics lab in Nelson, British Columbia.[13] It was probably the biggest DNA-based wildlife census in the world.

The lab results identified 545 individual grizzlies, consisting of 307 females and 238 males. That was not a total census, but it proved the presence of at least that many grizzlies. In other words, the area contained a minimum of 545 grizzlies—almost as many as the total population estimate for Yellowstone. Servheen was impressed by the numbers. A further analysis of how many bears showed up in the sample more than once—a sampling technique known as "mark and recapture"—would come closer to an accurate estimate of total population.

Biologists noticed several things about the results. First, the greater number of females identified suggested some bias in the sample. There was no reason to suspect that the sex ratio of bears was not 1:1, which meant that females must have been more attracted than males to the scent stations. Studies elsewhere had noted that female grizzlies seemed to take more interest than male grizzlies in certain scents, perhaps in the same way that women like Chanel and men prefer Old Spice. In this case it was cow's blood and rotten fish, but the principle was the same.

Of the 545 grizzlies, 245 grizzlies were inside Glacier National Park. Even though the park constituted only 13 percent of the study area, it provided 46 percent of the sampled bears. By contrast, the Bob Marshall Wilderness south of the park revealed substantially fewer bears.[14] Was the habitat that different, or did the highway and railroad between them discourage movement?

Impressive as it was, the DNA census offered only a snapshot in time. It could say nothing about population trends. To find out about trends, another phase of the study started in 2003, while the hair-snagging fieldwork was still under way. This effort was led by Rick Mace, a research biologist from the Montana Fish, Wildlife, and Parks agency. With a team of helpers, he used the DNA study to determine where he should concentrate his sampling. Then he and his team trapped fifteen female grizzlies at locations throughout the NCDE, fit them with GPS collars, and released them. He also coordinated with Canadian biologists, who had collared two bears that moved back and forth across the border. By tracking these bears via satellite signals over a period of years, the aim was to determine whether the population was growing or shrinking, how much bears were on the move, whether there were population "sinks" within the area where mortality was higher, and a wealth of other valuable information.

How long would all this take? Kate Kendall expected to release a final report on her DNA-based census, including an estimate of total grizzly population, by late 2007 or 2008. Rick Mace predicted in 2005 that it would take five years before his collaring and tracking produced any reliable trend estimate.[15] Because the recovery criteria for the NCDE required population data based on six-year averages, the same as in Yellowstone, Chris Servheen estimated it would be another seven years before anyone could draw conclusions about the population's recovery.[16] By this reckoning, the earliest possible date to consider delisting would be 2013.

This presupposed that Montana could keep funding its trend study for five consecutive years. In fact, in mid-2007 it warned that it was running out of money. This sent everyone scrambling, because the study would be valid only if it was continuous. A break in the data could invalidate everything. With no help from Washington DC, local Forest Service officials cobbled together enough money to keep the study going. A 2013 target to consider delisting also assumed that if the study was completed without a break the numbers would show that the grizzly population met the NCDE's recovery criteria.

Meanwhile, the debate that had raged in Yellowstone—numbers versus habitat—was not going away. The Great Bear Foundation sounded an early warning that it was not impressed with the apparent reliance on census and trending studies in the NCDE. "GBF has long cautioned that habitat, not numbers, is the important aspect of management and research."[17] This debate was still premature, however, because no one knew whether the numbers would even support recovery in the NCDE.

The NCDE recovery criteria set out in the grizzly bear recovery plan followed a format similar to Yellowstone's: number of females with cubs, percentage of habitat occupied by grizzlies, and human-caused bear mortality not exceeding certain limits. As in Yellowstone, the first two required a six-year average, and the mortality cap a three-year average. As in Yellowstone, the mortality cap could not be breached in two consecutive years.

The NCDE rules were more rigorous in two ways. First, they contained separate targets for females with cubs within Glacier National Park and for those outside the park. Inside the park, recovery required at least ten mothers with cubs, while areas outside the park had to have at least another twelve. The percentage of occupied habitat goal also contained a proviso that, no matter what the occupancy rates were in other parts of the NCDE, there could be no recovery unless the Mission Mountains were also occupied. No bears in the Missions would mean no delisting. Both special rules were designed to ensure a healthy bear population throughout the NCDE, so that strong results within the relatively secure national park could not mask shortcomings elsewhere. This meant higher goalposts than in Yellowstone, where the criteria drew no distinction between park and nonpark areas.

The highest goalpost of all was the limit on human-caused mortality. Within Glacier National Park, good management practices over the years had reduced bear-human conflicts so much that so-called problem bears were hardly a problem. The problems were outside the park. Mortality limits were set at the same rates as in Yellowstone—no more than 4 percent of the population, with no more than 30 percent of that mortality being females. Assuming a total population of six hundred grizzlies, that meant no more than twenty-four bears killed by humans each year, and of those only 7.2 could be females. Unless deaths stayed within these limits, by definition the mortality level was unsustainable, there was no recovery, and no possibility of delisting.

Through 2005, human-caused deaths in the NCDE had exceeded these limits for nine consecutive years, either in total bear deaths or deaths of females. The loss of females was the bigger worry because that limit was breached almost every year. "The population can't sustain such high losses without a decline," said Louisa Willcox of the Natural Resources Defense Council. "This should be setting off all sorts of alarm bells."[18]

These numbers did not count how many bears died from natural causes, such as berry crop failures or six years of drought. Such misfortunes mattered only if a hungry bear went looking for food in the wrong places and was shot. Mortality caps were a limit on human-caused mortality. Management control—the shooting by rangers or game officials of bears that had become incorrigible— had always been a leading cause of bear deaths. Wildlife managers had long recognized that these kinds of problems stem from unsecured garbage, backyard bird feeders, and the like. Attractions that produced problem bears were a big concern in the NCDE because of the number of people who lived within the recovery area along the Swan and Flathead river valleys. Residents were generally tolerant of grizzlies—some even liked the idea of living near them—but not all were careful about what it took for humans and bears to coexist.

Mistaken identity killings by hunters were another cause of death. Montana's spring and fall black bear seasons were a dangerous time for grizzlies. It was a federal crime for a hunter to shoot a grizzly, except in self-defense, but prosecutors did not press charges if hunters made a convincing case that they had mistaken a grizzly for a black bear. Montana required hunters to pass a bear identification test, but it was far from perfect. Trains also killed one to five grizzlies per year.[19] The railroad had improved its cleanup after grain spills, which especially attracted bears after rain fermented any spilled grain, but bears were also attracted to the carcasses of other animals hit by trains. Sometimes they just picked the wrong time to cross the tracks.

Poaching had become the biggest problem, and it greatly worried wildlife managers. Eleven of the twenty-five bear deaths recorded in 2005 were due to illegal killing, including one that appeared to be poisoning. These numbers were unprecedented and seemed to be rising. More bears were sighted in the open country east of the recovery area, but most of the killing was occurring on the west side. It seemed that someone had declared a private war against grizzlies. Poaching cases were especially hard to solve. Chris Servheen sounded a bit desperate. He called the perpetrators "a few unscrupulous people" and "vandal killers" who were "stealing a [public] resource."[20] He described the illegal killings as an emergency but complained that he lacked the resources to stop them. This, he warned, "is going to set back the population and recovery efforts for some time."[21] The Fish and Wildlife Service offered rewards, and Montana increased the fine for illegally killing a grizzly. But wildlife managers suspected that the killings were likely caused by the antibear, anti–federal government attitudes that seemed to flourish in some parts. Countering them would take a massive public education effort, and even that might not work. Ironically, whoever was doing the killing was sabotaging recovery and ensuring that the grizzly bear stayed under federal control even longer.

☙ ❧

Beyond these immediate worries about mortality, managers worried about the long-term effect of two developments. In the Swan Valley, Plum Creek Timber Company worked with the government for many years to ensure that its activities were wildlife-friendly. About 70 percent of the company's land in that valley included designated linkage zones between the Mission Mountains and Bob Marshall Wilderness. In 2006 Plum Creek decided to sell about ten thousand of its eighty thousand acres in the Swan for private residential development. It earmarked another fourteen thousand for sale to other timber companies or conservation buyers.[22]

Million-dollar homes started sprouting in the Swan like mushrooms after rain. Contractors punched in roads with fanciful names and felled trees so that new homeowners could enjoy panoramic vistas. The Fish and Wildlife Service scrambled to work out easement terms with Plum Creek to ensure that development within the wildlife corridors would be more sensitive, but it was unclear how much of this new invasion grizzlies would tolerate. If it cut off the Mission Mountains, the NCDE's recovery targets for bear dispersal might never be met.

The other big worry concerned mining proposals across the border in British Columbia. The valley of the north fork of Flathead River, which rose in the BC Rockies and flowed south along the western edge of Glacier National Park, was some of the best non-coastal grizzly habitat in North America.[23] Bears moved freely back and forth across the border, so those in the BC Flathead were really part of the same bear population. Anything that threatened the BC Flathead also threatened the NCDE.

Coal mining proposals in the BC Flathead first surfaced in the mid-1970s. Concerns over wildlife and water quality brought strong protests from Montana, leading to intervention by the International

Joint Commission, a body created by Canada and the United States to resolve transboundary water conflicts. The IJC eventually recommended against mining near the border, and plans for a mine were dropped in 1988.

But the mine idea kept coming back. In 2004 British Columbia considered a new request to mine within five miles of the border. Montana complained again, British Columbia backed down, and talk turned to coalbed methane drilling instead of an open pit mine. As that dispute rumbled on, the BC government granted an exploration permit for another mine, farther up the Flathead but still only twenty-two miles from Glacier. Like earlier proposals, it would be an open pit mine. Boundaries of a proposed Flathead National Park were gerrymandered to exclude these potential mining areas.

When the BC government finally invited comments from south of the border, the IGBC asked Chris Servheen to convey the committee's concerns. Servheen pointed out that a mine was sure to disturb grizzly bear habitat because mines come with people and heavy equipment running twenty-four hours a day, seven days a week. That kind of activity, he warned, had the potential to fracture grizzly bear habitat and movements in an area important to the NCDE.

Servheen was also concerned about a domino effect. Once mining started in one part of the Flathead, he wondered where it would stop. As he told a Montana reporter: "We fear it's the foot in the door."[24] Those fears appear to be justified.[25]

Whether one looked at the numbers or threats to the habitat, it did not appear that recovery and delisting of NCDE grizzlies was imminent. Nonetheless, everyone recognized that the NCDE had the only grizzly population outside of Yellowstone remotely near recovery. Given the constant drumfire in Washington DC from critics of the Endangered Species Act, no one doubted that the Fish and

Wildlife Service would keep pushing to delist. And no one doubted that the NCDE would be next even if there was no timetable. It was not a question of whether but when.

Ser005heen has made progress in the NCDE, even though he lacked much budget of his own. Relying on a graduate student to study road and railroad crossings cost Serveen very little beyond the time required to convince a university professor to urge a graduate student to do it. Serveen is a maestro at orchestrating efforts financed by others. He has to be. The studies needed in the NCDE were expensive because they were so comprehensive and required state-of-the-art equipment. The GPS collars fitted on bears for the tracking study cost $5,000 each, compared to $300 for the older telemetry models. That alone was a $75,000 budget item. The state of Montana picked up some of the costs, and other federal agencies covered some expense from their regular budgets, but Congress still had to make special appropriations of about $3 million for the NCDE studies. This prompted the Great Bear Foundation to complain: "We do wish that the huge amount of money herein involved could have been spent to protect habitat and corridors, especially where aimed to improve Selway/Bitterroots grizzly bear numbers."[26]

Giving the NCDE such priority removed any lingering doubt about the emphasis of the Fish and Wildlife Service on declaring recovery rather than doing much, aside from protesting Canadian mines, for actual recovery. This was painfully evident in those areas where grizzly survival was a bigger issue than grizzly recovery—the Cabinet-Yaak and the Selkirks, America's two smallest recovery areas.

20 | THE SMALL AREAS

The last two recovery areas are so small compared to all the others that they have been called "postage stamp ecosystems."[1] Combined, the Cabinet-Yaak and Selkirks comprise only 9 percent of the total US grizzly recovery area. Together the two of them are less than half the size of Yellowstone. They became recovery areas, despite their small size, because they were among the few federally managed areas that still had grizzly bears.

The Cabinet-Yaak, as its name implies, is really two areas—the Cabinet mountain range of northwestern Montana, which protrudes a short distance into Idaho—and the Yaak, which occupies the very northwest corner of Montana. The Kootenay River flows down the Rocky Mountain Trench out of Canada, changes its name to Kootenai, loops around between the Cabinet and Yaak areas, and then, having briefly visited the United States, returns to Canada and resumes its Canadian name. Historically, grizzlies swam this river to move back and forth between the Cabinet and Yaak. With US Highway 2 and the main line of the Burlington Northern Santa Fe Railroad now paralleling the river, travel for bears has become more precarious. Indeed, there is no evidence of bears crossing the Kootenai since the early 1980s.[2]

The north half of this area, the Yaak, is the southern end of the Purcell Mountains, which are much higher farther north in British Columbia. Because the Yaak abuts the Canadian border, Yaak grizzlies have dual citizenship. The effective northern edge of the Yaak, from a bear's perspective, is not the Canadian border, which is nothing more than a narrow clearing through the forest, but BC

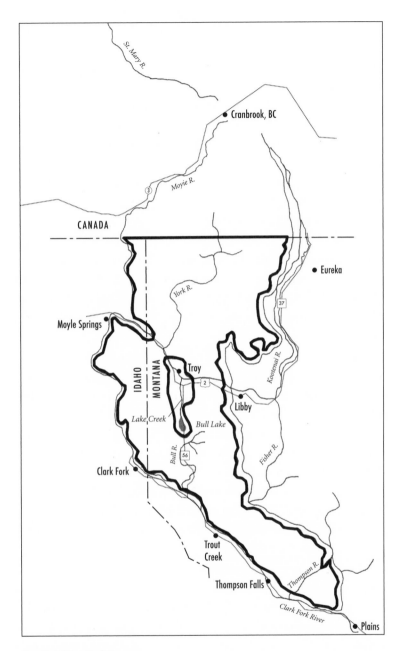

Map 8. Cabinet-Yaak Ecosystem

Highway 3, which cuts through the Purcells between Creston and Cranbrook. Genetic studies show that a few male grizzlies have braved this highway, but for many years no females have crossed it. For females, the Yaak is an island.[3]

Rick Bass, Montana's well-known nature writer, lives in the Yaak and writes eloquently about it. With great passion he pleads that saving the Yaak is the key to saving the Rockies, because it lies at a crossroads for plants and animals between the Canadian Rockies and interior ranges of the US Rockies as far south and west as Idaho and Oregon's Blue Mountains. According to Bass, the Yaak is the linchpin that holds it all together.[4]

The Selkirk Mountains recovery area, which straddles the border between the northeast corner of Washington and northern Idaho, is the southern end of another Canadian mountain range. The Selkirk Mountains split off from the Purcells near Revelstoke, British Columbia, and extend south into the United States to within sight of Spokane.

Like the Yaak, the Selkirk area also abuts Canada and hosts another population of dual-citizenship bears. Also like the Yaak, BC Highway 3 marks the effective northern end of this area. Unlike the Yaak, Highway 3 is more of a barrier in the Selkirks. Scientists have discovered that Selkirk grizzlies south of this highway, both male and female, are genetically isolated from those to its north.[5]

Whether the Cabinet-Yaak and Selkirks are actually two recovery areas is a subject of some debate. They were designated as two separate areas, and within the United States they are, but in the heat of a lawsuit the Fish and Wildlife Service decided that they were linked through British Columbia, so they really are one. As a result, the IGBC merged its two subcommittees and called the new subcommittee the Selkirk/Cabinet-Yaak.

No one disputes that if you go far enough north, the grizzly habitat in Canada ultimately merges. The Cabinet-Yaak and Selkirks are separate fingers of that habitat which extend down into the United States. By this reasoning, the Northern Continental Divide Ecosystem (NCDE) could also be called part of the same recovery area, for it too links farther north with habitat that ultimately links with the

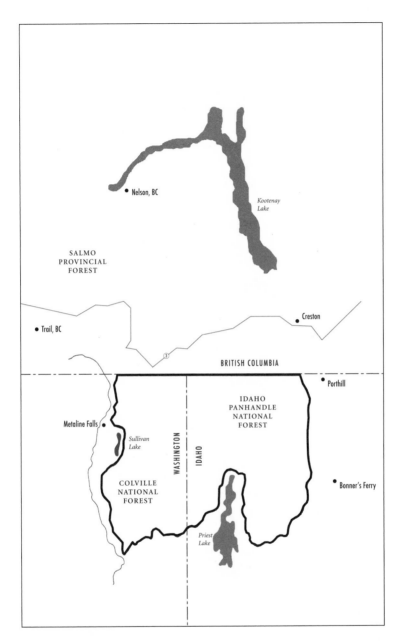

Map 9. Selkirks Ecosystem

Cabinet-Yaak and Selkirks. However, this ignores the distance and such formidable barriers as BC Highway 3, which effectively cut the southern tips of these fingers off from the rest of the hand.

Environmentalists viewed this "one area" claim with suspicion, because the Fish and Wildlife Service first unveiled it during a lawsuit in which it was seriously on the defensive. A federal judge had already chastised its refusal to uplist grizzlies in the Selkirks from threatened to endangered as "arbitrary and capricious,"[6] and was about to review its refusal a second time. The claim of a Canadian connection let the US government off the hook.

In fact, because the Selkirk and Yaak areas are physically separated from each other[7] and cut off from Canadian bears north of BC Highway 3, while the Cabinet and Yaak areas also seem to be cut off from each other by the Kootenai river-highway-railroad corridor, it is hard to see how these can be treated as one area. One male grizzly crossed Idaho's panhandle in 2006 from the Selkirks to the Cabinet-Yaak,[8] but that solo trek is the only fact contradicting strong evidence that the Selkirk/Cabinet-Yaak consists not of one grizzly recovery area but of three.

Jon Almack and Scott Fitkin, who tried so hard but never captured a grizzly in the North Cascades, would have loved the success of their colleagues in the Selkirks and Cabinet-Yaak. Starting in the early 1980s, state biologists with the Montana, Idaho, and Washington wildlife agencies, working with the US Fish and Wildlife Service, started trapping and radio-collaring grizzlies. They did not catch truckloads, but they did capture anywhere from one to six bears a year.

Trapping a grizzly bear in a leg snare or culvert trap makes the adrenaline pump in even the most seasoned biologist. The bear is frantic and angry, and the biologist is scared but has a lot to do between the time the tranquilizer, delivered in a dart from a blowgun or jab stick, takes effect and the time the bear is released and the biologist beats a hasty retreat. This short interval is the only occasion—Timothy Treadwell's fatal notions notwithstanding—on which a human being can with some degree of safety get up close to a live grizzly.

Several people typically work together with a trapped bear. They take blood and hair samples for later DNA analysis and extract a small tooth to determine the bear's age if its age is not obvious. They weigh the bear—no small feat with a large male—give it an ear tag and a lip tattoo, and fit it with a radio collar that includes spacers so it can expand as the bear grows. Then they pack up their gear, turn on the collar's transmitter, and clear out. If they figured the tranquilizer dosage right for the bear's size, they will be out of harm's way before it stirs.

As the number of radio-collared grizzlies grew, biologists began to monitor them, often from small planes fitted with antennae. Collared bears became so-called Judas bears, betraying the presence of other grizzlies. Tracing the movement of bears with collars and combining this with bear sightings from the ground began to answer questions about habitat use through the seasons, home ranges, distribution, and the effects of disturbances such as roads, logging, and wildfires. Like fog burning off in the sun, as the data grew, managers began to form a clearer picture of how many grizzlies they had, their sex and age, and where they were.

The Selkirk population was the largest, followed by the Yaak. Neither was large, but they were both better off than bears in the Cabinet Mountains, thanks in part to their connections to Canada. In the Cabinets, despite an extensive trapping effort, biologists captured only three grizzlies over seven years. All of them were old; indeed, one died before the fieldwork ended. Of the few other bears sighted, only one was a mother with cubs. For anyone who cared about the survival of the great bear in one of its few remaining redoubts, the picture was grim. Scientists concluded that grizzlies in the Cabinets were headed for extinction.[9]

The short-term answer was to augment that population quickly. As British Columbia's Bob Forbes had said of the Cascades, this was not rocket science. "Without transplants, that population will wink out." The Fish and Wildlife Service embarked in the Cabinets on a public process similar to that used later in the Bitterroots. There was still plenty of public opposition, although not as loud. One of Idaho's senators offered a rider in Congress to block funding for the effort. Concerns about human safety and conflicts with other land uses topped the list. The IGBC encouraged the creation of a citizens' committee to act as a liaison between scientists and local Montana communities. It produced a question-and-answer brochure and became a sounding board for local concerns. At its urging, wildlife managers delayed augmenting for a year and scaled it back to a "test" program of only four bears over five years.

British Columbia agreed to support this effort by supplying bears from its upper Flathead Valley, which was not far away. Between 1990 and 1994, biologists captured, radio-collared, and released into the Cabinet Mountains four subadult females from Canada. That was the first augmentation in the US grizzly bear recovery program.

It was not wildly successful. Three of the four bears stayed in the Cabinets. The fourth one left but was recaptured and brought back. One of the three that stayed was found dead from natural causes while she was still new to the neighborhood. Her infant cub probably died too. All the others lost their collars or radio signals, so biologists lost track of them. It was as if those bears walked off into the mist and simply faded away.

Over a decade later, DNA studies brought a surprise. They confirmed that at least one of the surviving trio had produced offspring, who had in turn produced cubs of their own. By 2006, Grandma Grizzly was fifteen years old, had three children and two grandchildren, was apparently still living in the Cabinet Mountains, and was probably unaware of her celebrity status among bear scientists.[10]

Still, it would take many more matriarchs to save bears in such vulnerable places as the Cabinet-Yaak and Selkirks. All the populations were small and, as scientists readily admitted, the size of a grizzly bear population is "one of the most powerful predictors" of its survival.[11] Bear managers were well aware of warnings from the

World Conservation Union that any animal population which falls below 250 adults is endangered, and an isolated population below fifty individuals is critically endangered.[12] Scientists warned that the process of extinction in small grizzly populations followed a pattern of isolation, habitat shrinkage, and excessive human-caused mortality.[13] The Fish and Wildlife Service conceded that grizzly bears in these small recovery areas warranted an upgrade from threatened to endangered, but other priorities precluded such a move.

The size of the areas itself was much of the problem. Even if every acre was pristine wilderness, were these areas really big enough to support a minimum viable population? Some scientists thought not.[14] And certainly not every acre was pristine wilderness. Yellowstone, the NCDE, even the North Cascades had the benefit of big national park cores managed mainly for natural conditions. The Bitterroots had no national park, but it was still mostly wild and scenic river country and wilderness. By contrast, the Selkirks and Cabinet-Yaak were "working forests" managed by the US Forest Service for multiple uses, including commercial timber production. They contained small wilderness and roadless areas, but nothing like the big core of other recovery areas.

Writer Rick Bass claimed the Yaak was being more intensively logged than any other national forest in the West.[15] He wanted 20 percent of the Yaak Valley set aside as a grizzly sanctuary, but there was no assurance he would succeed.

Adjoining British Columbia was a mixed blessing. Yes, it was a link to other bears, but logging was also active on the Canadian side. Studies showed that logging itself was only a temporary disturbance for grizzlies, but the roads that went with it were a real and permanent danger.[16] British Columbia also allowed grizzly hunting in much of the province, including areas adjoining the Selkirks and Yaak. It was frustrating for US bear biologists monitoring a vulnerable population to discover that members of it had wandered across the border and been shot.[17] Later British Columbia withdrew its part of both areas from grizzly hunting, the Yaak in the 1970s and the Selkirks in 1995.

Environmentalists did constant battle with the US Forest Service over roads. The conservationists won a major victory in 2006, when a federal judge in Missoula agreed with them that the Forest Service had relied on a flawed study in deciding to retain most of an 8,500-mile network of roads in the national forests, which covered the Selkirks and Cabinet-Yaak.

Forest Service biologists who had studied roads and access management in these areas concluded that closure of roads to the public enhanced grizzly habitat even if the total miles of roads continued to climb. They claimed 1987 was the worst year in terms of open motorized road density, but bear habitat and security had improved since then as the Forest Service decommissioned more roads or closed them to motorized access.[18] Skeptical environmentalists continued to sue the Forest Service, claiming that its road densities still exceeded acceptable limits for grizzly recovery.

The Cabinet Mountains, most vulnerable of the three areas, seemed to attract the most threats. The Rock Creek mine, first proposed in the 1980s, was in and out of court for years, with the Fish and Wildlife Service defending its biological opinions that the proposed copper and silver mine, with mitigating conditions attached to its approval, would not hurt grizzlies. So far, neither environmentalists nor the courts have been convinced. As the dispute drew national attention, Montana governor Brian Schweitzer even weighed in on the debate, warning in 2006 that his state would never approve permits unless Spokane-based Revette Minerals gave better assurances that the mine would not drain several high mountain lakes. Commenting on the mining company's willingness, as part of its mitigation, to fund the salary of a Montana bear biologist, grizzly author Bill Schneider likened it to "spending our money to measure the speed a ship sinks instead of buying more lifeboats."[19] Proposals for a second mine and a downhill ski area in the Cabinets raised concerns about further fragmention of the area.[20]

A DNA analysis released in 2003 brought new concerns to the Yaak and Selkirks. That was when scientists discovered how much BC Highway 3 cut off bears from larger populations to the north.[21] This was a particular blow to the Selkirks, where biologists had long assumed that the entire Selkirks Range, extending north to Nelson, British Columbia, and the West Arm of Kootenay Lake, hosted one relatively big, healthy bear population. It was a shock to realize that the highway split the Selkirk grizzlies into two groups isolated from each other. The only silver lining was that it provided a basis for the first reliable population estimates for grizzly bears in the Selkirks and Cabinet-Yaak. That news itself may not have caused any biologists to start dancing in the streets, but at least it took much of the mystery out of managing these recovery areas. When the number crunching was done, it showed a population of 105 grizzlies in the south Selkirks (north to BC Highway 3), thirty-five to fifty in the Yaak (also north to Highway 3), and fifteen in the Cabinet Mountains. These were estimates, but still the best estimates bear managers had ever seen. They also confirmed everyone's fear that "all three fragmented populations are small and likely have an elevated conservation risk."[22]

This was most obvious, again, in the Cabinet Mountains, and added a new urgency to the need to save its tiny population. A decade after the first augmentation "test" of four bears, locals were more relaxed about the idea of importing one or two more bears per year for several years, so long as they had not been in trouble somewhere else. The success story with Grandma Grizzly helped convince some locals that augmentation might hasten the day when grizzlies could come off the threatened species list.

A big project was underway in the NCDE to trap, collar, and release bears for that area's population trend study. This gave biologists a chance to consider bears that could be candidates for the Cabinet Mountains. A young adult female grizzly captured in the Flathead Valley under this program met all the criteria for relocation. The decision was made to do it. In October 2005 she was released into the Cabinet Mountains. Biologists picked the west side of that range as her new home, on the theory that if she started to head home to the Flathead, she would need to cross a lot of good grizzly habitat on the way. She stayed put.

This first augmentation in ten years went well. The bear's release was like a ceremony, with biologists, local officials, members of the media, and citizen group representatives all gathered for the occasion. They stood around congratulating each other until it was time, then they climbed into the safety of their vehicles to watch. When the gate opened on her culvert trap, the bear leaped from the back of the truck and dashed off at a dead run into the brush. In a moment she was gone. A local newspaper editorialized that her release in the Cabinets was "a milestone for common sense."[23] Politically, it did not hurt that the bear had been captured, moved, and released, all within the state of Montana, by Montana's wildlife agency. Politically, it probably also did not hurt that some environmentalists wanted to delay the transplant for more studies.

A year later, Montana moved a second female grizzly from the NCDE into the Cabinets. The second release was accompanied by less ceremony, although one county commissioner did attend. Jim Williams, regional wildlife manager for Montana Fish, Wildlife and Parks, told a local reporter, "We would like to do two this year, but we might not catch another female the entire summer that meets the criteria. We are being very selective."[24]

Moving bears from the NCDE seemed the best way to boost the Cabinet population. Even if the NCDE population had not recovered, it was clearly more robust than the beleaguered Cabinets. Robbing Peter to pay Paul in these circumstances made sense. In a jointly authored paper, Chris Servheen and others claimed that "augmentation can contribute significantly to the increased viability of small grizzly populations over the short term."[25] They proposed adding twelve subadult females to the Cabinet Mountains from 2004 to 2010.

But in the Yaak and Selkirks, in contrast to the Cabinets, they made a suggestion no one had made before. Instead of moving more bears from the NCDE, they proposed in 2004 that Canada add twenty bears each to the Yaak and Selkirk populations on its side of the border.[26] This was the first time US wildlife managers had suggested that Canada augment bear populations within Canada for the mutual benefit of transborder populations. They may have made this proposal partly because Canadian laws did not raise as many procedural hurdles for such actions as did America's National Environmental Policy Act. Biologists and wildlife officers in British Columbia moved bears more routinely than their US counterparts, and residents in bear country made no fuss about it. Fewer people lived near the Canadian sides of the Selkirks and Yaak, and no one on the US side would be in a position to complain about what Canadian biologists did in Canada, even if they knew about it.

Moreover, grizzly bear populations north of BC Highway 3 were healthy—they were even hunted—so British Columbia was in a better position than the United States to supplement the transborder populations that needed help. All they needed to do was move bears across the highway. For all these reasons, Canadian augmentation seemed like an astute idea.

Nonetheless, British Columbia did not adopt this suggestion. It decided instead to seek ways to improve the ability of grizzlies to cross the infamous Highway 3, so that bears could naturally disperse into the southern Selkirks and Yaak. It also closed hunting in areas to the north of those areas so that bear populations might grow enough to encourage some bears to cross the highway. If it became less of a barrier, this might achieve the same result as the suggested transplants but in a more natural way.

The Selkirks and Cabinet-Yaak grizzly populations were nowhere near the targets that define recovery. Augmentation could boost those numbers, but the same scientists who promote importing bears as a short-term solution also insist that it must be matched by a long-term commitment to link bear populations and cut human-caused mortality. It makes no sense to keep moving bears into places where they will be killed.

In 2006 the Cabinet-Yaak had exceeded allowable mortality limits in seven of the past twelve years, the Selkirks in eleven of the past twelve.[27] Breaking the limits in any two consecutive years would bar recovery, even if all the other numbers were right. The Cabinet-Yaak went for several years with no human-caused mortality, but then in 2005 it lost three grizzlies.

Most human-caused deaths occurred during hunting season. Hunters confused grizzlies with black bears, panicked during surprise encounters, or were charged when a grizzly claimed an elk carcass before a hunter returned the next day to retrieve it. A few hunters simply shot first and asked questions later. Trains killed a few bears, and grizzlies that ventured close to local residences sometimes disappeared under suspicious circumstances. As more people move into remote areas, this problem could worsen. Some studies suggested that the number of people living near grizzlies was more deadly for the bears than roads.[28] Fortunately for the bears, there was no evidence of the widespread poaching that plagued grizzly recovery in the NCDE. But with such small populations, any death was a major setback.

Some environmentalists claimed the Fish and Wildlife Service had written off the bear populations in the Selkirks and Cabinet-Yaak while it focused on higher priorities, such as Yellowstone and the NCDE.[29] Yet, on a per-bear basis, the feds and the state wildlife agencies probably were spending more on these two small grizzly recovery areas than any others. It was true that recovery efforts elsewhere sometimes conflicted with efforts in the small areas. In the NCDE, for instance, biologists were reluctant to relinquish captured and collared bears for transplant to the Cabinets because they also needed those bears for the NCDE trend study. Of approximately forty NCDE bears trapped in 2006, only one met the criteria for relocation to the Cabinets, partly because of this. In that sense, recovery in the Cabinet-Yaak took a backseat to the NCDE.[30]

Would delisting of grizzlies in the two biggest recovery areas shift attention to the small areas? At that point the Selkirks and Cabinet-Yaak might find themselves competing with the Bitterroots and North Cascades. By most accounts, the Bitterroots had no grizzlies and the Cascades very few. It was too soon to know if that would be a controlling issue, but the resident, albeit beleaguered grizzly bears in the Selkirks and Cabinet-Yaak were a compelling argument in their own favor.

Another dimension of this decision about where next to focus recovery efforts might be the effect in the United States of events that were unfolding in Canada.

PART 4
CANADA

21 | CANADA IS NO ARK

Grizzly bears are moving north in a drift of continental proportions. Two centuries ago they occupied Mexico's Sierra Madre Occidental, almost within sight of Guadalajara. Today, except for a pocket of possible survivors in Colorado, the southern edge of grizzly territory is Wyoming's Wind River Range just south of Yellowstone. As humans have advanced, bears have retreated to the north. Now with global warming, the northern edge of their range is also pushing north. As Arctic ice melts, grizzlies have been sighted in what was once the domain of polar bears.[1] A hunter on Banks Island in the Northwest Territories shot a hybrid bear in 2006, proving that where their ranges overlap, grizzlies and polar bears may interbreed.

Grizzlies extend across Canada's far north from Alaska to Hudson Bay. When David Thompson, the Canadian equivalent of Lewis and Clark, ventured west, grizzlies still roamed from the prairies of Alberta, Saskatchewan, and southern Manitoba to the Pacific. They occupied all of what became British Columbia except Vancouver Island and the Queen Charlotte Islands.

In subarctic Canada today, grizzlies remain only in British Columbia and along the spine of the Canadian Rockies, which divides British Columbia and Alberta. Together, these two provinces still host nearly eleven times as many grizzlies as in the lower 48 states. British Columbia estimates it has at least 13,000; Alberta claims another 750. These numbers are hotly disputed but are still of a magnitude so much larger than anything in the United States that Americans might be forgiven for regarding western

Canada as a landscape full of North America's biggest and best wildlife.

Canada is indeed a vast place, and it graciously and without moralizing has given a lot of wildlife to the United States. In this way it has helped stem the loss of some US animals. Woodland caribou transplanted to the Selkirks came from northern British Columbia. Lynx released in Colorado came from the Yukon. The first grizzlies brought to the Cabinet Mountains were from British Columbia's Flathead Valley. Wolves, the best-known imports, were delivered to Yellowstone and central Idaho from Alberta's William Switzer Provincial Park. For such generosity, Americans saw Canada as the Great White North, a wilderness stretching to the Arctic, an outdoor warehouse full of surplus animals. In wildlife terms, America was a cargo cult and Canada was its ark.

Indeed, British Columbia remains the most important home for North America's grizzlies outside of Alaska and Canada's far north. British Columbia is a huge province, longer than California and twice as wide. It hosts three-quarters of Canada's biodiversity. Matt Austin, who oversaw grizzly management in British Columbia, acknowledged that his province played "a continental role," with a responsibility to all of North America to protect the last of what was once a more mighty and awesome presence.

But that bastion of bears faces problems of its own. British Columbia's grizzly range has been fractured, with a big gap up through BC's center where grizzlies no longer live. Bears that depended on wildness have yielded to orchards, vineyards, and towns in the Okanogan Valley and to sawmills and cattle ranches in the Chilcotin as far north as Prince George. Nor were mountain bears in the southern half of the province much better off. The Great Bear Rainforest wildlife sanctuary, created in 2006, aimed to protect much of the remaining unlogged parts of BC's Pacific coast, where grizzly populations had been hit hard by industrial logging. Grizzlies survived in BC's Coast Range, but in an arc sweeping around Vancouver from Whistler Ski Resort to the Fraser River they faced growing pressure from people, roads, logging, and development.

BC's Cascades, east of Vancouver and adjoining the grizzly recovery area in Washington State, hosts a small endangered population of grizzlies. They are British Columbia's highest priority for bear recovery. East of the Okanogan, bear populations rose as one moved toward the Rockies. Their best range was in the upper Flathead Valley near BC's southeast corner, which had the densest population of inland grizzlies in North America.[2]

Follow the spine of the Canadian Rockies north from Montana up the British Columbia–Alberta border, and one passes along the edge of Waterton National Park and then the Castle-Crown Wilderness. Waterton, abutting Glacier National Park on the US side, is good bear habitat and a grizzly stronghold. The smaller Castle-Crown faces pressure from oil and gas development and heavy use by all-terrain vehicles.[3]

North of Castle-Crown, the going is even tougher for bears. Crowsnest Pass and the valleys approaching it are heavily developed and growing, especially on the Alberta side. The Highway 3 corridor over Crowsnest Pass has cut off grizzlies in the Glacier-Waterton-Castle-Crown region to the south from grizzlies farther north in Banff, Jasper, Kootenay, and Yoho national parks.[4] These four parks contain the crown jewels of the Canadian Rockies. In scenery and popularity, the Canadian Rockies are North America's answer to Europe's Alps. Rightfully proud, Canadians have clung to an image of their Rockies as a core refuge for grizzlies and other megafauna—big, wild mountains full of big, wild animals.

Scientists paint a different picture. They view these parks as only moderate grizzly habitat. The best habitat is out on the prairie, which people now dominate, and in the wider mountain valleys. But those valleys also carry trans-Canadian railroads and highways. Humans keep adding hotels, ski areas, golf courses, backcountry lodges, campgrounds, and hiking trails. Researchers warn that the 450 grizzlies left in Canada's central Rockies face a "dangerous decline."[5] Bear deaths from 1999 to 2005 exceeded sustainable limits for six straight years.[6] Parks Canada has resorted to closing some drainages to give bears some peace, and requiring hikers in others to visit only between certain hours or in groups of at least six when bears are present. Still, biologists warn that grizzlies in the most popular parks of the Canadian Rockies have reached the limits of their tolerance for so much human use.[7]

So the situation facing grizzly bears in Canada is more nuanced than Americans might expect. Most of the threats grizzlies face in western Canada are the same as they face in the western United States—human settlement, roads, and fragmented habitat. Outside the parks, add logging, mining, ranching, and recreation homes, in roughly that order.

Some people would also include hunting. Alberta suspended grizzly hunting in 2006 pending a scientific review of its bear population, but British Columbia continues to allow grizzly hunting. Since 1996 it has been on a quota basis, limited to those parts of the province where BC's Fish and Wildlife Branch concludes that bear populations are healthy. Not surprisingly, the BC grizzly hunt is a hot-button issue. The Fish and Wildlife Branch says it issues permits only in areas where hunting would have no negative effect on bear populations. The number of permits depends on the population, after factoring in growth rates, mortality from other causes, and hunter success rates. Environmentalists claim this is all based on suspect population assumptions and that hunting makes poaching easier. In an effort to garner green votes in a tight election, the provincial government in 2001 imposed a moratorium on grizzly hunting, but after it lost, the new government reinstated the hunt. In response, the European Union banned BC grizzly trophies.

British Columbia does not allow grizzly hunting in thirteen of its sixty bear units. Generally, they are in the southern part of the province, in places such as the Coast Range, around Vancouver, the Cascades, and the Granby, where bear populations are struggling. Hunting in the Yaak and southern Selkirks was phased out, starting in the 1970s and ending in 1995. Since then, the ministry has closed units adjoining those areas to encourage natural dispersal into them.

More than half of all British Columbians live within thirty miles of the US border, which puts more pressure on cross-border ecosystems. As Don Gayton, an American who moved to Nelson, BC, observed: "There is a curious development inversion that takes place around the border in this part of the world. Often the Canadian side is populated and developed, while the adjacent American side is hinterland."[8]

In 1995 the BC government released a conservation strategy for grizzly bears—a blueprint of what it needed to do. It identified the Cascades as its first priority to reverse the decline and recover a threatened bear population. This was followed by the Granby, east of the Okanogan and across the border from the Kettle River Range near Republic, Washington. In those two areas grizzlies were most threatened and recovery efforts were most likely to bring positive results.[9] Release of this strategy had no visible effect on activities in the Granby, where logging actually seemed to accelerate.[10] By contrast, the Cascades became the subject of an intense effort. It was a tough place to make a stand—so close to so many people, bisected by heavily traveled highways, next to logging and ranching country, where skepticism ran high. The Cascades became the test of British Columbia's will to reverse the forces that increasingly threatened its grizzly bears.

Matt Austin, head of the environment ministry's grizzly bear program, and members of his recovery team drafted a recovery plan for the Cascades in 1999.[11] It called for augmenting the Cascades population with five grizzlies a year for five years. Initial plans called for these bears to come from the dry side of the BC Coast Range near Chilko Lake. Later, the source area was changed to Wells Gray Provincial Park. Under this proposal, twenty-five new bears over five years would augment a resident grizzly population of something less than twenty-five bears between the US border and Fraser Canyon. BC biologists estimated that this starting population of about fifty bears would triple in fifty years, reaching 150 grizzlies in the BC Cascades by 2050. At that point, Cascades grizzlies would lose their threatened status. The plan predicted that eventually the BC Cascades could support about three hundred bears.

British Columbia urged the United States to join in this effort to recover transborder grizzlies in the Cascades. In August 1999, James Walker, British Columbia's assistant deputy minister for wildlife, habitat, and enforcement in what was then called the Ministry of Environment, Lands, and Parks, wrote Mike Dombeck, chief of the US Forest Service, urging that he accelerate grizzly recovery in the US Cascades. "I would like to enlist your support for increasing the profile of, and commitment to, recovery efforts in the North Cascades," Walker wrote. "I request that a strong message of support be sent to the IGBC . . . indicating that all reasonable efforts be made to recover this imperiled population." The US response was a study in creative ambiguity. The United States "remained committed" to grizzly recovery, it assured the Canadians. In the US Cascades, however, nothing changed. "It was very disappointing," Chris Servheen recalled. He had hoped the letter from a Canadian official might spur the US Fish and Wildlife Service to free up funds to start US recovery efforts in the Cascades. Instead, Servheen said, "British Columbia's letter had no effect."

The plan to bring bears into the BC Cascades also encountered resistance within British Columbia. Manning Provincial Park officials were openly hostile. Manning is a popular park, protecting the crest of the Cascades east of Vancouver, near the populous lower Fraser Valley. Manning Park rangers wanted nothing to do with grizzlies. Ranchers in the rainshadow country around Merritt, northeast of the Cascades, were also hostile. Loggers feared grizzly recovery might shut them down. And, needless to say, all the usual opponents were opposed. Even local environmentalists objected, but for reasons different from hikers and backpackers around Seattle. BC environmentalists hoped to use grizzly recovery as a lever to curtail logging. They argued that timber cutting north of Manning Park should be slowed or stopped before bringing in bears. Logging, they claimed, was not good for the bears. The truth was that they were more concerned about stopping logging than saving bears.

Austin and his team managed to weave their way through these minefields and stick with their plan. The first step was a major effort to identify and reduce hazards that could raise the risk of human-grizzly encounters. This meant bear-proofing campgrounds, garbage dumps, and the like, so that the new bears would never come near the slippery and lethal slope that starts when they first equate humans with food. Reducing hazards might also reduce objections from park managers.

This effort was barely into its second year when events took a bizarre turn. US interior secretary Norton had shelved the Bitterroots recovery plan. Hank Fischer, who had been a leading author of the citizens' plan that was endorsed by the Fish and Wildlife Service in the Bitterroots, was understandably bitter. He was also northwest representative for Defenders of Wildlife, perhaps the most effective nongovernmental advocate for grizzly recovery in America. When asked at a small informal gathering in 2001 about his group's views on grizzly recovery in the US Cascades, he replied, "Let 'em walk." As he explained, why spend a half-million dollars and years of effort on an augmentation plan in the US Cascades to end up with nothing, in the same way as had just happened in the Bitterroots, when British Columbia can move bears into the BC Cascades without all the legal fuss we face in the United States, and some of those bears will naturally and quietly disperse into the US Cascades?

Washington State's opponents of grizzly recovery never heard Fischer's proposal, and it never became official policy of the Defenders of Wildlife. Yet skeptics still suspected this was the hidden reason behind BC's recovery plan. They charged that Defenders of Wildlife was helping British Columbia—which it was, but not nearly to the extent they claimed—and that BC's plan to bring bears into the BC Cascades was merely a scheme to circumvent US rules and introduce grizzlies into the US Cascades through the back door. Austin adamantly denied it, as did BC's minister for the environment. "It is not our intention that grizzly bears will be released in a manner that is likely to result in them establishing home ranges in the United States," the minister declared.[12]

While conceding that some bears might drift south into the United States, the IGBC rejected any notion of relying on BC's recovery plan as a substitute for a US plan of its own. Aside from whether this approach would even be honorable, biologists were unanimous in their view that it would take too long anyway because grizzlies disperse so slowly. Unlike wolves, which biologists found could spread like wildfire before a wind, grizzly dispersal creeps like fog on a calm day. Male grizzlies can cover many miles, but females migrate no more than twenty miles per generation. In good habitat, where a mother bear needs less range and thus has less motive to move, it could be even less. When the girls stay behind, male forays are only reconnaissance.

Bill Gaines, Wenatchee Forest wildlife manager, explained: "I think [BC's] augmentation efforts are a great start towards recovery, given the social and political considerations. However, a population of grizzly bears that are distributed throughout the North Cascades, have established home ranges, show a positive population trend, and are numerous enough to study and regularly observe will not happen in my lifetime, and unless we are more aggressive in our recovery efforts, may not happen in my daughter's lifetime, and she is only two!"

The IGBC reckoned it would take more like two hundred years.

Policies and politics are intertwined, so it is little wonder that Canadian wildlife policies would be affected by the outcome of Canadian elections. It is the same the world over.

A major political difference between Canada and the United States is the relative power of provincial governments. In the US, the states can make a lot of noise, but Washington holds nearly all the cards. In Canada the provinces hold the final say on most land use and resource issues outside of national parks and military posts. Environmentalists decried Canada's species-at-risk law, for instance, for having no teeth except on federal lands. A spotted owl in British Columbia would be out of luck, quipped one cynic, unless it flew into a post office.

Hence, after British Columbians voted in 2001, wildlife policies underwent as profound a change within the province as the US election a year earlier had wrought within the United States. BC's Social Democrats, who had run British Columbia for a decade, were swept from office. The Liberals who replaced them, with strong backing from the resource industries, were well to the right of the national Liberal Party. The provincial Liberals claimed such a large majority in British Columbia's parliament that they basically could do whatever they liked.

One of their first moves was to end the moratorium on grizzly bear hunting. Then they doubled logging rates in central British Columbia, citing the need to stop a timber beetle outbreak. Skeptics called it a pretext to help forest industry supporters. Next the Liberals axed fourteen positions for staff studying endangered species. Then they eliminated the official post of environmental auditor, which they branded a Social Democrat gimmick to woo green votes. On similar grounds, the Liberals decided to review the election-eve creation of two provincial parks, and cut the environmental protection budget for the Ministry of Water, Land, and Air Protection by 24 percent. The new minister spoke of "market-oriented" funding sources—ideas like new taxes on outdoor equipment and wilderness access fees that raised hackles on Sierra Club members' necks. The Liberals expanded salmon farming, despite concerns about the damage to wild salmon runs. The government relaxed controls on the forest products industry, pressured BC Hydro to buy electricity from two big coal-fired power plants planned near Princeton, and campaigned to end Ottawa's moratorium on oil and gas drilling in sensitive waters off the Queen Charlotte Islands.

As the list grew, environmentalists expected the next headline to read "Grizzly Recovery Shelved in Cascades." On cue, the Cascades plan made the news. But it did not go quite as far as expected. The *Vancouver Sun* bannered: "Public Concerns Scale Back Cascades Grizzly Plan."[13] Matt Austin told reporters that instead of releasing five grizzlies per year in the Cascades, they would only release three per year. And they pushed back the first releases for a year. This would allow more time to complete reports, Austin explained, on habitat suitability and hazards, especially in Manning Park. "We had people tell us, 'Twenty-five scares me, but if it's ten I'm more comfortable with that,'" Austin said. In shades of similar reactions in the

US Cascades and Bitterroots, he conceded that residents around the BC Cascades were not as familiar with grizzly bears as folks elsewhere in the province, and because of that they voiced more fears. "We have to think about recovery of the bears, but also recovering the social and cultural experience of living with grizzly bears. That's part of the challenge," he said.

But the scaleback continued. A year later, the new minister wanted more input from local interests. She appointed a task force of "stakeholders" to review the Cascades plan. This group spanned the spectrum from ranchers and horsemen to Indians and environmentalists. After six months of debate and deliberation, all but two task force members agreed in early 2003 on a set of recommendations. The other two opposed any form of grizzly recovery. As the majority recommended, British Columbia further scaled back its augmentation target. Under the revisions approved late in 2003, British Columbia aimed to bring only three bears into the Cascades; if a review of that trial transplant was favorable, over the following four years it would add up to three more. The first new bears were set to arrive in 2004. British Columbia had gone from an initial plan to transplant twenty-five bears to one that would involve a maximum of six. "This is not intended as The Augmentation," Austin conceded to the IGBC. "It is more a demonstration of the technique."

That demonstration started, with the help of a helicopter rented by Defenders of Wildlife, by collaring six subadult female grizzlies in Wells Gray Provincial Park. The plan was to follow them for a year and see whether they moved to the streams during salmon migration. Because salmon were a distant memory in the Cascades, the recovery team was concerned that they not bring into the Cascades any salmon-dependent bears.

All the collared bears passed the test, but another season passed with no transplants. In June 2005 a new minister took over the environmental portfolio: Barry Penner, a lawyer from Chilliwack. Later that year, Austin told the IGBC that the new minister personally wanted to approve any augmentation before it started. Then a year later, Austin said the earliest date for approval would be 2007. The plan was obviously slipping.

In 2006, Minister Penner gave his clearest signal yet of what he thought about the Cascades recovery plan. He did not approve Austin's proposal to monitor the collared Wells Gray bears another year. Penner offered no explanation; he simply denied the request. Later that year, a colleague of Austin's in the Environment Ministry passed word along to the IGBC that Austin was busy on another project and Penner had decided not to proceed with the planned augmentation of grizzlies in the BC Cascades. Consequently, under BC's policies, collars were removed from the potential source bears in Wells Gray. Plans for augmentation in the Cascades, British Columbia's highest-priority grizzly recovery area, had gone from twenty-five bears to six to none.

Five years earlier Mike Rose, owner of Quilchena Cattle Company in Merritt, BC, had complained to reporters about plans to bring grizzlies into the Cascades. He said: "I'm still hoping this whole friggin' program will go away."[14] In 2006, it did.

This might not be the final word on British Columbia's commitment to grizzly bear recovery along the southern quarter of the province. A future government may have a different view. But it serves as a sober reminder to US wildlife officials of the responsibility they face to look after recovery of their own grizzly bears.

Brian Horejsi, a Calgary-based bear biologist, reminded an audience of environmentalists in Seattle that however bountiful the Canadian ark may once have been, it was no longer the easy answer to America's wildlife problems. "When it comes to endangered species now," Horejsi warned his US audience, "you're on your own."

CONCLUSION
A Race in Slow Motion

A child born the same year grizzly bears were listed is nearly old enough now to be a US president. How much has recovery of the great bear progressed during the time it took for a human to reach adulthood?

The US Fish and Wildlife Service launched its effort by creating four recovery areas, nominating three others, evaluating two of those three—the North Cascades and Bitterroots—and adding them to the list of refuges where it would attempt to save grizzly bears. Since then it has not expanded this list. Colorado's San Juans, the third nominee, was never evaluated and remains in limbo.

Fast-forward some thirty years to 2007, when the Fish and Wildlife Service announced, over vigorous objections, that Yellowstone's grizzlies had recovered. This was its first declaration of success in a long process marked by several defeats. Next up after Yellowstone, in a rush to make up time, it is overseeing a comprehensive study of grizzlies in the Northern Continental Divide Ecosystem (NCDE). This could lead, if human-caused bear mortality can be capped, to another declaration of success.

Grizzlies in the Cabinet-Yaak and Selkirk recovery areas were barely hanging on when those areas were first declared, and in many respects they are still only hanging on. Bear numbers are well below recovery levels. The Cabinet-Yaak hosts the only grizzly population that has been augmented with additional bears. And more are needed, either from other US bear populations or through natural dispersal from Canada. Those in charge of recovery in these small areas are encouraged that local tolerance for importing bears has improved.

In sum, the scorecard for the four original recovery areas reads: one recovered, one moving toward recovery, and two that are still very much works in progress. By contrast, the scorecard for the two newer areas shows no progress. The Bitterroots are the only recovery area other than the Cabinets where bear transplants have been planned, but that plan was shelved after objections from the state of Idaho. No one in the Fish and Wildlife Service would admit it, but the Bitterroots decision had a chilling effect on any notion of augmenting the grizzly population in the other new area—the North Cascades. In effect, neither the Bitterroots nor the Cascades have a plan. Any help that grizzlies in the US Cascades might have gained from Canada was dashed by British Columbia's own version of a Bitterroots decision. Both the Bitterroots and the Cascades areas on both sides of the border await political changes before much else is likely to happen.

The grizzly recovery plan calls for a review and evaluation of other potential recovery areas. Nothing is going to happen about those in the foreseeable future. Colorado's San Juans have waited in the wings for thirty years. Bear advocates are not shy about calling for expansion of the six recovery areas and for adding others where they think grizzlies could make a comeback. Their nominations include Hells Canyon on the Idaho-Oregon border, Utah's high Unitas, South Dakota's Black Hills, the Gila in New Mexico, the Siskiyous along the Oregon-California border, areas around Lassen National Park, and Los Padres National Forest, which overlooks California's Big Sur. Grizzlies once occupied all these areas, and most are federally managed wilderness. This may read like a list of the wildest places left in the West, but in a ranking of federal priorities for grizzly recovery, they are not even on the list. Until recovery is complete in all the currently selected areas—a day that is itself too far ahead to visualize—they will not be.

If recovery has little to show by way of progress, how well has the Fish and Wildlife Service done in husbanding the bear populations that already existed? In all the years that grizzly bears have been listed, no recovery areas that had grizzlies at the beginning have lost them. Compared to the decline grizzlies faced before listing, this is perhaps a measure of success. Keeping bears in the Cabinet Mountains required human intervention, as it will in the Cascades, where the survivors are prophetically called "ghost grizzlies."

Estimates suggest that bear numbers have grown in Yellowstone, the NCDE, and the Selkirks. Partly this may be a mirage based on better data than when earlier estimates were made. In other words, populations may not have grown as much as we think, because they were larger than we thought in the first place. Grizzlies are not easy to count, but there is no denying the remarkable comeback they made in Yellowstone in relatively few years after the dumps were closed. And there is no denying what this shows about their ability to multiply, despite low reproductive rates, when they start from a sufficiently large base in an adequate habitat.

Declaring success in Yellowstone has raised several new issues. Before the government started declaring success, the same legal protections applied to a grizzly inside or outside a recovery area. With the delisting decision in Yellowstone, a new question arises about the status of bears outside an area after bears inside that area are taken off the endangered species list.

The "outside" bear may have been outside all along or moved there, in the pessimist's view, in search of better habitat or, in the optimist's view, to escape crowding inside the recovery area. Either way, young male grizzlies are particularly prone to wander and may end up in improbable places, such as on the northern outskirts of Spokane. During a presentation to the IGBC on western Montana's bear management plan, the state's regional wildlife manager told the committee, "Bears are expanding and can be expected to show up anywhere in western Montana, including the Bitterroot."[1] The roaming teenager makes an exciting addition to the local evening news, but expansion of grizzly range by both male and female bears is more complex. As communities in western Wyoming have demonstrated, this expansion is not always welcome.

By ignoring boundaries, the bears themselves are making recovery areas outdated. As a result, Montana has changed its policy on where to release captured grizzlies. No longer will it return all bears to designated recovery areas. "It doesn't make sense," a wildlife manager explains, "to pack them all into a few small areas and expect them to stay put."[2]

This poses questions about the status of "outside" bears when "inside" bears are delisted. The "inside" bear has lost protection under the Endangered Species Act; does the "outside" bear as well? Does an "inside" bear regain protection if it crosses the recovery area boundary and becomes an "outside" bear? The Fish and Wildlife Service would say no, because it delisted a "distinct population segment" consisting of all bears within a more or less contiguous area that included a recovery area core—much like saying that separately incorporated Santa Monica is also part of the Los Angeles metropolitan area. But how far does this go, and how does it apply to the adventuresome bear that strikes off for parts unknown?

Both Montana and Wyoming will allow hunting of some "outside" grizzlies under plans the federal government approved when it delisted Yellowstone. That may be acceptable for a population that has recovered, but how does hunting mesh with the need for linkage zones and wildlife corridors between Yellowstone and, say, the Bitterroots?

Grizzlies outside of recovery areas are in something of a legal limbo, a point the Fish and Wildlife Service seems to acknowledge. It has launched a review of its policy on distinct populations, designed to tie the policy closer to science. In deciding whether a bear population is distinct enough for separate treatment, it will analyze each bear group's genetics and movement, and the significance of its habitat and available range. This exercise, slated for completion in 2008, could bring some changes in recovery area boundaries and the uplisting of some bear populations, such as in the North Cascades, from threatened to endangered.[3]

Importantly, this policy review must find some way to reconcile the delisting of "outside" bears with the need for wildlife corridors as links between recovery areas. Bear scientists and wildlife managers all repeat the mantra about how important these links are to long-term recovery, but no one has found the magic formula to ensure that they work. Linkage zones raise a host of sociopolitical, legal, and practical issues about private landowner attitudes, adequate wildlife cover, conflicting uses on public lands, and how to entice bears to cross over or under busy highways. The Yukon-to-Yellowstone proposed wildlife corridor, dubbed "Y2Y,"[4] may inspire managers to try harder, but creating and keeping these linkage zones intact is all about site-specific details, and no part of this work is very glamorous.[5] If linkage zones fail to deliver the genetic interchange that all recovery areas need, those genes will have to come from culvert traps on the back of trucks. No island population can survive forever without bears being on the move, either naturally or artificially.

Yellowstone also opened another chapter about returning grizzly bear management to the states. Given how strongly states opposed a federal takeover when grizzlies were first listed, the prospect of handing control back to the states, even under federally approved plans, has caused heartburn among environmentalists. It has not helped that some ranchers and even state officials have gloated publicly at the prospect, saying, as if their patience had run out, that they finally may have a chance to shoot a grizzly.

It is too early to tell how well the states will handle their new responsibility. The state biologists and wildlife managers are professionals. If they are left alone to do their job, with adequate funds to do it, environmentalists might eventually have to admit that their fears were overblown. The key questions are how much elected state officials will pressure wildlife staff to bend their judgment in ways that may not be in the best interest of bears, and how far the US Fish and Wildlife Service will allow bear management to unravel before it intervenes. If populations fall below certain numbers, that could automatically trigger federal review, but who will be in charge of gathering the numbers?

This assumes the worst, and early signs do not necessarily point that way. The Wyoming Game and Fish Department steered its way through heated hearings about the expanding Yellowstone grizzly population and emerged with a plan that at least protected half the Wind River Range. Idaho's Fish and Game Department, despite antipredator rhetoric from officials in Boise, kept a bear biologist in

Bonners Ferry working steadily for grizzlies in the Idaho parts of the Cabinet and Selkirk recovery areas.

Montana's Fish, Wildlife, and Parks agency has set the standard for other states to match. It contributed critical manpower and resources to the NCDE bear surveys. It has handled the capture and relocation of grizzlies from the NCDE to the Cabinet Mountains. It responds to rancher complaints, investigates poaching, tracks collared grizzlies, and talks to landowners about coexisting with bears. Montana has become so active that it appears for most intents and purposes to be managing its own grizzly bears. As if to prove it, the state has developed its own grizzly bear management plan for western Montana. While it has coordinated with the feds, Montana has taken most of these steps on its own. Partly this is because Montana has so many grizzlies, especially in comparison to other states. Someone needs to manage them. But Fish and Wildlife Service funding is so short that little would happen unless the state took this initiative. Of course, Montana's funding is not endless either, but at least it tries.

For similar reasons, nongovernmental organizations have assumed a greater role. The principle that nature abhors a vacuum even applies to wildlife management. If the feds cannot or will not do it, and the states are short of commitment or money, others are likely to step up. These groups vary from one area to another, but almost every recovery area has its local champions. Government officials sometimes grumble about whether they are champions or detractors, because these groups do not march to the government's tune. They may buy timber or grazing rights to defuse conflicts, provide fieldwork volunteers, and lobby Congress for funds—which all privately please agency officials—but the next day they may turn around and sue those same officials for not doing their job.

Defenders of Wildlife and the National Wildlife Federation have augmented official efforts in nearly all the recovery areas. They took the lead in developing a citizens' plan for grizzly recovery in the Bitterroots, a plan adopted with little change by the Fish and Wildlife Service but later nixed for reasons that had nothing to do with its origins. Defenders paid for helicopters so that British Columbia could capture, collar, and track candidate grizzlies for its Cascades recovery project, another effort aborted for unrelated reasons.

Defenders of Wildlife is best known for its compensation programs, which pay ranchers for livestock losses due to predation by protected species such as wolves and grizzlies. Since it took over this program in 1997, Defenders has paid out $142,000 for losses due to grizzlies. Ranchers grumble that Defenders sets too high a standard of proof for establishing what killed the cow or sheep before it will pay, but that is a different argument from the outright howls ranchers might wail if they were paid nothing.

Nor is the compensation intended as get-lost money. Defenders recognizes that the burdens of saving endangered species are not borne equally and it is unfair to ask those whose livelihoods are at stake to bear those burdens by themselves.[6] The limits of this philosophy will be tested in Yellowstone, where the organization must decide whether to keep compensating ranchers after the delisting of grizzlies.

Defenders of Wildlife spends even more under a separate proactive conservation fund. It pays ranchers to take steps aimed at preventing livestock losses in the first place—such things as guard dogs for sheep flocks and fencing—and buys out grazing permits in areas where predators and livestock do not mix. Defenders has spent over half a million dollars on some 150 projects, mainly in the Northern Rockies, aimed at stemming predation by both wolves and bears. More than half of this served to head off potential conflicts with grizzly bears. In like fashion, the National Wildlife Federation has paid ranchers to retire twenty-five grazing allotments, representing half a million acres, around Yellowstone.

Ironically, the Bush administration encouraged nongovernmental groups to take greater initiative, by encouraging them to pick up the slack left by underfunding federal agencies and by funding private groups directly. In Montana, for instance, the Fish and Wildlife Service made a so-called stewardship grant of nearly $100,000 to the Blackfoot Challenge, an umbrella organization for six groups and forty-five landowners. The funds, which required a 10 percent match in nonfederal dollars or in-kind contributions, were earmarked to reduce conflicts between grizzly bears and ranchers by temporarily fencing calving areas and other means. One could debate whether such programs deliver the best bang for the buck, but they reflected a federal policy of working with local and private groups—the partial privatization of grizzly recovery.

According to the Fish and Wildlife Service box score at the end of 2007, 566 animals were listed as threatened or endangered within the United States. Eighty-one of these were mammals. Another 138 animals were candidates for listing. Since adoption of the Endangered Species Act, forty-six plants and animals have been delisted. Some came off the list after taxonomic study revealed that they were not separate species and thus should not have been listed in the first place. Nine listed animals went extinct. The rest recovered. The big success stories are the American alligator, the gray wolf, and the bald eagle.

Comparing the pace of grizzly recovery with the progress of recovery in other success stories may be unfair because grizzlies reproduce more slowly. Even if everything is done right, it takes longer to see results. Wolves, introduced in the Rockies well after the grizzly program started, have already left the list. The reproductive rates of wolves and grizzlies are like the difference between high-speed Internet and dialing on an old phone line. Threats to bears can multiply at the high speed of modern life, but grizzlies live according to an ancient and slower rhythm. In the ways we measure time, it is slow motion. How well can such a slow-motion animal cope in such a fast-paced world?

As the Yellowstone debate demonstrates, habitats only stay the same in fairy tales. Change is one of nature's few certainties. But changes due to global warming and a growing human presence are faster than normal change in nature. These changes suggest that quality habitat in the core areas is eroding, yet we have little knowledge about how seriously. We know what grizzlies prefer, but we do not know the limits of their tolerance. Fortunately for the bears, their diverse diets provide some built-in cushion against habitat change.[7]

Even if Servheen is right that recovery is best measured by demographics rather than habitat, in the short term bear numbers do not address such issues as genetic diversity—the lack of which can be a silent killer. Without it, a species simply stops reproducing. Some scientists warn of a fifty- to four-hundred-year lag between habitat fragmentation and population extinction—a worrisome concept called "extinction debt."[8] In other words, the clock could be ticking without us even knowing it.

Is change happening faster than bears are able to adapt? Some people think so and predict that grizzlies may be extinct in the lower 48 states within thirty-five years.[9] In *Mark of the Grizzly*, Scott McMillion calls extinction a "disgrace to God." This verdict may be at one end of a spectrum of possible futures that ranges from doomsday to success, but where are the grizzlies on that scale?

Given the speed of change and how long grizzly recovery could take at its current slow-motion rate, one has to ask whether the pace of change is itself a cause for concern. Does it matter how long grizzly recovery takes?

In the case of the Cascades and Cabinet-Yaak, recovery sooner rather than later would mean needing to add fewer bears. Every surviving resident bear equals one less bear that a dwindling population needs. Preserving the genes of those resident survivors would also add to important genetic variety. It is too late to do this in the Bitterroots, because the local genes are already gone.

Recovery in more areas would also stabilize the species overall. Grizzly recovery today has a poor eggs-to-baskets ratio. Yellowstone and the NCDE can serve, like two big warehouses, as sources for bears used to augment the smaller or more precarious recovery areas for some time. But how stable is a species that relies indefinitely on one or two populations to keep all the others alive?

Larger populations are inherently more resilient. Scientists warn again and again that small and isolated populations are vulnerable.[10] Nudged the wrong way by a poor berry crop, a big wildfire, or too much inbreeding, such groups can spin into an "extinction vortex."[11] The sooner recovery occurs for all grizzlies, the fewer 911 calls they will require.

The final reason for pressing ahead more quickly is the inherent danger in moving slowly. In an observation that combines sociopolitical and biological wisdom, Chris Servheen warns that a recovery program that is not moving forward invites defeat. "Without a strategic and proactive approach, a management program continuously responds to ongoing conservation threats," he says. "Such a defensive and reactive approach is doomed to failure."[12] Grizzly recovery is an odd mixture of both. On the one hand it has "a strategic and proactive" plan that spells out in more detail than a cake recipe what needs to be done, but it also follows "a defensive and reactive approach."

Time and again Servheen has said he would launch various initiatives "tomorrow" if he had the funds. But he does not. Yet, like everything else about grizzlies, the amount actually spent trying to save them is a matter of some dispute. Congress asked the Fish and Wildlife Service midway through the Bush term to calculate how much all federal and state agencies spent in a year on endangered species. After some investigation, the agency replied that the total was $1.4 billion. It included everything from scientific research and public meetings to law enforcement, planning, and the most mundane paperwork—everything that could be identified as some type of endangered species activity.[13] Skeptics questioned the figure and wondered how much it had been inflated to justify not spending more. Critics cited it as proof of how much taxpayer money already was being wasted. Servheen was surprised at the report's claim that $7.7 million was spent annually on grizzly bears. He did not know the source of that number and could not reconcile it with his own budget, which was around $400,000 per year.[14] Spending by other federal and state agencies could hardly make up the difference, which suggested that the estimate was either way off or included a lot of salaries for a lot of senior officials in Washington DC.

Closer to the ground, the list of projects postponed for lack of funds is almost endless—management work in the Selkirks, tracking studies in the NCDE, a revived citizen committee in the

Bitterroots, an augmentation plan for the Cascades. A subcommittee of the IGBC discussed in November 2006 what to do about this chronic shortage of funding. The group included regional managers from the US Fish and Wildlife Service, Park Service, Forest Service, Geological Survey, and Montana's Fish, Wildlife, and Parks agency—all of them involved in grizzly recovery. They agreed that base funding had been inadequate to implement Yellowstone's postrecovery management and simultaneously monitor the NCDE. They had filled the shortfalls with congressional earmarks and add-ons, a practice that Congress plans to stop because of its misuse for pork barrel projects.

Yellowstone funding for the next fiscal year was adequate, the group concluded, but no one had found the funds needed to complete the NCDE's tracking project. "Given the flat or declining budgets at the regional and forest level, along with increasing fixed costs," the group noted, "it is increasingly difficult to fund these and other recovery efforts."[15] The subcommittee discussed various strategies to improve reliable funding. Their brightest idea seemed to be for Congress to fund a trust dedicated to grizzly management, with its annual income spent to fund the work. They concluded, in remarks intended not for the public but as a warning to the IGBC: "To a very real extent, failure to increase funding for grizzly bear recovery and conservation has jeopardized delisting in Yellowstone, recovery in the NCDE, and the continued existence of grizzly bears in other ecosystems."[16] This sounds more like an indictment one might expect from the Sierra Club than from a group of government managers.

Even if $7.7 million accurately estimates how much all state and federal agencies spent in one year on grizzly recovery, compare that with the federal government's total spending that same year of $2.2 trillion. The budget process is byzantine, but the end product reflects America's commitments, or lack of them, on an array of issues, including saving endangered species.

Ultimately, funding is the measure of public resolve. How we allocate public funds tells more than what we say. Budgets may be an imperfect measure, but over the years they are a more reliable gauge than pronouncements by policy makers. In this case, however, the conclusions from both are much the same. Both reveal America's ambivalence about the recovery of grizzly bears. People are divided over whether to save grizzlies at all, and how much to spend doing it. The sums needed are not huge; they are like a bushel in a trainload of wheat. But when the public keeps debating whether it wants grizzlies, it is hard to justify spending more.

Bill Paleck, supervisor of North Cascades National Park, retired in 2006, after fourteen years on the IGBC's North Cascades subcommittee. Wistfully, he spoke of an era when America might move beyond this conflicted ambivalence. "Working on this committee has been one of my biggest frustrations," Paleck confessed. "We have progressed so little because the public is so impassioned on the subject of grizzly bears. People are impassioned either by zeal or by fear. This issue won't be resolved so long as folks are that way. Somehow we need to inspire the public to think instead that we are nobler because grizzlies live among us."

NOTES

Many of the articles cited here are from *Ursus*, the official publication of the International Association for Bear Research and Management. To order copies, contact Terry White, Southern Appalachian Field Laboratory, 274 Ellington Hall, University of Tennessee, Knoxville, TN 37996; e-mail: tdwhite@utk.edu.

INTRODUCTION: "I WON'T SAY IT WASN'T"

1. Fred Becky, *Cascade Alpine Guide: Stevens Pass to Rainy Pass*, vol. 2 (Seattle: Mountaineers Books, 1989): 132–33.
2. Stephen Herrero, *Bear Attacks: Their Causes and Avoidance* (New York: Lyons and Burford, 1985): 146.
3. Douglas Chadwick, "Grizz," *National Geographic* (July 2001): 2.
4. Christopher Servheen, "Conservation of Small Bear Populations through Strategic Planning," *Ursus* 10 (1998): 69.

1 | AN END TO THE KILLING

1. *Title 16, U.S. Code*, §§ 1531–43.
2. Wildlife in the dry Columbia Basin was described as "meager." D. W. Meinig, *The Great Columbia Plain* (Seattle: University of Washington Press, 1968): 19–20. Grizzlies generally did not favor desert ecoregions. David Mattson and Troy Merrill, "Extirpations of Grizzly Bears in the Contiguous United States, 1850–2000," *Conservation Biology* 16 (August 2002): 1123.
3. A grizzly was shot on Vancouver Island in May 2006. British Columbia's environment minister, Barry Penner, said that grizzlies are not native to the island but occasionally swim over from the mainland.
4. Charles Churcher and Alan Morgan, "A Grizzly Bear from the Middle Wisconsin of Woodbridge, Ontario, Canada," *Canadian Journal of Earth Science* 13 (1976): 341–47. An Oregon cave revealed a grizzly fossil over fifty

thousand years old. Richard Hill, "Ice-Age Jaguar among Fossil Finds," *OregonLive.com*, December 13, 2006.

5. Tsutomu Mano, "Harvest History of Brown Bears in the Oshima Peninsula, Hokkaido, Japan," *Ursus* 10 (1998): 173–80.

6. Andreas Zedrosser, Bjorn Dahle, Jon Swenson, and Norbert Gerstl, "Status and Management of the Brown Bear in Europe," *Ursus* 12 (2001): 9; Michael Kohn and Felix Knauer, "Phylogeography of Brown Bears in Europe and Excremental PCR: The New Tool in the Genetic Analysis of Animals in the Wild," *Ursus* 10 (1998): 315–21.

7. T. McTaggart Cowan, "The Status and Conservation of Bears (*Ursidae*) of the World—1970," *Bears: Their Biology and Management* (1972): 343–67.

8. Robert Rausch, "Geographic Variation in Size in North American Brown Bears (*Ursus arctos*) as Indicated by Condylobasal Length," *Canadian Journal of Zoology* 41 (1963): 33–45.

9. Alec Rekow, "Telling about Bear in Scott Momaday's 'The Ancient Child,'" *Wicazo Sa Review* (Spring 1997): 155–60; Lydia Black, "Bear in Human Imagination and in Ritual," *Ursus* 10 (1998): 343; Lisa Whitehead, "The Medicine Grizzly: The Bear among the Blackfeet," *Independent Grizzly Bear Report* (published by Earth First!, Spring 1988): 2; Scott McMillion, *Mark of the Grizzly* (Helena, MT: Falcon Publishing, 1999): 240.

10. Paul Cutright, *Lewis and Clark: Pioneering Naturalists* (Lincoln: University of Nebraska Press, 1989).

11. Robert Cleland, *This Reckless Breed of Men* (New York: Alfred A. Knopf, 1952): 10.

12. On the basis of the Lewis and Clark journals, some scientists argue that native northwestern tribes overhunted ungulates within their territories. The journals report a scarcity of game in proximity to tribes but abundant game in the no-man zones between tribes. Paul Martin and Christine Szuter, "War Zones and Game Sinks in Lewis and Clark's West," *Conservation Biology* 13 (February 1999): 36. Others argue that biogeographic history, habitat differences, and climatic change had as much to do with these differences as did humans. Lee Lyman and Steve Wolverton, "The Late Prehistoric–Early Historic Game Sink in the Northwestern United States," *Conservation Biology* 16 (February 2002): 73. This debate continues. See Paul Martin and Christine Szuter, "Game Parks before and after Lewis and Clark: Reply to Lyman and Wolverton," *Conservation Biology* 16 (February 2002): 244.

13. Hiram Chittenden, *The American Fur Trade of the Far West* (Stanford, CA: Academic Reprints, 1954): 10.

14. Ibid., 824–25.

15. Various tallies on the number of grizzly bear hides are contained in Meinig, *The Great Columbia Plain*, 86; US Fish and Wildlife Service, *North Cascades Ecosystem Recovery Plan Chapter* (Washington DC: US Fish and Wildlife Service, 1997): 2; Sally Portman, *The Smiling Country: A History of the*

Methow Valley (Winthrop, WA: Sun Mountain Resorts, 1993): 313. For a more comprehensive report, see Paul Sullivan, "A Preliminary Study of Historic and Recent Reports of Grizzly Bears in the North Cascades Area of Washington" (Olympia: Washington Department of Game, 1983).

16. Cleland, *This Reckless Breed of Men*, 44.
17. Fred Becky, *Range of Glaciers* (Portland: Oregon Historical Society Press, 2003): 101.
18. Becky, *Range of Glaciers*, 346.
19. Bob Spring, Ira Spring, and Harvey Manning, *The North Cascades National Park* (Seattle: Superior Publications, 1969): 3.
20. Doug Devin, *Mazama: The Past 100 Years* (Seattle: Peanut Butter Publishing, 1997): 76.
21. Portman, *The Smiling Country*, 313.
22. For a summary of the last recorded grizzly bear in various states, see Gary Brown, *The Great Bear Almanac* (New York: Lyons and Burford, 1993): 280.
23. A hunter killed the bear in self-defense. That incident and the search for more recent proof of grizzlies in the San Juans are described in David Petersen, *Ghost Grizzlies* (New York: Henry Holt, 1995). See also David Brown, *The Grizzly in the Southwest* (Tucson: University of Arizona Press, 1985).
24. Colorado grizzlies have been back in the news after a sighting, described by wildlife officials as "credible," of a female grizzly with two cubs near Independence Pass, southeast of Aspen. "Colorado Wildlife Officials Investigate Grizzly Sighting East of Aspen," Associated Press, September 29, 2006.
25. Brian Horejsi, "A Future for the Grizzly," *Bear News* (published by the Great Bear Foundation, Spring 2001): 11.
26. The former range is based on the combined area of Arizona, California, Colorado, Idaho, Montana, Nevada, New Mexico, Utah, and Wyoming, and parts of Kansas, Oklahoma, Nebraska, North Dakota, South Dakota, Texas, and Washington. The five areas of presently occupied range are: Yellowstone (9,500 sq. mi.), Northern Continental Divide (9,600 sq. mi.), Cabinet-Yaak (2,000 sq. mi.), Selkirks (1,081 sq. mi.), and North Cascades (9,565 sq. mi.). These totals do not include continuous portions of these ecosystems in Canada.
27. Bruce McLellan, "Maintaining Viability of Brown Bears along the Southern Fringe of Their Distribution," *Ursus* 10 (1998): 607.

2 | A TENTATIVE START

1. The National Marine Fisheries Service within the US Department of Commerce implements the Endangered Species Act for marine species.
2. Some still argue that the recovery areas are too small. Michael Bader,

"Distribution of Grizzly Bears in the U.S. Northern Rockies," *Northwest Science* 74 (2000): 325; Michael Bader, "Spatial Needs of Grizzly Bears in the U.S. Northern Rockies," paper presented at the Society for Conservation Biology meeting, June 12, 2000.

3. Jonathan Bjorklund, "Preliminary Investigation of the Feasibility of Reestablishing a Grizzly Bear Population in the North Cascades National Park Complex," Misc. Research Paper NCT-8, North Cascades National Park (1978); Jonathan Bjorklund, "Historical and Recent Grizzly Bear Sightings in the North Cascades," Misc. Research Paper NCT-13, North Cascades National Park (1980); Jonathan Bjorklund, "Species, Subspecies, and Distribution of Mammals in the North Cascades," Misc. Research Paper NCT-14, North Cascades National Park (1981).

4. Interagency Grizzly Bear Committee, *Grizzly Bear Compendium* (Missoula, MT: US Fish and Wildlife Service, 1987): 102.

3 | WHO NEEDS IT ANYWAY?

1. Aldo Leopold, "A Biotic View of Land," *Journal of Forestry* 37 (September 1939): 727.

2. Daniel Simberloff, "Biodiversity and Bears: A Conservation Paradigm Shift," *Ursus* 11 (1999): 24; Robert Naiman and Kevin Rogers, "Large Animals and System-Level Characteristics in River Corridors," *BioScience* 47 (September 1997): 521.

3. McMillion, *Mark of the Grizzly*, 231–32.

4. Grant Hilderbrand, Sean Farley, Charles Robbins, Thomas Hanley, Kimberley Titus, and Christopher Servheen, "Use of Stable Isotopes to Determine Diets of Living and Extinct Bears," *Canadian Journal of Zoology* 74 (1996): 2080.

5. Mary Willson, Scott Gende, and Brian Marston, "Fishes and the Forest," *BioScience* 48 (1998): 455; Grant Hilderbrand, Thomas Hanley, Charles Robbins, and Charles Schwartz, "Role of Brown Bears (*Ursus arctos*) in the Flow of Marine Nitrogen into a Terrestrial Ecosystem," *Oecologia* 121 (1999): 546.

6. Ian Huggett, "Salmon-Grizzlies-Trees," *Bear News* (October–December 1998): 12.

7. Petersen, *Ghost Grizzlies*, 182–83.

8. Grizzlies are not efficient predators. Derek Craighead, "An Integrated Satellite Technique to Evaluate Grizzly Bear Habitat Use," *Ursus* 10 (1998): 198. Grizzly diet is discussed in Interagency Grizzly Bear Committee, *Grizzly Bear Compendium*, 24–25.

9. Bear scavenging of cougar kills is discussed in Kerry Murphy, Gregory Felzien, Maurice Hornocker, and Toni Ruth, "Encounter Competition between Bears and Cougars: Some Ecological Implications," *Ursus* 10 (1998): 55.

10. Grizzly–black bear relations are discussed in Interagency Grizzly Bear Committee, *Grizzly Bear Compendium*, 77–78.

11. Peyton Curlee and Tim Clark, "Nature's Movers and Shakers," *Defenders* 70 (Spring 1995): 22.

12. Reed Noss, Howard Quigley, Maurice Hornocker, Troy Merrill, and Paul Paquet, "Conservation Biology and Carnivore Conservation in the Rocky Mountains," *Conservation Biology* 10 (1996): 949; Simberloff, "Biodiversity and Bears," 21–22; Roman Gula, Witold Frackowiak, and Kajetan Perzanowski, "Current Status and Conservation Needs of Brown Bears in the Polish Carpathians," *Ursus* 10 (1998): 85.

13. Humans benefit from the wilderness that grizzlies require. John Mills, ed., *Impressions of the North Cascades* (Seattle: Mountaineers Books, 1996): 190.

14. Alan Thein Durning, *Green-Collar Jobs* (Seattle: Northwest Environment Watch, 1999): 12–14.

15. Edward Wilson, *The Diversity of Life* (Cambridge, MA: Belknap Press, 1992); Edward Wilson and Frances Peter, eds., *Biodiversity* (Washington DC: National Academy Press, 1988).

16. Scott Brennan, cited in Mills, *Impressions of the North Cascades*, 189. Brennan is executive conservation fellow with the National Parks and Conservation Association.

17. Center for Biodiversity and Conservation, *Biodiversity, Science, and the Human Prospect* (New York: American Museum of Natural History, 1997): 5.

18. Larry Pynn, "Grizzly Viewing a Boon to BC Ecotourism," *Vancouver Sun*, August 4, 2001.

19. Suzanne Miller, Sterling Miller, and Daniel McCollum, "Attitudes toward and Relative Value of Alaskan Brown and Black Bears to Resident Voters, Resident Hunters, and Nonresident Hunters," *Ursus* 10 (1998): 357, 373.

20. Stephen Stringham, *Bear Viewing in Alaska* (Guilford, CT: Globe Pequot Press, 2007).

21. Michael Gibeau, Stephen Herrero, Bruce McLellan, and John Woods, "Managing for Grizzly Bear Security Areas in Banff National Park and the Central Canadian Rocky Mountains," *Ursus* 12 (2001): 127–28.

22. Doug Peacock, "Making the West Safe for Grizzlies," *Audubon* (November–December 1997): 50.

23. David Petersen, "Old Ephraim's Last Stand," *Mother Earth News*, August 15, 2005.

24. See Peacock, "Making the West Safe for Grizzlies."

4 | SAVE IT SOMEWHERE ELSE

1. The secretary of the interior may declare a population "experimental" on a determination that it is not essential to the continued existence of an endangered or threatened species, but the designation will further conser-

vation of that species. Experimental designation has several consequences. It relieves the Fish and Wildlife Service from a duty to identify and manage critical habitat for an endangered species, and may allow the "taking" (harassing or killing) of individual animals without threat of criminal penalty under conditions specified by agency regulations. See *Title 16, U.S. Code* § 1539 (j); *Title 50, Code of Federal Regulations—U.S. Fish and Wildlife Service*, Subpart H, section 17.80 et. seq.

2. *United States v. McKittrick*, 142 F.3d 1170 (9th Cir. 1998).

3. *Wyoming Farm Bureau Federation v. Babbitt*, 987 F.Supp. 1349 (D.C. Wyo. 1997).

4. Ibid., 199 F.3d 1224 (10th Cir. 2000).

5. Both these studies are summarized in Interagency Grizzly Bear Committee, *Grizzly Bear Compendium*, 88–89.

6. John Fialka, "In a Montana Valley, Grizzlies Are Closer Than People Think," *Wall Street Journal*, August 4, 2004, A6.

7. Suzanne Miller, Sterling Miller, and Daniel McCollum, "Attitudes Toward and Relative Value of Alaskan Brown and Black Bears," 357.

8. Emily Miller, "Salmon Says No Bears, No Way," *High Country News*, October 7, 1997, 4.

9. The effect of roads on grizzly habitat is discussed generally in Lowell Suring, Kim Barber, Charles Schwartz, Theodore Bailey, William Shuster, and Michael Tetreau, "Analysis of Cumulative Effects on Brown Bears on the Kenai Peninsula, Southcentral Alaska," *Ursus* 10 (1998): 111; Bruce McLellan, "Dynamics of Grizzly Bear Population during a Period of Industrial Resource Extraction. II: Mortality Rates and Causes of Death," *Canadian Journal of Zoology* 67 (1988): 1861.

10. Brian Horejsi, "Endangered Granby-Gladstone Grizzly Bear Population," *Bear News* (Summer 1999): 14.

11. Wayne Kasworm and Timothy Manley, "Road and Trail Influences on Grizzly Bears and Black Bears in Northwest Montana," *International Conference on Bear Research and Management* 8 (1990): 79.

12. Arnold Dood, Robert Brannon, and Richard Mace, *Final Environmental Impact Statement: The Grizzly Bear in Northwest Montana* (Helena: Montana Department of Fish, Wildlife, and Parks, 1986): 22.

13. David Mattson and Richard Knight, "Effects of Access on Human-Caused Mortality of Yellowstone Grizzly Bears," Interagency Grizzly Bear Study Team Report 1991B (Missoula, MT: National Park Service, 1991).

14. Michael Jamison, "Forest Road Gates Ineffective, Report Finds," *Missoulian*, February 18, 2005; *Bear News* (Spring 2005): 16.

15. Stressing the need to close roads after logging, see Bruce McLellan, "Relationships between Human Industrial Activity and Grizzly Bears," *International Conference on Bear Research and Management* 8 (undated): 62–63; J. A. Mills, "The Grizzly and the Hand of Man," *American Forests* (January–February 1989): 29–30.

16. Kerry Gunther and Hopi Hoekstra, "Bear-Inflicted Human Injuries in Yellowstone National Park, 1970–1994," *Ursus* 10 (1998): 377.

17. Steve Gniadek and Katherine Kendall, "A Summary of Bear Management in Glacier National Park, Montana 1960–1994," *Ursus* 10 (1998): 158.

5 | THE CASCADES BECOME OFFICIAL

1. The Endangered Species Act directs all federal agencies to seek to conserve endangered or threatened species and to avoid actions that might jeopardize those species or damage their critical habitat. *Title 16, U.S. Code* §§ 1531(c)(1) and 1536(a)(2). In addition, the National Forest Management Act specifically requires the Forest Service to protect plants and animals in preparing its national forest plans. *Title 16, U.S. Code* §1600 (Note), section 6.

2. The early work is described in Jon Almack, *North Cascades Grizzly Bear Project, Annual Report* (Olympia: Washington Department of Game, 1986).

3. This effort was described in William Gaines, Robert Naney, Peter Morrison, James Eby, George Wooten, and Jon Almack, "Use of Landsat Multispectral Scanner Imagery and Geographic Information Systems to Map Vegetation in the North Cascades Grizzly Bear Ecosystem," *International Conference on Bear Research and Management* 9 (1994): 533. Habitat mapping has since become even more sophisticated. See Erik Ness, "The Electronic Grizzly," *Discover* (September 2003): 48.

4. See US Fish and Wildlife Service, *North Cascades Ecosystem Recovery Plan Chapter*, 5.

5. I. R. Franklin, "Evolutionary Change in Small Populations," in Michael Soule and Bruce Wilcox, eds., *Conservation Biology: An Evolutionary-Ecological Perspective* (Sunderland, MA: Sinauer Associates, 1980): 135; Michael Lynch and Russell Lande, "The Critical Effective Size for a Genetically Secure Population," *Animal Conservation* 1 (1998): 70; I. R. Franklin and R. Frankham, "How Large Must Populations Be to Retain Evolutionary Potential?" *Animal Conservation* 1 (1998): 69.

6. Derek Craighead, "An Integrated Satellite Technique to Evaluate Grizzly Bear Habitat Use," 199.

7. The female's range varies with whether she has cubs and their size. Art Pearson, *The Northern Interior Grizzly Bear* (Ottawa: Environment Canada, 1975); Glen Cole, "Preservation and Management of Grizzly Bears in Yellowstone National Park," *Bears: Their Biology and Management* (1972): 274. The adult male's range also varies, with males covering the largest area during mating season. Generally a male's range is two to four times larger than that of females. See Pearson, *The Northern Interior Grizzly Bear*; Frank Craighead, "Grizzly Bear Ranges and Movement as Determined by Radio-Tracking," *Bears: Their Biology and Management* (1976): 97.

8. Typical grizzly diet is described in Interagency Grizzly Bear Committee, *Grizzly Bear Compendium*, 24–25; Petersen, *Ghost Grizzlies*, 181–82.

9. Maurice Hornocker, "Population Characteristics and Social and Reproductive Behavior of the Grizzly Bear in Yellowstone National Park," master's thesis, University of Montana, Missoula, 1962; Allan Egbert and Allen Stokes, "The Social Behavior of Brown Bears on an Alaskan Salmon Stream," *Bears: Their Biology and Management* 41 (1976). Adult males are typically at the top of the hierarchy. John Craighead, Jay Sumner, and John Mitchell, *The Grizzly Bears of Yellowstone: Their Ecology in the Yellowstone Ecosystem, 1959–1992* (Washington DC: Island Press, 1995).

10. Derek Craighead, "An Integrated Satellite Technique to Evaluate Grizzly Bear Habitat Use," 195–97.

11. Their conclusions were stated in Technical Review Team, *Evaluation of the Bitterroot and North Cascades to Sustain Viable Grizzly Bear Populations* (Boise, ID: Interagency Grizzly Bear Committee, 1991). For their final report, see Jon Almack, William Gaines, Peter Morrison, James Eby, Robert Naney, George Wooten, Scott Fitkin, and E.R. Garcia, *North Cascades Ecosystem Evaluation: Final Report* (Missoula, MT: Interagency Grizzly Bear Committee, 1993).

7 | THE PUBLIC VOICES ITS FEARS

1. The Fish and Wildlife Service adopts such plans to specify how a designated recovery area should be managed to promote survival and recovery of a threatened or endangered species. Such plans usually contain specific objectives and population targets and individual actions needed to reach those targets. The Grizzly Bear Recovery Plan contains directions applicable to grizzly bear recovery overall, followed by separate chapters with site-specific management prescriptions for individual recovery areas, such as the North Cascades. The mandate for recovery plans comes from the *Endangered Species Act, Title 16, U.S. Code* § 1533(f).

2. Emily Miller, "Salmon Says No Bears, No Way," 4.

3. Letter to the editors, *Seattle Times*, September 26, 1988.

4. See Emily Miller, "Salmon Says No Bears, No Way."

5. B. J. Williams, "Grizzlies in the North Cascades," *Washington* (1989): 49.

6. Interagency Grizzly Bear Committee, North Cascades Subcommittee, *Grizzly Bear Recovery in the North Cascades: Questions and Answers* (November 1993).

7. *Okanogan Valley Gazette-Tribune* (Oroville, WA), June 17, 1993.

8. Unpublished letter from Backcountry Horsemen of Washington to Robert Becker, May 19, 1994.

9. Editorial, *Backcountry Horsemen of America* (March 1994): 1.

10. A private Canadian group has adopted a variation on this idea, creating a Web site where users can check and report grizzly sightings in Banff National Park. See www.trailex.org.

11. See Edward Grumbine, *Ghost Bears: Exploring the Biodiversity Crisis* (Washington DC: Island Press, 1992): 80.
12. Guest editorial, *Signpost* (March 1992): 33.
13. Letter from the Mountaineers to the US Fish and Wildlife Service, February 7, 1994.
14. "Group Says Bear Plan Won't Limit Recreation," *Seattle Post-Intelligencer*, July 20, 1994; Matt Norton, "Grizzly Recovery Plan," *Northwest Conservation* (Summer 1994): 6.
15. Mills, *Impressions of the North Cascades*, 211.
16. Associated Press, "Animal Group Sues to Stop Government's Grizzly Recovery Plan," *Seattle Times*, May 22, 1994, B3.
17. See Alliance for the Wild Rockies, *Conservation Biology Alternative*, Special Report No. 8 (Missoula, MT: Alliance for the Wild Rockies, 1996).
18. Alistair Bath, "The Role of Human Dimensions in Wildlife Resource Research in Wildlife Management," *Ursus* 10 (1998): 351.
19. Ibid., 352.
20. Ibid.
21. Danny Westneat, "Residents Like Grizzlies in Cascades," *Seattle Times*, November 29, 1996, B3.
22. Reported in Brian Peck, "Bitterroot Recovery 'Bushwacked,'" *Bear News* (Summer 2001): 3.
23. Christopher Servheen, "Conservation of Small Bear Populations through Strategic Planning," *Ursus* 10 (1998): 67.

8 | ARE THEY STILL THERE?

1. Nicholas Geranios, "It's Official Now: Grizzlies Have Found a Home in Cascades," *Seattle Times*, October 17, 1993, B1.
2. Class 1 is definitely a grizzly; class 2 probably is. Both require confirmation by a trained biologist. Class 3 means the information is inadequate to tell one way or the other. Class 4 means it definitely is not a grizzly. These criteria are discussed in Almack et al., *North Cascades Ecosystem Evaluation: Final Report.*
3. Gaines reports that twenty-two of these were class 1 or confirmed sightings. William Gaines, "Grizzly Bears in the North Cascades: A Population Close to Extinction," *Environmental Review: An Independent Newsletter of Environmental Science, Human Health & Natural History* (October 1994): 8.
4. This view is supported by studies in Glacier National Park, which concluded that sightings are an unreliable indicator of bear population trends. Gniadek and Kendall, "A Summary of Bear Management in Glacier National Park," 157, 158.
5. The grizzly's rear paw is almost as distinctive. Its heel is pointed at the back with no instep. The black bear's rear paw, with an eerie resemblance to a

human foot, has a rounded heel and a noticeable instep. Diagrams depicting these differences are contained in various government booklets and pamphlets. See North Cascades National Park, *Bears and You in the North Cascades* (1995): 4; North Cascades Ecosystem Subcommittee, *Grizzly Bear Recovery in the North Cascades* (November 1993): 8; US National Park Service, US Forest Service, and Washington Department of Wildlife, "Grizzly Bears in the North Cascades? What You Should Know" (undated pamphlet).

6. Jon Almack and Scott Fitkin, *Grizzly Bear and Gray Wolf Investigations in Washington State, 1994–1995* (Olympia: Washington Department of Fish and Wildlife, 1998).

7. British Columbia North Cascades Grizzly Bear Recovery Team, *Recovery Plan for Grizzly Bears in the North Cascades of British Columbia: Consensus Recommendation Draft for Consultation* (Victoria: British Columbia Ministry of Environment, Lands, and Parks, 2001): 7.

8. Joel Connelly, "Fewer Grizzly Bears Roaming British Columbia," *Seattle Post-Intelligencer*, September 17, 1992, A13.

9. Europe's brown bear populations in 1996 are depicted in Sybille Klenzendorf and Michael Vaughn, "An Overview of Brown Bear Management in Six European Countries," *Ursus* 11 (1999): 163.

10. "Bears Are Back in Switzerland," *Environmental News Network*, July 26, 2005.

11. Claudio Groff, Angelo Caliari, Enrico Dorigatti, and Alberto Gozzi, "Selection of Denning Caves by Brown Bears in Trentino, Italy," *Ursus* 10 (1998): 275.

12. "There's No Such Thing as a Picky Grizzly Bear," *Physorg.com*, February 22, 2007.

13. Charles Russell, Maureen Enns, and Fred Stenson, *Grizzly Heart: Living without Fear among the Brown Bears of Kamchatka* (Toronto: Random House Canada, 2002).

14. Herrero, *Bear Attacks*, 206.

15. Ibid., chapter 4; US Fish and Wildlife Service, *Grizzly Bear Recovery Plan* (Washington DC: US Fish and Wildlife Service, 1993): 13; Djuro Huber, Josip Kusak, and Alojzije Frkovic, "Traffic Kills of Brown Bears in Gorski Kotar, Croatia," *Ursus* 10 (1998): 167; Jon Swenson, "Does Hunting Affect the Behavior of Brown Bears in Eurasia?" *Ursus* 11 (1999): 157.

16. Warren Guntheroth, letter to the editor, *Signpost* (May 1998): 6.

17. Andreas Zedrosser, Bjorn Dahle, Jon Swenson, and Norbert Gerstl, "Status and Management of the Brown Bear in Europe," *Ursus* 12 (2001): 17. For this conclusion, the authors also relied on an earlier study of wolf management in North America.

9 | ISLANDS IN THE SKY

1. Stephen Bown, "The Historic Adventures of Milton and Cheadle," *Beautiful British Columbia* (Summer 2001): 30, 33.
2. Genetic research shows that Highway 3 in eastern British Columbia is causing a demographic separation of grizzly populations. Michael Proctor, Bruce McLellan, and Curtis Strobeck, "Population Fragmentation of Grizzly Bears in Southeastern British Columbia," *Ursus* 13 (2002): 153, 157. This study is described in Brian Peck, "River of Bears Running Dry?" *Bear News* (Winter 2002): 12.
3. Gary Turback, "Highway Madness," *Wildlife Conservation* 103 (February 2000): 11.
4. Mark Matthews, "Wildlife Crossings Cut Down on Roadkill," *High Country News*, November 23, 1998, 3.
5. Ed Struzik, "Life Lines," *Equinox* (August–September 1998): 46.
6. Matthews, "Wildlife Crossings Cut Down on Roadkill."
7. *Columbia Falls Hungry Horse News*, March 15, 2006. This study is also described in Matthews, "Wildlife Crossings Cut Down on Roadkill" and "Grizzly Study," *Bear News* (April–June 1998): 16.
8. One such purchase is described by Perry Backus, "Foundation Negotiates Conservation Easement with Rancher to Protect Grizzly Corridor," *Missoulian*, January 13, 2006.
9. Peter Singleton, William Gaines, and John Lehmkuhl, "Landscape Permeability for Grizzly Bear Movements in Washington and Southwest British Columbia," *Ursus* 15 (2004): 90, 98.
10. Joe McWilliams, "Grizzly Research Project Reaches into Swan Hills, Alberta," *Lakeside Leader* (Alberta), April 15, 2006. See also Michael Proctor, Christopher Servheen, Sterling Miller, Wayne Kasworm, and Wayne Wakkinen, "A Comparative Analysis of Management Options for Grizzly Bear Conservation in the U.S.-Canada Trans-Border Area," *Ursus* 15 (2004): 145, 146; Proctor, McLellan, and Strobeck, "Population Fragmentation of Grizzly Bears in Southeastern British Columbia," 157.

10 | CAN THEY SURVIVE ON THEIR OWN?

1. *Okanogan Valley Gazette-Tribune* (Oroville, WA), June 17, 1993.
2. Letter to the editor, *Signpost* (December 1992): 6.
3. Douglas Chadwick, "Helping a Great Bear Hang On," *National Wildlife* (December 1998–January 1999): 25.
4. Males mature in 5.5 years. Don White, James Berardinelli, and Keith Aune, "Reproductive Characteristics of the Male Grizzly Bear in the Continental United States," *Ursus* 10 (1998): 497. Another study concluded 4.5 years.

Hornocker, "Population Characteristics and Social and Reproductive Behavior of the Grizzly Bear in Yellowstone National Park."

Females are at sexual maturity from 3.5 to 8.5 years, with an average of 5.5 years in areas studied in the lower 48 states. Hornocker, "Population Characteristics and Social and Reproductive Behavior of the Grizzly Bear in Yellowstone National Park"; John Craighead, Maurice Hornocker, and Frank Craighead, "Reproductive Biology of Young Female Grizzly Bears," *Journal of Reproduction and Fertility,* supp. 6 (1969): 447. All studies caution that maturity varies significantly based on nutrition. See Richard Russell, J. W. Nolan, N. G. Woody, G. H. Anderson, and Art Pearson, *A Study of the Grizzly Bear (*Ursus arctos*) in Jasper National Park* (Edmonton: Canadian Wildlife Service, 1978).

5. US Fish and Wildlife Service, *Grizzly Bear Recovery Plan* (Washington DC: US Fish and Wildlife Service, 1993): 12.

6. D. Arapaho, "A Natural History of Ursus Horribilis," *Independent Grizzly Bear Report* (Spring 1988): 4.

7. Ibid.

8. For a review of grizzly bear reproductive rates, see Stephen Herrero, "A Comparison of Some Features of the Evolution, Ecology and Behavior of Black and Grizzly Bears," *Carnivore* 1 (1978): 7.

9. Interagency Grizzly Bear Committee, *Grizzly Bear Compendium,* 108–9.

10. Mark Shaffer, "Determining Minimum Viable Population Sizes for the Grizzly Bear," *Bears: Their Biology and Management* 5 (1983): 133, discussed in Grumbine, *Ghost Bears,* 38.

11. Small, isolated populations are vulnerable to natural disasters. Mark Shaffer and Fred Samson, "Population Size and Extinction: A Note on Determining Critical Population Sizes," *American Naturalist* 125 (1985): 144. The same point is made in Grumbine, *Ghost Bears,* 36.

12. Tom Caro, *Cheetahs of the Serengeti Plains* (Chicago: University of Chicago Press, 1994): 366; Tom Caro, "An Elegant Enigma," *Wildlife Conservation* 99 (May–June 1996): 47; M. Kelly, M. Laurenson, and Tom Caro, "Demography of the Serengeti Cheetah (*Acinonyx jubatus*) Population: The First 25 Years," *Journal of Zoology* 244 (April 1998): 473.

13. M. Kelly, "Lineage Loss in Serengeti Cheetahs: Consequences of High Reproductive Variance and Heritability of Fitness on Effective Population Size," *Conservation Biology* (February 2001): 137.

14. Gregory Wilker and Victor Barnes, "Responses of Brown Bears to Human Activities at O'Malley River, Kodiak Island, Alaska," *Ursus* 10 (1998): 557.

15. Proctor, McLellan, and Strobeck, "Population Fragmentation of Grizzly Bears in Southeast British Columbia," 157.

16. Lisette Waits, "Molecular Genetic Applications for Bear Research," *Ursus* 11 (1999): 257.

17. David Paetkau and Curtis Strobeck, "Ecological Genetic Studies of Bears Using Microsatellite Analysis," *Ursus* 10 (1998): 299, 302, 337; Soule and Wilcox, *Conservation Biology*: 151–69; Horejsi, "A Future for the Grizzly," 11.

18. David Quammen, "The Newmark Warning: Why Our National Parks Are Resembling Desert Isles," in Deborah Clow and Donald Snow, eds., *Northern Lights: A Selection of New Writing from the American West* (New York: Vintage Books, 1994): 81; Grumbine, *Ghost Bears*, 41–43. High human density around parks also poses a significant threat to animal survival. S.A. Parks and A.H. Harcourt, "Reserve Size, Local Human Density, and Mammalian Extinctions in U.S. Protected Areas," *Conservation Biology* 16 (June 2002): 800.

19. Paetkau and Strobeck, "Ecological Genetic Studies of Bears Using Microsatellite Analysis," 303–4.

20. Ibid., 303.

21. Lisette Waits, David Paetkau, Curtis Strobeck, and Richard Ward, "A Comparison of Genetic Diversity in North American Brown Bears," *Ursus* 10 (1998): 311–12.

22. Paetkau and Strobeck, "Ecological Genetic Studies of Bears Using Microsatellite Analysis," 303–4.

23. Waits, Paetkau, Strobeck, and Ward, "A Comparison of Genetic Diversity in North American Brown Bears," 311.

24. Others share this pessimism, claiming that conservation areas can be refuges from extinction but none are large enough to hold the full range of genetic diversity. Thus, they warn, long-term survival is in doubt. Lance Craighead, David Paetkau, Harry Reynolds, Curtis Strobeck, and Ernest Vyse, "Use of Microsatellite DNA Analyses to Infer Breeding Behavior and Demographic Processes in an Arctic Grizzly Bear Population," *Ursus* 10 (1998): 327. This has prompted calls for larger recovery areas in the Northern Rockies and wildlife corridors to link them. Bader, "Spatial Needs of Grizzly Bears in the U.S. Northern Rockies."

25. The Yukon to Yellowstone conservation initiative is described in Struzik, "Life Lines," 38. Metapopulations are more resilient in the face of catastrophes. Bruce Rieman and John McIntyre, *Demographic and Habitat Requirements for Conservation of Bull Trout*, General Technical Report INT-302 (Ogden, UT: US Dept. of Agriculture, Forest Service, Intermountain Research Station, 1993). Modeling has shown that linking populations would significantly improve the prospects for grizzly bears. Mark Boyce, "Metapopulation Analysis for the Bitterroot Population," appendix 21C in *Grizzly Bear Recovery in the Bitterroot Ecosystem, Final Environmental Impact Statement* (Missoula, MT: US Fish and Wildlife Service, 2000).

11 | NEW BLOOD

1. Mark Hume, "Looking for Mr. Goodbear," *Vancouver Sun*, reprinted in *Pack and Paddle* (April 1993): 18, 19.
2. "Canadian Grizzly May Advance Habitat Knowledge," *Vancouver Sun*, reprinted in *Okanogan Valley Gazette-Tribune*, November 5, 1992.
3. Augmentation criteria are discussed in Interagency Grizzly Bear Committee, *Grizzly Bear Compendium*, 97–101; Wayne Kasworm, Timothy Thier, and Christopher Servheen, *Cabinet Mountain Grizzly Bear Population Augmentation: 1991 Progress Report* (Missoula, MT: US Fish and Wildlife Service, 1992), reports on actual augmentation experience in the Cabinet-Yaak recovery area.
4. Interagency Grizzly Bear Committee, *Grizzly Bear Compendium*, 98.
5. Joel Connelly, "B.C. Grizzlies Could be Idaho-Bound," *Seattle Post-Intelligencer*, May 20, 2000, 1, reports on BC opposition to exporting grizzlies to the United States.
6. Grumbine, *Ghost Bears*, 80.
7. Proctor et al., "A Comparative Analysis of Management Options for Grizzly Bear Conservation in the U.S.-Canada Trans-Border Area," 154.
8. Differences in augmentation and reintroduction techniques are discussed in Interagency Grizzly Bear Committee, *Grizzly Bear Compendium*, 102–3.
9. Joseph Clark, Djuro Huber, and Christopher Servheen, "Bear Reintroductions: Lessons and Challenges," *Ursus* 13 (2002): 340.
10. John Craighead, leading bear biologist, also concluded that augmentation was more acceptable to the public than reintroduction. Petersen, *Ghost Grizzlies*, 47.

12 | IMPORT BANS

1. Associated Press, "State Officials Oppose Transfer Plan for Grizzlies," *Seattle Post-Intelligencer*, August 23, 1992.
2. Ibid.
3. "Morton Measures Would Keep Grizzly Bears at Bay," *Okanogan Valley Gazette-Tribune*, February 11, 1993.
4. Interagency Grizzly Bear Committee, *Grizzly Bear Compendium*, 102.
5. Catherine Lutz, "State Says No to New Wildlife," *High Country News*, May 10, 1999, 5.
6. "New Hampshire Bans Wolves," *Defenders* (Spring 1999): 25.
7. Jim Robbins, "Group Sues over Montana Bear Hunt," *New York Times*, April 29, 1991.
8. Betsy Marston, "Heard around the West," *High Country News*, April 13, 1998, 15.
9. Becky Bohrer, "Feds to Seek Delisting of Yellowstone Grizzlies as Early as July," *Billings Gazette*, June 10, 2005.

10. Letter, *High Country News*, August 2, 1999, 11.
11. Servheen, "Conservation of Small Bear Populations through Strategic Planning," 67. See also Christopher Servheen, "The Grizzly Bear Recovery Program: Current Status and Future Considerations," *Ursus* 10 (1998): 595.

13 | A TOUGH CHOICE

1. Marco Restini and John Marzluff, "Funding Extinction? Biological Needs and Political Realities in the Allocation of Resources to Endangered Species Recovery," *BioScience* 52 (2002): 169.
2. "Grizzly Recovery in the North Cascades: Budgeting for NEPA in FY 2002," attachment to July 17, 2000, memo from Fish and Wildlife Service Manager for Western Washington office to Assistant Regional Director, Ecological Services, Portland, OR.
3. Waits, Paetkau, Strobeck, and Ward, "A Comparison of Genetic Diversity in North American Brown Bears," 311–12.
4. Under the Endangered Species Act, a distinct population segment may be separately listed if it is threatened or endangered. See *Title 16, U.S. Code* § 1532 (16). In 1996 the US Fish and Wildlife Service refined this by explaining that a population segment is distinct if it is substantially isolated reproductively from other population units and it represents an important component in the evolutionary legacy of that species. See *Federal Register* 61 (February 7, 1996): 4722. This gave rise to the term *evolutionary significant unit*, or ESU.
5. David Reed and Richard Frankham, "Correlation between Fitness and Genetic Diversity," *Conservation Biology* 17 (February 2003): 230; Paetkau and Strobeck, "Ecological Genetic Studies of Bears," 299; and Michael Soule, "Thresholds for Survival: Maintaining Fitness and Evolutionary Potential," in Soule and Wilcox, *Conservation Biology*, 151–69. Genetic variability becomes even more critical in small populations, where inbreeding reduces the natural mutation rate that would otherwise renew genetic diversity. Paetkau and Strobeck, "Ecological Genetic Studies of Bears," 302–3; Denis Couvert, "Deleterious Effects of Restricted Gene Flow in Fragmented Populations," *Conservation Biology* 16 (April 2002): 369.
6. "West Nile Virus Takes Startling Toll on Wildlife," *Seattle Times*, December 29, 2002, A5. Other potential catastrophes could be extended drought and major food source failures (David Mattson and John Craighead, "The Yellowstone Grizzly Bear Recovery Program: Uncertain Information, Uncertain Policy," in Tim Clark, Richard Reading, and Alice Clarke, eds., *Endangered Species Recovery: Finding the Lessons, Improving the Process* [Washington DC: Island Press, 1994]: 101–29) or large habitat disturbances such as wildfires (David Mattson, "Changes in Mortality in Yellowstone's Grizzly Bears," *Ursus* 10 [1998]: 129). If habitat was already confined, the harmful effects of more habitat loss could escalate (Horejsi, "A Future for the Grizzly," 11).

7. This process is discussed in Hank Fischer and Michael Roy, "New Approaches to Citizen Participation in Endangered Species Management: Recovery in the Bitterroot Ecosystem," *Ursus* 10 (1998): 603.

8. For insights into this process, see James Peek, "Experiences with a Committee of User Groups Examining Grizzly Bear Restoration in Idaho," *Ursus* 10 (1998): 613.

9. Fish and Wildlife Service managers still admit that the Cabinet-Yaak recovery area north of the Bitterroots needs more grizzlies. Wayne Kasworm, Timothy Thier, and Christopher Servheen, "Grizzly Bear Recovery Efforts in the Cabinet/Yaak Ecosystem," *Ursus* 10 (1998): 153.

10. Joe Kane, "One Man's Wilderness," *Sierra* 85 (March–April 2000): 51. Others support this concept (Bader, "Spatial Needs of Grizzly Bears in the U.S. Northern Rockies"). Larger areas have a multiplier benefit for wide-ranging species such as grizzlies (Gary Meffe and C. Ronald Caroll, *Principles of Conservation Biology* [Sunderland, MA: Sinauer Associates, 1994]). Linking recovery areas would significantly improve grizzly bear prospects (Boyce, "Metapopulation Analysis for the Bitterroot Population").

11. See Restini and Marzluff, "Funding Extinction?"

14 | HOLDING PATTERN

1. The Loomis Forest conflict is described by one of the participants in Mills, *Impressions of the North Cascades*, 214.

2. Interagency Grizzly Bear Committee, *Interagency Grizzly Bear Guidelines* (Missoula, MT: US Forest Service, 1998).

3. This was the second such petition. The first, in 1990, is described in Grumbine, *Ghost Bears*, 81.

4. Reported in Rob Hazen and Rosemary Jackson, "North Cascades Grizzlies and Cutworm Moths," *Bear News* (1999): 14.

5. For detailed descriptions of this technique, see Andrew Rebmann, David Edward, Marcella Sorg, et al., *Cadaver Dog Handbook: Forensic Training and Tactics for the Recovery of Human Remains* (Boca Raton, FL: CRC Press, 2000); Jack Robicheaux and John Jons, *Basic Narcotic Detection Dog Training* (Houston, TX: J.A.R. Jons, 1996); Lue Button, *Practical Scent Dog Training* (Loveland, CO: Alpine Publications, 1990); Milo Pearsall and Hugo Verbruggen, *Scent, Training to Track, Search, and Rescue* (Loveland, CO: Alpine Publications, 1982).

15 | RESISTANCE GROWS

1. *Defenders* (Fall 2000): 5.

2. Jon Margolis, "These Legislative Riders Sit Low in the Saddle," *High Country News*, August 31, 1998, 5.

3. Carl Pope, "Ghost Riders," *Sierra* (September–October 1998): 18.
4. Secretary Babbitt apparently first used this term during testimony before the Fisheries and Wildlife Subcommittee of the US Senate Environment and Public Works Committee on June 15, 1994, when the subcommittee was beginning to consider reauthorization of the Endangered Species Act.
5. The agency's authority for a "warranted but precluded" declaration stems from *Title 16, U.S. Code* § 1533 (b)(3)(B) of the Endangered Species Act.
6. Politics also play a major role in the way endangered species funds are spent. One study shows that 1 percent of the listed species receive 50 percent of the recovery funds. Expenditures do not track what some biologists view as the most urgent recovery priorities because of lawsuits, as well as institutional, political, and social pressures, which result in earmarking congressional appropriations for specific species. See Restini and Marzluff, "Funding Extinction?" 169.
7. Some biologists claim that species from areas with more political clout enjoy better funding. As far as overall vulnerability is concerned, they argue, recovery work for charismatic animals such as the gray wolf and grizzly bear is overfunded in comparison to the efforts being made on behalf of such obscure species as the Red Hills salamander. Restini and Marzluff, "Funding Extinction?"
8. Ed Marston, "Interior View," *High Country News*, February 12, 2001, 8, 11.

16 | "W" DOES NOT STAND FOR "WILDLIFE"

1. The presidential election of 1876 between Rutherford B. Hayes and Samuel Jones Tilden was almost a dead heat. Tilden won the popular vote, but a special commission was formed to resolve disputes over who had won in South Carolina, Louisiana, Oregon, and Florida. In an 8–7 decision, the commission gave the electoral votes from all four states to Hayes. As a result, Hayes was elected president by one electoral vote.
2. Natural Resources Defense Council, *Rewriting the Rules: The Bush Administration's Assault on the Environment* (New York: Natural Resources Defense Council, 2002).
3. Rodger Schlickeisen, "Bush's Extinction Policy," *Defenders* (Summer 2001): 5.
4. Editorial, *Northwest Conservation* (Summer 2001): 3.
5. Natural Resources Defense Council, *The Bush Administration's Assault on the Environment* (New York: Natural Resources Defense Council, 2003).
6. Katherine Pfleger, "U.S. Signals a Shift for Forest Rules," *Seattle Times*, December 30, 2001, A3.
7. Joan Lowy, "From Air to Sewage, Bush Has Reshaped Agenda," *Seattle Post-Intelligencer*, December 23, 2002, A1.
8. Natural Resources Defense Council, "Rewriting the Rules" (entry for September 21, 2001, "Wetlands").

9. Environmental Protection Agency, Office of the Inspector General, *EPA's Response to the World Trade Center Collapse: Challenges, Successes, and Areas for Improvement*, Report No. 2003-P-00012 (Washington DC: US Environmental Protection Agency, 2003), 17.

10. "Follow-up," *High Country News*, June 9, 2003, 3.

11. Craig Welch, "Bush Switches Nation's Tack on Protecting Species," *Seattle Times*, September 27, 2004, A1.

12. Julie Elliott, "Habitat Protection Takes a Critical Hit," *High Country News*, April 15, 2002, 4.

13. Greg Hanscom, "Environmental Issues Disappear into Election-Season Smog," *High Country News*, October 25, 2004, 19.

17 | BACK TO GO IN THE BITTERROOTS

1. Dan Hanson, "Kempthorne to Grizzlies: Keep Out!" *Spokesman-Review* (Spokane, WA), November 17, 2000.

2. US Fish and Wildlife Service, Denver Regional Office, "U.S. Fish and Wildlife Service Completes Plan for Bitterroots Reintroduction," news release, November 2000.

3. The process leading to this plan is discussed in Fischer and Roy, "New Approaches to Citizen Participation in Endangered Species Management," 603. See also Hank Fischer, "New Home for the Griz," *Defenders* (Winter 1993–94): 14.

4. US Fish and Wildlife Service, news release, November 2000.

5. Jeff Woods, "Norton vs. the Environment," *Defenders* (Summer 2002): 10.

6. Sherry Devlin, "Grizzlies Invited Back to the Bitterroot," *High Country News*, December 4, 2000, 3.

7. *Palila v. Hawaii Dept of Land and Natural Resources,* 471 F.Supp. 985 (D.Hawaii 1979), held that the Endangered Species Act was authorized under the Constitution's authority for Congress to adopt laws relating to treaties, such as those involving migratory birds, and its broad authority to regulate interstate commerce. This decision was affirmed on appeal. The court did not refer to Congress's authority under the Constitution to "make all needful rules and regulations respecting . . . property belonging to the United States," which also authorizes laws regulating what happens on federal lands.

8. In an interview, Secretary Norton was asked about her decision in the Bitterroots. She replied, "Predators make it much more difficult to find consensus. It's a lot easier to agree about birds and plants than about animals that endanger people and livestock." Alex Pasquariello, "A Conversation with Interior Secretary Gale Norton," *High Country News*, May 24, 2004, 6.

9. Bill Schneider, *Where the Grizzly Walks* (Helena, MT: Falcon Publishing, 2004): 43.

10. Reprinted in *High Country News*, December 23, 2002, 15.

11. These statistics compiled by the Fish and Wildlife Service are summarized in John Schoen and Sterling Miller, "New Strategies for Bear Conservation: Collaboration between Resource Agencies and Environmental Organizations," *Ursus* 13 (2002): 365.

12. IGBC North Cascades subcommittee meeting, September 27, 2007.

13. These views are collected in Bader, "Spatial Needs of Grizzly Bears in the U.S. Northern Rockies." The omnibus recovery plan for grizzly bears addresses the need to connect populations in different recovery areas. See generally, Servheen, "The Grizzly Bear Recovery Program," 592. A study published two years after Norton's decision concludes that the Centennial Mountains on the Montana-Idaho border offer a potential link between Yellowstone and the Bitterroots that is even better than previously thought. Troy Merrill and David Mattson, "The Extent and Location of Habitat Biophysically Suitable for Grizzly Bears in the Yellowstone Region," *Ursus* 14 (2003): 171.

14. US Fish and Wildlife Service, news release, November 2000.

18 | YELLOWSTONE: HOW SHOULD WE MEASURE SUCCESS?

1. Frederick Vosburgh, "Fabulous Yellowstone," *National Geographic* (June 1940): 788.

2. Gunther and Hoekstra, "Bear-Inflicted Human Injuries in Yellowstone National Park, 1970–1994," 377.

3. The incidents are described in Jack Olsen, *Night of the Grizzlies* (New York: Signet Books, 1969).

4. John Craighead, "Status of the Yellowstone Grizzly Bear Population: Has It Recovered, Should It Be Delisted?" *Ursus* 10 (1998): 597, 598. The highest mortality was among large males, who had dominated the dumps. Charles Robbins, Charles Schwartz, and Laura Felicetti, "Nutritional Ecology of Ursids: A Review of Newer Methods and Management Implications," *Ursus* 15 (2004): 166–67.

5. Mary Meagher and Jerry Phillips, "Restoration of Natural Populations of Grizzly and Black Bears in Yellowstone National Park," *Int. Conf Bear Res. and Management* 5 (1983): 152–58.

6. John Craighead, "Status of the Yellowstone Grizzly Bear Population."

7. Mike Stark, "Wyoming Senators Press for Wolf, Grizzly Delisting," *Jackson Hole Star-Tribune*, October 14, 2005.

8. Ibid.

9. "Wyoming Governor Impatient for Delisting," *Billings Gazette*, November 3, 2005.

10. US Fish and Wildlife Service, "FWS Proposes Delisting Grizzly Bear Recovery in Yellowstone," press release, November 17, 2005.

11. US Fish and Wildlife Service, *Grizzly Recovery Plan,* Part II, p. 26. The dispersal requirement is stated in terms of mothers with young occupying sixteen of eighteen bear management units, which equals 88.9 percent if the bear management units are equal in size.

12. Brian Peck, "Yellowstone Delisting—Grizzly Lite," *Bear News* (Spring 2005): 7.

13. John Craighead, "Status of the Yellowstone Grizzly Bear Population."

14. Mattson, "Changes in Mortality of Yellowstone's Grizzly Bears," 129.

15. Becky Bohrer, "Yellowstone Delisting in 2005," Associated Press, December 24, 2004.

16. These were the Wyoming and Salt River ranges south of Jackson Hole.

17. Brodie Farquhar, "Wyoming Grizzly Plan Draws Fire from Left and Right," *Casper Star-Tribune,* June 26, 2005.

18. Mattson, "Changes in Mortality of Yellowstone's Grizzly Bears"; Cory Hatch, "New Yellowstone Bear Census," *Jackson Hole News and Guide,* October 18, 2006. Servheen questioned this correlation, arguing that the majority of bears dying during poor pine cone years already live in habitats where mortality risks are higher. Brodie Farquhar, "Good Pine Nut Years Help Bears," *Jackson Hole Star-Tribune,* August 1, 2007.

19. Scientists fear that Yellowstone grizzlies are threatened by the loss of whitebark pine. David Mattson and Troy Merrill, "Extirpations of Grizzly Bears in the Contiguous United States, 1850–2000," *Conservation Biology* 16 (August 2002): 1123. Before the beetles reached epidemic proportions, a blister rust was attacking whitebark pine, and 44 percent of these trees in Grand Teton National Park were already dead by 2001. Schneider, *Where the Grizzly Walks,* 63.

20. Scott McMillion, "Global Warming Allows Beetles to Attack Whitebark Pines," *Bozeman Daily Chronicle,* March 31, 2005.

21. Minutes of IGBC Winter Meeting, November 28–29, 2006.

22. Charles Petit, "In the Rockies, Pines Die and Bears Feel It," *New York Times,* January 30, 2007, D1.

23. Brodie Farquhar, "Grizzly Plan Draws Fire at Cody Hearing," *Jackson Hole Star-Tribune,* January 15, 2006.

24. Dustin Bleizeffer, "Feds Assure Grizzly Progress," *Casper Star-Tribune,* November 18, 2006.

25. Michael Martinez, "Debate over Delisting Grizzlies," *Chicago Tribune,* November 30, 2006.

26. Some scientists raised questions about the effect of Yellowstone's wildfires on grizzly bear food sources. Shannon Podruzny, Daniel Reinhart, and David Mattson, "Fire, Red Squirrels, Whitebark Pine, and Yellowstone Grizzly Bears," *Ursus* 11 (1999): 131. Biologists have since noted changes in elk migration patterns as a likely result of the fires, but no noticeable effect on grizzlies.

27. Brodie Farquhar, "Agency Revises Grizzly Methods," *Casper Star-Tribune*, March 14, 2007.
28. Servheen, "Conservation of Small Bear Populations through Strategic Planning," 67; Servheen, "The Grizzly Bear Recovery Program," 593; Proctor et al., "A Comparative Analysis of Management Options for Grizzly Bear Conservation in the U.S.-Canada Trans-Border Area," 157.
29. These questions are explored in Bader, "Spatial Needs of Grizzly Bears in the U.S. Northern Rockies."
30. IGBC Summer Meeting minutes, July 25–26, 2001.
31. Doug Peacock, "Tough Grizzlies Still Need Human Help," *Los Angeles Times*, April 5, 2006.
32. The Fish and Wildlife Service appears to be uneasy about its own policy. In 2007 it planned to launch a review of its distinct population segment approach to grizzly recovery. See "Proposed Process for a Status Review of Grizzly Bears outside the Greater Yellowstone Area," minutes of IGBC Winter Meeting, November 28–29, 2006.

19 | GLACIER IS NEXT

1. Schneider, *Where the Grizzly Walks*, 182.
2. See Rupert Pilkington, "Crisis in the Castle," *Bear News* (July 1998): 1; Martha Green, "Continental Divides," *Nature Conservancy* (January–February 2000): 18, 22. Genetic research shows that grizzlies north and south of BC Highway 3, which crosses Crowsnest Pass, are losing demographic connectivity. Proctor, McLellan, and Strobeck, "Population Fragmentation of Grizzly Bears in Southeastern British Columbia," 157. This study is described in Brian Peck, "River of Bears Running Dry?" *Bear News* (Winter 2002): 12.
3. Grizzlies in the NCDE have more genetic diversity than those in Yellowstone or the east slope of the Canadian Rockies. Waits et al., "A Comparison of Genetic Diversity in North American Brown Bears," 312.
4. Sonja Lee, "Berry Crop Failure Pushing Hungry Bears East," *Great Falls Tribune*, August 21, 2004. Cooperative efforts with ranchers are discussed in Douglas Chadwick, "Ranching with Grizzlies," *Defenders* (Spring 2005): 9.
5. "Bear Scare Shuts Montana School," Associated Press, May 6, 2005.
6. Mike Stark, "The Stench Would Buckle Your Knees," *Billings Gazette*, September 17, 2004.
7. Sonja Lee, "Lack of Funding Keeps Many Montana Animals on Threatened or Endangered Lists," *Great Falls Tribune*, February 6, 2005.
8. Perry Backus, "Different Issues in NCDE than Yellowstone," *Missoulian*, December 1, 2005.
9. Becky Bohrer, "Two Studies of Grizzly Population," *Billings Gazette*, May 13, 2006.

10. IGBC North Cascades subcommittee meeting, October 12, 2005.

11. The results of Waller's dissertation are described in "Grizzlies Mostly Cross Highway 2 at Night," *Columbia Falls Hungry Horse News*, March 15, 2006.

12. Gniadek and Kendall, "A Summary of Bear Management in Glacier National Park, Montana 1960–1994," 157.

13. This study is described in Jim Mann, "Grizzly Census Wraps Up," *Daily Inter Lake* (Kalispell), September 17, 2004; and Jim Mann, "Early Results of NCDE Population Studies," *Daily Inter Lake* (Kalispell), January 27, 2006.

14. Pending publication of these results, they have been described most comprehensively in Jim Mann, "DNA Study Tallies 545 Grizzlies," *Daily Inter Lake* (Kalispell), November 16, 2006.

15. Jim Mann, "Female Grizzlies Tracked to Study Population Trends in NCD," *Daily Inter Lake* (Kalispell), September 4, 2005.

16. Sonja Lee, "NCDE Unaffected by Yellowstone Delisting," *Great Falls Tribune*, November 16, 2005.

17. Editors of *Bear News*, reply to Jim Mann, "DNA Study Tallies 545 Grizzlies," *Bear News* (Fall 2006): 3.

18. Becky Bohrer, "Lack of Resources to Deal with Bear Killings," Associated Press, January 6, 2006.

19. Brian Peck, "NCDE Grizzly Mortalities Hit Another Record," *Bear News* (Fall 2004): 1, 9.

20. Sonja Lee, "Poachers Put Bite on NCDE Grizzly Recovery," *Great Falls Tribune*, January 22, 2006.

21. Ibid.

22. Perry Backus, "Timber in Transition: Development of Plum Creek Land Creates Roadblock for Wildlife," *Missoulian*, February 5, 2007.

23. Early studies showed that the area had the densest population of inland grizzlies in North America. Brian Peck, "Paving Paradise?" *Bear News* (Summer 1999): 1; Jim Robbins, "Where the Bears and the Wolverines Prey," *New York Times*, July 16, 2002, Science, p. 1.

24. Chris Peterson, "Canada Seeks Input on North Fork Coal," *Hungry Horse News*, December 13, 2006.

25. By mid-2007, Cline Mining Corporation of Ontario was proposing to develop a metallurgical coal mine called Lodgepole in the Flathead, while BP Canada Energy Company of Calgary hoped to explore and ultimately develop a coalbed methane project north of the mine. BC and Montana officials were trying to agree on how to assess the environmental impacts of these proposals. Don Whiteley, "B.C.'s Coal Bed Dreams," *Toronto Globe and Mail*, August 8, 2007.

26. See the editors of *Bear News*, reply to Jim Mann, "DNA Study Tallies 545 Grizzlies," *Bear News* (Fall 2006).

20 | THE SMALL AREAS

1. Jim Robbins, "A Battle for Turf Where Threatened Grizzlies Still Roam," *New York Times*, September 9, 2003.

2. Michael Proctor, "Genetic Analysis of Movement, Dispersal, and Population Fragmentation of Grizzly Bears in Southwestern Canada," Ph.D. diss., University of Calgary, Calgary, 2003, discussed in Proctor et al., "A Comparative Analysis of Management Options for Grizzly Bear Conservation in the U.S.-Canada Trans-Border Area," 145.

3. Ibid.

4. Rick Bass, "Thunder and Lightning," in John A. Murray, ed., *American Nature Writing: 1999* (San Francisco: Sierra Club Books, 1999): 23.

5. See Proctor, "Genetic Analysis of Movement, Dispersal, and Population Fragmentation."

6. *Carlton v. Babbitt*, 26 F.Supp.2d 102, 112 (D.D.C. 1998).

7. The actual distance between the two is only some forty miles, but that is across a heavily settled valley that includes Bonners Ferry, Idaho, and Creston, British Columbia, with farms and busy roads. Creston is a regional center big enough to brew one of western Canada's most popular beers.

8. Brian Peck, "The State of Grizzly Recovery: 2006," *Bear News* (Fall 2006): 5.

9. Wayne Kasworm, Timothy Thier, and Christopher Servheen, "Grizzly Bear Recovery Efforts in the Cabinet/Yaak Ecosystem," *Ursus* 10 (1998): 150.

10. Jim Mann, "Evidence of Griz Cubs in the Cabinet Mountains," *Bear News* (Fall 2006): 1.

11. Proctor et al., "A Comparative Analysis of Management Options for Grizzly Bear Conservation in the U.S.-Canada Trans-Border Area," 145.

12. See ibid., 155.

13. Sterling Miller and Thomas France, "Small Populations of Grizzly Bears in the U.S.-Canada Transborder Region," *Ursus* 15 (2004): 62.

14. Michael Bader, "Unless Their Habitat Area Is Increased Greatly, Grizzly Bears Won't Survive," *Bear News* (Spring 2001): 7.

15. Joel Connelly, "Great Natural Zoo Has Become an 'Extinction Zone,'" *Seattle Post-Intelligencer*, September 18, 2002, A2.

16. McLellan, "Dynamics of a Grizzly Bear Population during a Period of Industrial Resource Extraction," 1856, 1865.

17. Studies confirm that this happened. See Kasworm, Thier, and Servheen, "Grizzly Bear Recovery Efforts in the Cabinet/Yaak Ecosystem," 151.

18. Bob Summerfield, Wayne Johnson, and David Roberts, "Trends in Road Development and Access Management in the Cabinet-Yaak and Selkirk Grizzly Bear Recovery Zones," *Ursus* 15 (2004): 115.

19. Bill Schneider, "Rock Creek Mine Decision Sells Grizzly's Future," *New West*, October 26, 2006.

20. See Kasworm, Thier, and Servheen, "Grizzly Bear Recovery Efforts in the Cabinet/Yaak Ecosystem," 152.

21. See Proctor, "Genetic Analysis of Movement, Dispersal, and Population Fragmentation of Grizzly Bears in Southwestern Canada."

22. Proctor et al., "A Comparative Analysis of Management Options for Grizzly Bear Conservation in the U.S.-Canada Trans-Border Area," 146.

23. "Give a Boost to Cabinet Grizzlies," *Daily Inter Lake* (Kalispell), October 9, 2005.

24. Jim Mann, "Second Grizzly Moved to Cabinets," *Daily Inter Lake* (Kalispell), August 18, 2006.

25. See Proctor et al., "A Comparative Analysis of Management Options for Grizzly Bear Conservation in the U.S.-Canada Trans-Border Area," 151.

26. See ibid., 156.

27. See Peck, "The State of Grizzly Recovery: 2006," 4–5.

28. David Mattson and Troy Merrill, "A Model-Based Appraisal of Habitat Conditions for Grizzly Bears in the Cabinet-Yaak Region of Montana and Idaho," *Ursus* 15 (2004): 76.

29. Schneider, *Where the Grizzly Walks*, 55.

30. Selkirk/Cabinet-Yaak subcommittee report, IGBC Winter Meeting, November 28–29, 2006.

21 | CANADA IS NO ARK

1. The 2003 sighting on Melville Island in the Arctic Ocean was confirmed as a grizzly by University of Alberta researchers. Peter Calamai, "Grizzlies Invade Polar Bear Territory," *Toronto Star*, March 12, 2005.

2. Brian Peck, "Paving Paradise?" *Bear News* (Summer 1999): 1; Jim Robbins, "Where the Bears and the Wolverines Prey."

3. "Grizzlies 'Barely Hanging On' in Alberta's Castle-Crown," *Canadian Press*, August 19, 2004; Rupert Pilkington, "Crisis in the Castle," *Bear News* (July 1998): 1.

4. Proctor, McLellan, and Strobeck, "Population Fragmentation of Grizzly Bears in Southeast British Columbia," 157; Martha Green, "Continental Divides," *Nature Conservancy* (January–February 2000): 22.

5. Michael Gibeau, "Grizzly Bear Habitat Effectiveness Model for Banff, Yoho, and Kootenay National Parks, Canada," *Ursus* 10 (1998): 240.

6. Jeff Gailus, "Banff Park Officials Ignore Own Rules," *Toronto Globe and Mail*, September 30, 2005.

7. Gibeau et al., "Managing for Grizzly Bear Security Areas in Banff National Park and the Central Canadian Rocky Mountains," 121.

8. Don Gayton, *Landscapes of the Interior* (Gabriola Island, BC: New Society Publications, 1996): 48.

9. BC Ministry of Environment, Lands, and Parks, *A Future for the Grizzly: British Columbia Grizzly Bear Conservation Strategy* (Victoria: BC Ministry of Environment, Lands, and Parks, 1995).

10. Nadine Dechiron, "Granby Park's Traverse Creek to Be Clearcut," *Kettle Range Highlands News* 4 (Winter 1998–99): 4; "Study Shows U.S. Can't Rely on Canada to Protect Grizzly Bear Habitat," *Kettle Range Highlands News* 4 (Summer 1999): 12.

11. North Cascades Grizzly Bear Recovery Team, BC Ministry of Environment, Lands, and Parks, *Recovery Plan for Grizzly Bears in the North Cascades of British Columbia, Consensus Recommendation Draft for Consultation* (Victoria: BC Ministry of Environment, Lands, and Parks, 2001). At time of publication, this was the plan's most current form.

12. IGBC North Cascades Subcommittee meeting, March 13, 2003.

13. Larry Pynn, "Public Concerns Scale Back Cascades Grizzly Plan," *Vancouver Sun*, October 5, 2001.

14. Ibid.

CONCLUSION: A RACE IN SLOW MOTION

1. IGBC Winter Meeting minutes, November 28–29, 2006, 3. In fact, in 2007 a male grizzly did wander into the Bitterroots, where it was mistakenly shot by a hunter. To the surprise of wildlife officials, the bear's DNA traced it to the Selkirks. Michael Jamison, "Bitterroot Griz Logged at Least 140 Miles," *Missoulian*, October 5, 2007.

2. Michael Jamison, "Bruins Abound in Region," *Missoulian*, September 23, 2007.

3. IGBC North Cascades subcommittee meeting, September 27, 2007.

4. The Yukon to Yellowstone proposal is described in Ed Struzik, "Life Lines," *Equinox* (August–September 1998): 40.

5. For an analysis of this complex process, see Steve Primm and Seth Wilson, "Reconnecting Grizzly Bear Populations: Prospects for Participatory Projects," *Ursus* 15 (2004): 104.

6. Defenders of Wildlife does not pay in states such as Wyoming, which has its own state-funded compensation program. Wyoming's plan covers losses due to grizzlies and several other predators, but not wolves. Accordingly, Defenders pays Wyoming ranchers for wolf predation.

7. "There's No Such Thing as a Picky Grizzly Bear," *Physorg.com*, February 22, 2007.

8. Horejsi, "A Future for the Grizzly," 11.

9. Petersen, "Old Ephraim's Last Stand."

10. Proctor et al., "A Comparative Analysis of Management Options for Grizzly Bear Conservation in the U.S.-Canada Trans-Border Area," 145; Shaffer and Samson, "Population Size and Extinction," 144; Grumbine, *Ghost Bears*, 36.

11. Michael Gilpin and Michael Soule, "Minimum Viable Populations: Processes of Species Extinction," in Michael Soule, ed., *Conservation Biology: The Science of Scarcity and Diversity* (Sunderland, MA: Sinauer Associates, 1986): 19.

12. Servheen, "Conservation of Small Bear Populations through Strategic Planning," 69.

13. Mike Stark, "Protecting One Bear Costs $6K/Year per FWS Estimate," *Billings Gazette*, January 26, 2006.

14. Ibid.

15. IGBC Winter Meeting minutes, November 28–29, 2006, 8.

16. Ibid.

BIBLIOGRAPHY

This bibliography lists the major sources relied upon in this book, as well as additional materials for readers interested in pursuing these subjects. Sources for this book not listed here include interviews and communications by the author with approximately twenty-five individuals identified in the text. These interviews and communications occurred between 1997 and 2007. The author also relied on personal notes of meetings attended with the Interagency Grizzly Bear Committee and its North Cascades subcommittee, official minutes of the same committee and subcommittee, and newspaper and other periodical accounts identified in the notes.

Alliance for the Wild Rockies. *Conservation Biology Alternative.* Missoula, 1999.

Almack, Jon. *North Cascades Grizzly Bear Project, Annual Report.* Olympia: Washington Department of Game, 1986.

Almack, Jon, and Scott Fitkin. *Grizzly Bear and Gray Wolf Investigations in Washington State, 1994–1995.* Olympia: Washington Department of Fish and Wildlife, 1998.

Almack, Jon, William Gaines, Peter Morrison, James Eby, Robert Naney, George Wooten, Scott Fitkin, and E. R. Garcia. *North Cascades Ecosystem Evaluation: Final Report.* Missoula, MT: Interagency Grizzly Bear Committee, 1993.

Bader, Michael. "Spatial Needs of Grizzly Bears in the U.S. Northern Rockies." Paper presented at the Society for Conservation Biology meeting. June 12, 2000.

———. "Distribution of Grizzly Bears in the U.S. Northern Rockies." *Northwest Science* 74 (2000): 325–34.

Bath, Alistar. "The Role of Human Dimensions in Wildlife Resource Research in Wildlife Management." *Ursus* 10 (1998): 349–55.

Becky, Fred. *Cascade Alpine Guide.* 3 vols. Seattle: Mountaineers Books, 1989.

———. *Range of Glaciers.* Portland: Oregon Historical Society Press, 2003.

Bjorklund, Jonathan. *Preliminary Investigation of the Feasibility of Reestablishing a Grizzly Bear Population in the North Cascades National Park Complex.* Misc. Research Paper NCT-8, North Cascades National Park, 1978.

———. *Historical and Recent Grizzly Bear Sightings in the North Cascades.* Misc. Research Paper NCT-13, North Cascades National Park, 1980.

———. *Species, Subspecies, and Distribution of Mammals in the North Cascades.* Misc. Research Paper NCT-14, North Cascades National Park, 1981.

Boyce, Mark. "Metapopulation Analysis for the Bitterroot Population," appendix 21C in *Grizzly Bear Recovery in the Bitterroot Ecosystem, Final Environmental Impact Statement.* Missoula, MT: US Fish and Wildlife Service, 2000.

British Columbia Ministry of Environment, Lands, and Parks. *A Future for the Grizzly: British Columbia Grizzly Bear Conservation Strategy.* June 1995.

British Columbia North Cascades Grizzly Bear Recovery Team. *Recovery Plan for Grizzly Bears in the North Cascades of British Columbia: Consensus Recommendation Draft for Consultation.* January 19, 2001.

Brown, David. *The Grizzly in the Southwest.* Tucson: University of Arizona Press, 1985.

Brown, Gary. *The Great Bear Almanac.* New York: Lyons and Burford, 1993.

Center for Biodiversity and Conservation. *Biodiversity, Science, and the Human Prospect.* New York: American Museum of Natural History, 1997.

Chadwick, Douglas. "Grizz." *National Geographic* (July 2001): 2–25.

Chittenden, Hiram. *The American Fur Trade of the Far West.* Stanford, CA: Academic Reprints, 1954.

Clark, Joseph, Djuro Huber, and Christopher Servheen. "Bear Reintroductions: Lessons and Challenges." *Ursus* 13 (2002): 335–45.

Clark, Tim, Richard Reading, and Alice Clarke, eds. *Endangered Species Recovery: Finding the Lessons, Improving the Process.* Washington DC: Island Press, 1994.

Craighead, Derek. "An Integrated Satellite Technique to Evaluate Grizzly Bear Habitat Use." *Ursus* 10 (1998): 187–201.

Craighead, Frank. *Track of the Grizzly.* San Francisco: Sierra Club Books, 1979.

Craighead, John. "Status of the Yellowstone Grizzly Bear Population: Has It Recovered, Should It Be Delisted?" *Ursus* 10 (1998): 597–602.

Craighead, John, Maurice Hornocker, and Frank Craighead. "Reproductive Biology of Young Female Grizzly Bears." *Journal of Reproduction and Fertility,* Supp. 6 (1969): 447–75.

Craighead, John, Jay Sumner, and John Mitchell. *The Grizzly Bears of Yellowstone: Their Ecology in the Yellowstone Ecosystem, 1959–1992.* Washington DC: Island Press, 1995.

Craighead, Lance, David Paetkau, Harry Reynolds, Curtis Strobeck, and Ernest Vyse. "Use of Microsatellite DNA Analyses to Infer Breeding Behavior and Demographic Processes in an Arctic Grizzly Bear Population." *Ursus* 10 (1998): 323–27.

Cutright, Paul. *Lewis and Clark: Pioneering Naturalists.* Lincoln: University of Nebraska Press, 1989.

Dood, Arnold, Robert Brannon, and Richard Mace. *Final Environmental Impact Statement: The Grizzly Bear in Northwest Montana.* Helena: Montana Department of Fish, Wildlife, and Parks, 1986.

Fischer, Hank, and Michael Roy. "New Approaches to Citizen Participation in Endangered Species Management: Recovery in the Bitterroot Ecosystem." *Ursus* 10 (1998): 603–6.

Franklin, I. R., and R. Frankham. "How Large Must Populations Be to Retain Evolutionary Potential?" *Animal Conservation* 1 (1998): 69–70.

Gaines, William, Robert Naney, Peter Morrison, James Eby, George Wooten, and Jon Almack. "Use of Landsat Multispectral Scanner Imagery and Geographic Information Systems to Map Vegetation in the North Cascades Grizzly Bear Ecosystem." *International Conference on Bear Research and Management* 9 (1994): 533–47.

Gibeau, Michael, Stephen Herrero, Bruce McLellan, and John Woods. "Managing for Grizzly Bear Security Areas in Banff National Park and the Central Canadian Rocky Mountains." *Ursus* 12 (2001): 121–30.

Gniadek, Steve, and Katherine Kendall. "A Summary of Bear Management in Glacier National Park, Montana, 1960–1994." *Ursus* 10 (1998): 155–59.

Green, Martha. "Continental Divides." *Nature Conservancy* (January–February 2000): 18–25.

Grumbine, Edward. *Ghost Bears: Exploring the Biodiversity Crisis.* Washington DC: Island Press, 1992.

Gunther, Kerry, and Hopi Hoekstra. "Bear-Inflicted Human Injuries in Yellowstone National Park, 1970–1994." *Ursus* 10 (1998): 377–84.

Herrero, Stephen. "A Comparison of Some Features of the Evolution, Ecology and Behavior of Black and Grizzly Bears." *Carnivore* 1 (1978): 7–17.

———. *Bear Attacks: Their Causes and Avoidance.* New York: Lyons and Burford, 1985.

Horejsi, Brian. "A Future for the Grizzly." *Bear News* (Spring 2001): 11.

Hornocker, Maurice. "Population Characteristics and Social and Reproductive Behavior of the Grizzly Bear in Yellowstone National Park." Master's thesis, University of Montana, Missoula, 1962.

Interagency Grizzly Bear Committee. *Grizzly Bear Compendium.* Missoula, MT: US Fish and Wildlife Service, 1987.

———. *Interagency Grizzly Bear Guidelines.* Missoula, MT: US Forest Service, 1998.

———. Meeting minutes, 1997–2007.

Interagency Grizzly Bear Committee, Technical Review Team. *Evaluation of the Bitterroot and North Cascades to Sustain Viable Grizzly Bear Populations.* 1991.

IGBC North Cascades Subcommittee. *Grizzly Bear Recovery in the North Cascades: Questions and Answers.* November 1993.

———. Meeting minutes, 1997–2007.

Kasworm, Wayne, and Timothy Manley. "Road and Trail Influences on Grizzly Bears and Black Bears in Northwest Montana." *International Conference on Bear Research and Management* 8 (1990): 79–84.

Kasworm, Wayne, Timothy Thier, and Christopher Servheen. *Cabinet Mountain Grizzly Bear Population Augmentation: 1991 Progress Report.* Missoula, MT: US Fish and Wildlife Service, 1992.

———. "Grizzly Bear Recovery Efforts in the Cabinet/Yaak Ecosystem." *Ursus* 10 (1998): 147–53.

Lynch, Michael, and Russell Lande. "The Critical Effective Size for a Genetically Secure Population." *Animal Conservation* 1 (1998): 70–72.

Mattson, David. "Changes in Mortality in Yellowstone's Grizzly Bears." *Ursus* 10 (1998): 129–38.

Mattson, David, and Richard Knight. "Effects of Access on Human-Caused Mortality of Yellowstone Grizzly Bears." Interagency Grizzly Bear Study Team Report 1991B. Missoula, MT: National Park Service, 1991.

Mattson, David, and Troy Merrill. "Extirpations of Grizzly Bears in the Contiguous United States, 1850–2000." *Conservation Biology* 16 (August 2002): 1123–36.

———. "A Model-Based Appraisal of Habitat Conditions for Grizzly Bears in the Cabinet-Yaak Region of Montana and Idaho." *Ursus* 15 (2004): 76–89.

McLellan, Bruce. "Dynamics of Grizzly Bear Population during a Period of Industrial Resource Extraction. II: Mortality Rates and Causes of Death." *Canadian Journal of Zoology* 67 (1988): 1861–64.

———. "Maintaining Viability of Brown Bears along the Southern Fringe of Their Distribution." *Ursus* 10 (1998): 607–11.

McMillion, Scott. *Mark of the Grizzly.* Helena, MT: Falcon Publishing, 1999.

McNamee, Thomas. *The Grizzly Bear.* New York: Alfred A. Knopf, 1984.

Meffe, Gary, and C. Ronald Caroll. *Principles of Conservation Biology.* Sunderland, MA: Sinauer Associates, 1994.

Merrill, Troy, and David Mattson. "The Extent and Location of Habitat Biophysically Suitable for Grizzly Bears in the Yellowstone Region." *Ursus* 14 (2003): 171–87.

Miller, Sterling, and Thomas France. "Small Populations of Grizzly Bears in the U.S.-Canada Transborder Region." *Ursus* 15 (2004): 61–64.

Miller, Suzanne, Sterling Miller, and Daniel McCollum. "Attitudes toward and Relative Value of Alaskan Brown and Black Bears to Resident Voters, Resident Hunters, and Nonresident Hunters." *Ursus* 10 (1998): 357–76.

Mills, John, ed. *Impressions of the North Cascades.* Seattle: Mountaineers Books, 1996.

Murphy, Kerry, Gregory Felzien, Maurice Hornocker, and Toni Ruth. "Encounter Competition between Bears and Cougars: Some Ecological Implications." *Ursus* 10 (1998): 55–60.

Murray, John, ed. *The Great Bear.* Seattle: Alaska Northwest Books, 1992.

Naiman, Robert, and Kevin Rogers. "Large Animals and System-Level Characteristics in River Corridors." *BioScience* 47 (September 1997): 521–29.

Natural Resources Defense Council. "Rewriting the Rules: The Bush Administration's Assault on the Environment." New York: Natural Resources Defense Council, April 2002 and January 2003 editions.

North Cascades National Park. *Bears and You in the North Cascades.* 1995. Available at http://www.nps.gov/noca/naturescience/bear-safety.htm.

Noss, Reed, Howard Quigley, Maurice Hornocker, Troy Merrill, and Paul Paquet. "Conservation Biology and Carnivore Conservation in the Rocky Mountains." *Conservation Biology* 10 (1996): 949–63.

Olsen, Jack. *Night of the Grizzlies.* New York: Signet Books, 1969.

Paetkau, David, and Curtis Strobeck. "Ecological Genetic Studies of Bears using Microsatellite Analysis." *Ursus* 10 (1998): 299–306.

Peacock, Doug. "Making the West Safe for Grizzlies." *Audubon* (November–December 1997): 46–51, 102–3.

Peacock, Doug, and Andrea Peacock. *The Essential Grizzly: The Mingled Fates of Men and Bears.* Guilford, CT: Lyons Press, 2006.

Pearson, Art. *The Northern Interior Grizzly Bear.* Ottawa: Environment Canada, 1975.

Peck, Brian. "The State of Grizzly Recovery: 2006." *Bear News* (Fall 2006): 4–5.

Peek, James. "Experiences with a Committee of User Groups Examining Grizzly Bear Restoration in Idaho." *Ursus* 10 (1998): 613–14.

Petersen, David. *Ghost Grizzlies.* New York: Henry Holt, 1995.

Primm, Steve, and Seth Wilson. "Re-connecting Grizzly Bear Populations: Prospects for Participatory Projects." *Ursus* 15 (2004): 104–14.

Proctor, Michael. *Genetic Analysis of Movement, Dispersal, and Population Fragmentation of Grizzly Bears in Southwestern Canada.* Ph.D. diss., University of Calgary, 2003.

Proctor, Michael, Bruce McLellan, and Curtis Strobeck. "Population Fragmentation of Grizzly Bears in Southeastern British Columbia." *Ursus* 13 (2002): 153–60.

Proctor, Michael, Christopher Servheen, Sterling Miller, Wayne Kasworm, and Wayne Wakkinen. "A Comparative Analysis of Management Options for Grizzly Bear Conservation in the U.S.-Canada Trans-Border Area." *Ursus* 15 (2004): 145–60.

Restini, Marco, and John Marzluff. "Funding Extinction? Biological Needs and Political Realities in the Allocation of Resources to Endangered Species Recovery." *BioScience* 52 (2002): 169–77.

Robbins, Charles, Charles Schwartz, and Laura Felicetti. "Nutritional Ecology of Ursids: A Review of Newer Methods and Management Implications." *Ursus* 15 (2004): 161–71.

Russell, Charles, Maureen Enns, and Fred Stenson. *Grizzly Heart: Living without Fear among the Brown Bears of Kamchatka.* Toronto: Random House Canada, 2002.

Russell, Richard, J. W. Nolan, N. G. Woody, G. H. Anderson, and Art Pearson. *A Study of the Grizzly Bear (Ursus arctos) in Jasper National Park.* Edmonton: Canadian Wildlife Service, 1978.

Schneider, Bill. *Where the Grizzly Walks.* Helena, MT: Falcon Publishing, 2004.

Schoen, John. "Introduction to a Panel Discussion: Recovery of Threatened Grizzly Bear Populations in North America." *Ursus* 10 (1998): 589.

Schoen, John, and Sterling Miller. "New Strategies for Bear Conservation: Collaboration between Resource Agencies and Environmental Organizations." *Ursus* 13 (2002): 361–67.

Servheen, Christopher. "Conservation of Small Bear Populations through Strategic Planning." *Ursus* 10 (1998): 67–73.

———. "The Grizzly Bear Recovery Program: Current Status and Future Considerations." *Ursus* 10 (1998): 591–96.

Shaffer, Mark. "Determining Minimum Viable Population Sizes for the Grizzly Bear." *Bears: Their Biology and Management* 5 (1983): 133–39.

Shaffer, Mark, and Fred Samson. "Population Size and Extinction: A Note on Determining Critical Population Sizes." *American Naturalist* 125 (1985): 144–52.

Simberloff, Daniel. "Biodiversity and Bears—A Conservation Paradigm Shift." *Ursus* 11 (1999): 21–28.

Singleton, Peter, William Gaines, and John Lehmkuhl. "Landscape Permeability for Grizzly Bear Movements in Washington and Southwest British Columbia." *Ursus* 15 (2004): 90–103.

Soule, Michael, ed. *Conservation Biology: The Science of Scarcity and Diversity.* Sunderland, MA: Sinauer Associates, 1986.

Soule, Michael, and Bruce Wilcox, eds. *Conservation Biology: An Evolutionary-Ecological Perspective.* Sunderland, MA: Sinauer Associates, 1980.

Sullivan, Paul. *A Preliminary Study of Historic and Recent Reports of Grizzly Bears in the North Cascades Area of Washington.* Olympia: Washington Department of Game, 1983.

US Fish and Wildlife Service. *Grizzly Bear Recovery Plan.* Washington DC: US Fish and Wildlife Service, 1993.

———. *North Cascades Ecosystem Recovery Plan Chapter.* Washington DC: US Fish and Wildlife Service, 1997.

US Geologic Survey, North Rocky Mountain Science Center. *North Divide Grizzly Bear Project.* Available at http://www.nrmsc.usgs.gov/projects/ DNA_NCDE.htm.

US National Park Service, US Forest Service, and Washington Department of Wildlife. "Grizzly Bears in the North Cascades? What You Should Know." Undated pamphlet.

Waits, Lisette. "Molecular Genetic Applications for Bear Research." *Ursus* 11 (1999): 253–60.

Waits, Lisette, David Paetkau, Curtis Strobeck, and Richard Ward. "A Comparison of Genetic Diversity in North American Brown Bears." *Ursus* 10 (1998): 307–14.

White, Don, James Berardinelli, and Keith Aune. "Reproductive Characteristics of the Male Grizzly Bear in the Continental United States." *Ursus* 10 (1998): 497–501.

Wilson, Edward. *The Diversity of Life.* Cambridge, MA: Belknap Press, 1992.

Wilson, Edward, and Frances Peters, eds. *Biodiversity.* Washington DC: National Academy Press, 1988.

INDEX

Access management standards:
adoption of, in North Cascades,
138–39
Alberta, 142, 188, 217, 218, 219, 220
Almack, Jon, 8, 53, 57; on augmentation, candidate bears for, 114;
on character of North Cascades
grizzlies, 89; and conflict with
state officials, 63–70, 87, 133;
departure of from North Cascades, impact of, 132; and evaluation of North Cascades, 53–55,
57–61; on grizzlies and ecosystems, 34, 36; on grizzlies and
rival species, 33; and mapping of
vegetation in North Cascades,
57–58; on mortality rate of adolescent male grizzlies, 102; and
population estimate for North
Cascades, 86–87; and search for
grizzlies in North Cascades, 8,
58–59, 133; on small populations,
104; and stealth bear theory, 89
Augmentation, 92, 114–16; in
British Columbia, 210–11,
221–24, 226–27; in Cabinet-Yaak,
205–6, 209–10, 228; candidate
bears for, 114–15; compared to
reintroduction, 92, 116–17; as
first step in recovery, 116; impact
of Bitterroots decision on, 229;

in North Cascades, 80, 107, 108,
110, 118–19, 129, 162, 229, 238;
and small population vitality,
210; and Washington State
import ban, 119–21, 123; in
Yellowstone, 185

Babbitt, Bruce (interior secretary):
and Endangered Species Act,
efforts to protect, 148–55; use of
"warranted but precluded" provision (of ESA), 152
BC Highway 3, 95, 202, 204, 208–9,
211, 219
Bear-human relations, 41, 49–50,
51–52; and stealth bear theory,
88–90. *See also* Public attitudes
toward grizzlies
Biodiversity: importance of, 37–39
Bitterroots, 61, 164–74; adoption of
recovery plan in, 61, 79–80,
164–67; evaluation of as recovery
area, 27–30, 46–47, 52, 56; as
funding priority versus North
Cascades, 128–32, 134–35, 143,
155; and funding shortages,
237–38; importance of to grizzly
recovery, 29, 171–72; and isolation of grizzly populations, 99,
107–8, 171–72, 184; map of, 166;
proposed suspension of recovery

plan for, 163, 167–71; and public attitudes toward grizzlies, 50, 73–74, 76, 80–81, 92; recovery area created in, 61; reintroduction temporarily blocked in, 149–50, 153; search for grizzlies in, 48–49; suspension of recovery plan for, effects of, 173, 223, 229

Black bears, 8, 32, 51, 106, 109, 133, 141; compared to grizzlies, 6, 33, 85–86, 102, 105, 142

Braaten, Anne: and recovery efforts in North Cascades, 68–69, 138, 139, 142

Breeding habits (of grizzlies), 101–3, 106, 178, 183

British Columbia, 218; augmentation proposed in, 210–11; coal mining proposals in, 197–98; coastal ecosystem collapse in, 36–37; conservation strategy (1995) of, 221; election (2001) in, 224–25; Granby area of, 221; grizzly population of, 217; highways in, effect of, 94–98, 202; hunting policy in, 220, 225; importance of to grizzly recovery, 218; and proposed augmentation in North Cascades, 221–27; relocation of grizzlies in, 112; and US need for self-sufficiency, 227. See also Fraser Canyon; Winston

Brown bears, 17, 24, 40, 88, 92, 105. See also Kodiak bears

Bush, George W., 156, 159, 160–61, 163, 167. See also Bush administration

Bush administration, 156–63, 171; backdoor tactics of, 160–61; and Bitterroots plan, 167; compared to Clinton administration, 157–58, 159, 160; environmental rollbacks under, 156–59; funding

cutbacks under, 160; impact of on grizzly recovery, 162–63; and 9/11, effects of, 159, 160; and public opinion on environmental policy, 159; and shift in approach to recovery, 168, 186–87; use of lawsuits by, 157, 160, 161; and Yellowstone delisting, 163, 186–87. See also Norton, Gail

Cabinet-Yaak, 115, 126, 200-213, 236; augmentation in, 205–6, 209–11; and BC hunting policy, 207, 220; combined with Selkirks, 202, 204; compared to other recovery areas, 207; grizzly mortality in, 211–12; grizzly population of, 184, 205–6, 209, 228; impact of BC Highway 3 on, 202, 208–9; as island, 99, 107, 131, 171; and logging, 207; map of, 201; mining proposals in, 208

Canada, 52, 65–66, 71, 91, 188, 198, 217–27; and augmentation in Cabinet-Yaak and Selkirks, 210–11; grizzly populations in, 217; hunting policy in, 220; as link between Cabinet-Yaak and Selkirks, 99, 126, 202, 205; national parks of, as grizzly habitat, 219–20; provincial power in, 224; as source of wildlife exports, 218; and US need for self-sufficiency, 227. See also British Columbia

Cascades. See North Cascades

Clinton administration, 147–48, 157, 160, 186; contrasted with Bush administration, 159, 160, 161; and funding for endangered species, 154; and riders to appropriations bills, 149–50. See also Babbitt, Bruce

Colorado, 121–22, 217, 218. *See also* San Juan Mountains

Conservation Northwest. *See* Northwest Ecosystem Alliance

Corridors. *See* Wildlife corridors

Defenders of Wildlife, 72, 126, 147, 173, 226; and Bitterroots campaign, 130–31, 134, 164, 165; and Bush administration, opinions concerning, 157, 173; compensation programs of, 234; North Cascades strategy of, 223; as source of funding, 163

Diet (of grizzlies), 22, 32–33, 58, 140, 181

DNA studies, 140–42, 192–94, 205, 208–9

Earthjustice: and Yellowstone delisting, 179, 182

Ecosystems: effect of grizzlies on, 31–36

Ecotourism: bear watching as, 39–40, 175

Endangered Species Act, 26, 31, 75, 76, 81; Babbitt's approach to, 148–55; and Bush administration, 160, 163, 167–68, 198; congressional attacks on, 147–50, 161; "experimental" population designation under, 47–49; and Fish and Wildlife Service, 56; and Forest Service, 55, 56; grizzlies protected under, 9, 15, 25, 176, 231; and Idaho challenge to Bitterroots plan, 168; and import bans, 119, 120, 122; and North Cascades grizzlies, 62, 138; relative success of, 235; "threatened" versus "endangered" listings under, 25, 184; "warranted but precluded" provision of, 138,

152, 155; and Yellowstone grizzlies, 179, 182–85, 231–32

Evaluation area: criteria for, 46–47

"Experimental" populations, 47–49, 92, 165

Fish and Wildlife Service. *See* US Fish and Wildlife Service

Forest Service. *See* US Forest Service

Fraser Canyon (British Columbia): as barrier to grizzly travel, 93–98; and grizzly populations, 87, 112–13, 114, 221; map of, 96

Funding: for augmentation in Cabinet-Yaak, 206; and Bush administration, 160, 162–63, 233–34; cutbacks in, impact of on grizzly recovery, 237–38; of Endangered Species Act, 26; and Fish and Wildlife Service budget, 126–27, 152–53; for grizzly recovery in BC, 225; for North Cascades versus Bitterroots, 128–29, 134, 136–37, 143, 155; of trend study in NCDE, 194; and Yellowstone delisting, 181, 184; as zero-sum game, 135

Fur trade, 18–21

Gaines, Bill: on augmentation in BC, 224; and evaluation of North Cascades, 58–59, 61, 65, 69, 143; on funding loss in North Cascades, impact of, 132, 137–39; on isolation of North Cascades grizzlies, 99, 107–8, 116; and population modeling, approaches to, 103–4, 107–8; on public attitudes toward grizzlies, 73, 79, 82; on resistance to grizzly recovery, 69, 173

Genetic diversity: importance of, 26, 104–6, 129–30, 236; and minimum viable population, 59; and

reintroduction, 116, 171; in Selkirks, 202; and wildlife corridors, 231–32; in Yellowstone, 181, 185. *See also* Highways
Genetic drift, 105, 129, 171
Glacier National Park. *See* Northern Continental Divide Ecosystem
Grand Tetons. *See* Yellowstone
Great Bear Foundation, 126; and Bitterroots recovery plan, opinion of, 167; and search for grizzlies in Bitterroots, 48–49; and trend study in NCDE, reservations concerning, 194, 199
Grizzly habitat, 7, 22, 24, 30, 32, 79, 202, 207; Bitterroots as, 172; and breeding, 101–2, 230; in Canada, 219–20; changes in, consequences of, 181, 183, 235–36; Colockum wildlife area as, 66; in evaluation area, criteria for, 47; logging and roads as threat to, 51, 137–38, 208; and national forest policy, 55, 139; North Cascades as, 53, 57–61, 115; in Northern Continental Divide, 188, 194, 197; protective function of, 35; and reintroduction, 92, 114; relation of to recovery areas, 26–27, 99, 230–31; Yellowstone as, 178, 180–83, 194. *See also* Numbers versus habitat debate
Grizzly mortality rates, 51, 195, 211–12; of cubs and adolescents, 102. *See also* Hunting policy; Killing; Recovery goals
Grizzly populations, 24; and BC conservation strategy (1995), 221; in Bitterroots, as "experimental," 48–49, 165; as distinct population segments, 183–85, 231–32; and genetic diversity, need for, 105–6, 129–30, 236;

growth rates of, 102–3; historical, 15–17; historical range, map of, 16; as metapopulation, 108; and need for wildlife corridors, 231–32; in North Cascades, survival estimates for, 103–4, 106–8; recovery of, relative success of, 228–30; resident populations, as issue, 47, 48–49; in Rockies, 126; small, 103–4, 105; as "threatened," 15, 26, 70, 114, 176, 187, 209, 221; as "threatened" versus "endangered," 128, 183–84, 204, 207, 231; in Yellowstone, 115, 163, 174. *See also* Population estimates
Grizzly range, 60–61, 91, 141, 188, 217, 224, 230; in BC, 219; historical, map of, 16; of subadults, 102; in Yellowstone, 178

Habitat. *See* Grizzly habitat
Habitat protection plans: and Babbitt, 154
Highways: in BC, 94–96, 98, 100, 202, 204; as genetic barriers, 95–99, 191–92, 202, 208–9; in North Cascades, effect of, 13, 15; reaction of grizzlies to, 51. *See also* BC Highway 3; Trans-Canada Highway
Hunting policy, 15, 90, 133, 196, 220; in BC, 207, 220, 225; and ecotourism, 40; and state autonomy, 122; and stealth bear theory, 90; and Yellowstone delisting, 180, 231

Idaho, 26, 29, 232–33; and attitudes toward grizzlies, 50, 55, 73–74, 75, 81, 130–31; and augmentation in Cabinet-Yaak, 206; and Bitterroots recovery plan, 164,

Fish and Wildlife funding priorities, 153; as source of support for recovery efforts, 233, 234; and Yellowstone delisting, 181

Native Americans: attitudes of toward grizzlies, 17–18; and fur trade, 18–20

Natural Resources Defense Council, 126; and antienvironmental actions of Bush administration, 156–57; on grizzly mortality in NCDE, 195

North Cascades, 9, 13–15, 24, 29, 45–46; augmentation needed in, 107–8, 116; and BC recovery plan, 223; Cabinet-Yaak and Selkirks compared to, 207; census efforts in, 140–42; and Colockum wildlife area, 66–67; and core area management standards, 139; evaluation of, 28, 30, 53–54, 66–67; funding requests for, 155, 162; and funding shift to Bitterroots, 128–29, 132–35; and funding shortages, consequences of, 143, 238; as grizzly habitat, suitability of, 27, 29, 47, 57–58, 61, 66, 78; grizzly range in, 60–61; importance of to grizzly recovery, 29; improvement in federal attitudes toward, 136–39; killing of grizzlies in, 13–15, 20–23; and "Let 'em walk" strategy, 223; loss of remnant population in, implications of, 116–17; map of, 64; mapping of vegetation in, 57–58; minimum viable population in, 59–61, 106–7; and opposition from federal land managers, 52, 54–55; population estimate for, 86–87; and public concerns regarding grizzlies, 71–79, 81; as separate gene pool

from Rockies, 129–30; sighting of grizzlies in, 84–86; survival of grizzlies in, 27–28, 58–59, 83–92; and suspension of Bitterroots plan, impact of, 172–73, 223. *See also* Almack, Jon; British Columbia

Northern Continental Divide Ecosystem, 188–99; and augmentation in Cabinet-Yaak, 212; and BC coal mining proposals, 197–98; Cabinet-Yaak and Selkirks compared to, 207; census efforts in, 189, 192–93, 230; compared to Yellowstone, 189; funding of trend study in, 194; and funding shortages, consequences of, 237–38; grizzly killings in, 195–97; grizzly range in, 188–89; housing construction as threat to, 197; map of, 190; poaching as threat in, 196; possible delisting of, 189; recovery criteria for, 194–95; as source of bears, 236; and study of US Highway 2, 191–93; trend study in, 193–94

Northwest Ecosystem Alliance: and Bush administration, opinion concerning, 157; and lawsuit over Loomis logging, 133, 137; and recovery efforts in North Cascades, 131, 138, 140, 153, 155; and survival of grizzlies in North Cascades, 90, 92; and trail closures, impact of, 78; and Washington State import ban, 119; and wildlife corridors, 98

Norton, Gail (interior secretary): and Bitterroots plan, suspension of, 167–71; resignation of, 173–74

Numbers versus habitat debate, 176, 181–83, 186, 194

Okanogan Valley, 98; and hostility toward grizzlies, 72–73, 117; logging in, 51

debate concerning, 207–8; territory covered by, 202; uplisting proposal for, 184, 204; and Washington State import ban, 120

Selway-Bitterroot. *See* Bitterroots

Servheen, Chris (US coordinator for grizzly recovery), 53, 126, 127, 151, 199; on adaptability of grizzlies, 183; as advocate of wildlife corridors, 184; and augmentation in Cabinet-Yaak and Selkirks, 210; on BC mining proposals, 198; on conservation as warfare, 9; decision of to fund Bitterroots over North Cascades, 128–29, 137; on "dual-citizenship" grizzlies in North Cascades, 87; on funding needs for Bitterroots and North Cascades, 134, 143; minimum viable population estimate of, for North Cascades, 59; on need for proactive approach to recovery, 237; on need for standards in Forest Service management plans, 182; and numbers versus habitat debate, 183, 236; on poaching, 196; on public attitudes toward grizzlies, 50, 74, 75, 82, 123; reaction of to federal report on expenditures, 237; and recovery efforts in North Cascades, 53–54, 61, 66, 68, 111, 118, 138, 143, 222; and recovery efforts in Northern Continental Divide, 189, 191–94, 196, 198, 199; and state participation in recovery, views on, 121, 123; and suspension of Bitterroots plan, reaction to, 169; and uplist petitions, opposition to, 183–84; on US reaction to BC proposal for North Cascades, 222; and

Yellowstone delisting, 178, 179, 183, 191

Sexual maturity (of grizzlies), 101–2

State agencies: commitment of to recovery in North Cascades, 132–34, 136–37; and evaluation of North Cascades, 54–55, 65–70, 87, 118; and IGBC, 29–30; importance of to recovery, 56–57; and import bans, 120–23; as source of funding for recovery, 163, 237; and Yellowstone delisting, 176–79, 184, 186, 232–33

State legislation: and hunting of bears around Yellowstone, 231; and import bans, 119–23; and motives of politicians, 122–23; and resistance to federal programs, 120–23, 168–69

State management plans: in aftermath of Yellowstone delisting, 179–80, 232–33

Stealth bear theory, debate concerning, 88–90

Territory. *See* Grizzly range

Timber industry. *See* Logging

Trans-Canada Highway, 94, 96–97, 108, 111

Umbrella species: defined, 35

US Fish and Wildlife Service, 15, 235; and Babbitt's efforts to protect the ESA, 148, 150–51, 154–55; and Bitterroots recovery plan, 164, 165, 167, 170, 172, 233; budget of for endangered species, limiting of, 152–53; and Bush administration, 156–57, 160, 162–63; and creation of recovery areas, 25–29, 99, 201, 203, 228; and estimate of total expenditures for endangered species,

237–38; and funding for EIS in North Cascades, 143, 153; and funding for grizzly recovery, 126–28, 153, 173, 191, 234–35, 237; geographical regions of, 125–28; and IGBC, 29–30; and protection of grizzlies, 229–31, 232; and public opposition to grizzly recovery, 75, 78, 82; and recovery efforts in Cabinet-Yaak, 204, 206, 207, 208, 212; and recovery efforts in North Cascades, 118, 129, 132–33, 138, 143, 155, 222, 229; and recovery efforts in Northern Continental Divide, 189, 196, 197, 198–99; and reintroduction of species, 47–48, 121–22; and shift of funding to Bitterroots, 131–32; and state agencies, relations with, 56–57, 121, 148; and "warranted but precluded" provision of ESA, use of, 138, 152; and Yellowstone delisting, 176–77, 178–80, 182–83, 185–87. *See also* Servheen, Chris; Zimmer, Doug

US Forest Service: and Bush administration, 160, 162; and concerns of hikers, 77, 167; and early recovery areas, 46; geographical regions of, 125; and logging industry, 51, 151, 207; and recovery efforts in North Cascades, 30, 54, 57–58, 132, 136–37, 138, 139–40, 222; and resistance to recovery programs, 52, 54–55, 56, 157–58; and road density debate in Cabinet-Yaak and Selkirks, 207–8, 211; and rules governing national forests, impact on Yellowstone, 182; as source of funding for NCDE trend study, 194

"Warranted but precluded" provision of ESA: uses made of, 138, 152

Washington (state), 26, 29; and congressional resistance to recovery, 150, 153; Department of Natural Resources of, 67, 69, 133; Fish and Wildlife Department of, 56, 63, 67, 132; as grizzly habitat, 9, 17, 27, 115, 130; import ban in, 119–21, 123; and recovery efforts in North Cascades, 30, 46, 53, 63, 66, 68–70, 175; statewide poll in, 81–82

Wildlife corridors: Bitterroots as, 29; and delisting of specific populations, 184; and highways, impact of, 97–98; and hunting, 231; importance of, 26, 79–80, 184, 231–32; and isolation of North Cascades, 98–99; in Northern Continental Divide, threats to, 197; Servheen as advocate of, 184; Y2Y proposal for, 108, 232

Wind River Range, 217; and Wyoming's bear management plan, 179–80, 181–82, 232

Winston, travels of, 109–13

Wyoming, 29, 217; and augmentation in North Cascades, 115; hunting policy in, 231; and import bans, 122; and "outside" bears, 230; and state autonomy, 176, 179–80; and Yellowstone delisting, 176–78, 179–80, 181–82, 232

Yellowstone, 24, 26, 32, 175–87, 188, 217; and Bitterroots as corridor, 29, 131, 171; and Bush administration, relation of to delisting, 163, 174, 186–87; Cabinet-Yaak and Selkirks compared to, 200, 207; and classification of grizzlies as distinct population segment, 183–85; closure of garbage dumps in, 175–76; closure of hiking trails in, 77, 78–79; decision to delist grizzlies in, 176–82; delisting decision, implications of, 191, 230, 232, 234; ecotourism in, 39, 175; and Forest Service rules governing national forests, 182; and funding shortages, consequences of, 238; genetic isolation of grizzlies in, 106, 129, 181, 185; growth rate of grizzly population in, 112; habitat change in, debate concerning, 181–83, 235; and human-bear relations, 51, 52; and hunting policy, 231; and lawsuits, 161, 182; map of, 177; North Cascades compared to, 89; Northern Continental Divide compared to, 188–89, 198; population estimates for, 126, 176, 178, 230; as precedent for future delistings, 185–86, 228; and recovery criteria, debate concerning, 178–79; and recovery criteria for NCDE, 193–95; reintroduc-

tion of wolves in, 34, 47–48, 81, 117, 122, 147, 150, 218; state management plans for, 179–80; as source of bears, 236; and Wyoming, role of in delisting, 176–78, 179–80, 181, 182; and Y2Y wildlife corridor proposal, 108

Yukon-to-Yellowstone (Y2Y) corridor, 108, 232

Zimmer, Doug (FWS information specialist), 71; on changed attitude of Forest Service toward North Cascades, 137; on loss of funding for North Cascades, 133; on North Cascades as clean ecosystem, 89–90; on pace of recovery as national policy issue, 163; on public attitudes toward grizzlies, 49, 71, 74; on recovery in North Cascades, official viewpoints concerning, 54–55, 68–69, 70; on remnant population of grizzlies in North Cascades, 117; on stealth bears, 88; as target of hostility at Okanogan public meeting, 72–73